D1696039

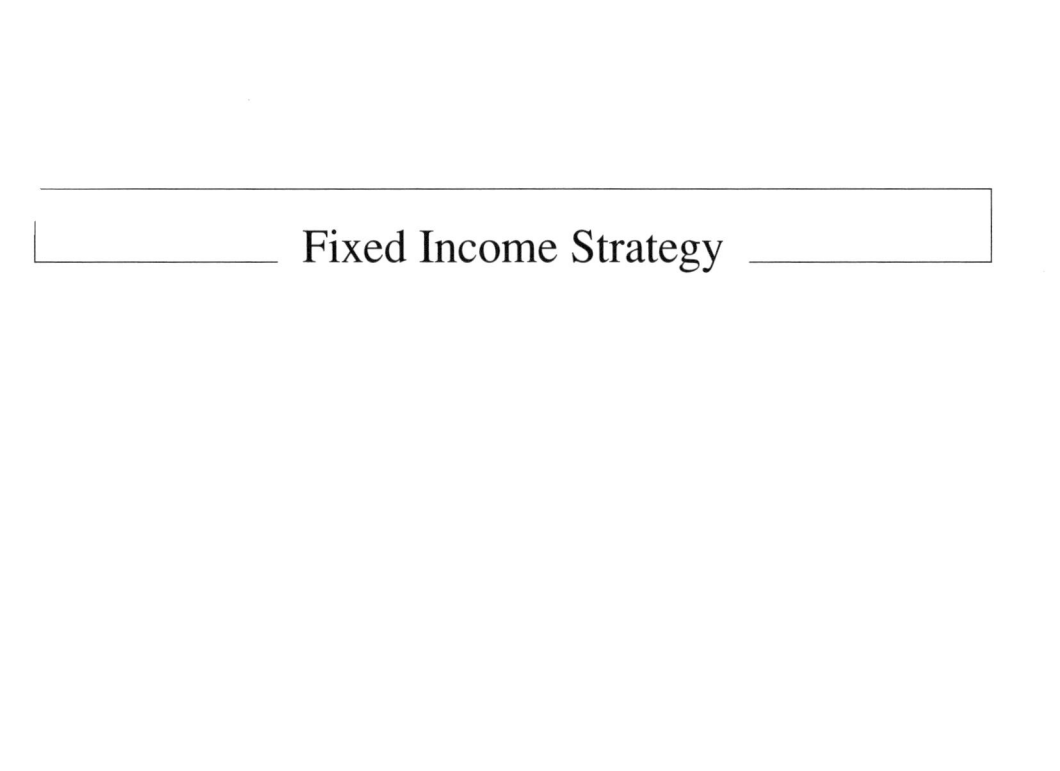

Fixed Income Strategy

Wiley Finance Series

Fixed Income Strategy: The Practitioner's Guide to Riding the Curve
Tamara Mast Henderson

Active Investment Management
Charles Jackson

Option Theory
Peter James

The Simple Rules of Risk: Revisiting the Art of Risk Management
Erik Banks

Capital Asset Investment: Strategy, Tactics and Tools
Anthony F. Herbst

Brand Assets
Tony Tollington

Swaps and other Derivatives
Richard Flavell

Currency Strategy: The Practitioner's Guide to Currency Trading, Hedging and Forecasting
Callum Henderson

The Investor's Guide to Economic Fundamentals
John Calverley

Measuring Market Risk
Kevin Dowd

An Introduction to Market Risk Management
Kevin Dowd

Behavioural Finance
James Montier

Asset Management: Equities Demystified
Shanta Acharya

An Introduction to Capital Markets: Products, Strategies, Participants
Andrew M Chisholm

Hedge Funds: Myths and Limits
Francois-Serge Lhabitant

The Manager's Concise Guide to Risk
Jihad S Nader

Securities Operations: A guide to trade and position management
Michael Simmons

Modeling, Measuring and Hedging Operational Risk
Marcelo Cruz

Monte Carlo Methods in Finance
Peter Jäckel

Building and Using Dynamic Interest Rate Models
Ken Kortanek and Vladimir Medvedev

Structured Equity Derivatives: The Definitive Guide to Exotic Options and Structured Notes
Harry Kat

Advanced Modelling in Finance Using Excel and VBA
Mary Jackson and Mike Staunton

Operational Risk: Measurement and Modelling
Jack King

Advance Credit Risk Analysis: Financial Approaches and Mathematical Models to Assess, Price and Manage Credit Risk
Didier Cossin and Hugues Pirotte

Interest Rate Modelling
Jessica James and Nick Webber

Volatility and Correlation in the Pricing of Equity, FX and Interest-Rate Options
Riccardo Rebonato

Risk Management and Analysis vol. 1: Measuring and Modelling Financial Risk
Carol Alexander (ed)

Risk Management and Analysis vol. 2: New Markets and Products
Carol Alexander (ed)

Interest-Rate Option Models: Understanding, Analysing and Using Models for Exotic Interest-Rate Options (second edition)
Riccardo Rebonato

Fixed Income Strategy

The Practitioner's Guide to Riding the Curve

Tamara Mast Henderson

WILEY

Copyright © 2003   John Wiley & Sons Ltd, The Atrium, Southern Gate, Chichester,
West Sussex PO19 8SQ, England

Telephone   (+44) 1243 779777

Email (for orders and customer service enquiries): cs-books@wiley.co.uk
Visit our Home Page on www.wileyeurope.com or www.wiley.com

All Rights Reserved. No part of this publication may be reproduced, stored in a retrieval system or transmitted in any form or by any means, electronic, mechanical, photocopying, recording, scanning or otherwise, except under the terms of the Copyright, Designs and Patents Act 1988 or under the terms of a licence issued by the Copyright Licensing Agency Ltd, 90 Tottenham Court Road, London W1T 4LP, UK, without the permission in writing of the Publisher. Requests to the Publisher should be addressed to the Permissions Department, John Wiley & Sons Ltd, The Atrium, Southern Gate, Chichester, West Sussex PO19 8SQ, England, or emailed to permreq@wiley.co.uk, or faxed to (+44) 1243 770620.

This publication is designed to provide accurate and authoritative information in regard to the subject matter covered. It is sold on the understanding that the Publisher is not engaged in rendering professional services. If professional advice or other expert assistance is required, the services of a competent professional should be sought.

Other Wiley Editorial Offices

John Wiley & Sons Inc., 111 River Street, Hoboken, NJ 07030, USA

Jossey-Bass, 989 Market Street, San Francisco, CA 94103-1741, USA

Wiley-VCH Verlag GmbH, Boschstr. 12, D-69469 Weinheim, Germany

John Wiley & Sons Australia Ltd, 33 Park Road, Milton, Queensland 4064, Australia

John Wiley & Sons (Asia) Pte Ltd, 2 Clementi Loop #02-01, Jin Xing Distripark, Singapore 129809

John Wiley & Sons Canada Ltd, 22 Worcester Road, Etobicoke, Ontario, Canada M9W 1L1

Wiley also publishes its books in a variety of electronic formats. Some content that appears in print may not be available in electronic books.

British Library Cataloguing in Publication Data

A catalogue record for this book is available from the British Library

ISBN 0-470-85063-9

Typeset in 10/12pt Times by TechBooks, New Delhi, India
Printed and bound in Great Britain by TJ International Ltd, Padstow, Cornwall, UK
This book is printed on acid-free paper responsibly manufactured from sustainable forestry in which at least two trees are planted for each one used for paper production.

To Callum

Contents

Acknowledgments	xi
Biography	xiii
Introduction	xv
PART I BASIC TOOLS FOR ESTABLISHING A FIXED INCOME STRATEGY	1

1 Fixed income basics — 3
  1.1 Pricing a bond — 3
  1.2 Market risk: The price–yield relationship — 5
  1.3 Yield curve risk: The yield–maturity relationship — 9
  1.4 Beyond theoretical value: Other sources of risk — 13
  1.5 Sources of return — 15
  1.6 Summary — 16
  Notes — 16
  Recommended reading — 17

2 Fixed Income Securities: Beyond the Basics — 19
  2.1 Spread risk: Evaluating bonds of different quality — 19
  2.2 Volatility risk: Evaluating bonds with embedded options — 21
  2.3 Interest rate derivatives — 27
    2.3.1 Futures — 27
    2.3.2 Options — 29
    2.3.3 Swaps — 32
  Notes — 36
  Recommended reading — 37

3 Economic Fundamentals — 39
  3.1 The building blocks of economic analysis — 39
  3.2 Interest rate theories: Forecasting market direction — 44
  3.3 Yield curve models: Forecasting movements in the yield curve — 50
  3.4 Spread theories: Anticipating changes in the risk premium — 54

3.5	Volatility models: Anticipating changes in volatility	57
3.6	The efficient markets hypothesis	58
3.7	Chaos theory	59
3.8	Economic fundamentals: Uses and misuses	60
Notes		61

PART II ENHANCED TOOLS FOR ESTABLISHING A VIEW ON INTEREST RATES — 63

4 Government policy: The interface between economics and politics — 65
- 4.1 The political economy perspective — 65
  - 4.1.1 Political business cycles — 65
  - 4.1.2 Budget deficits and monetary policy — 67
  - 4.1.3 Central bank independence — 68
  - 4.1.4 Policy objectives — 68
  - 4.1.5 The monetary policy mechanism — 69
- 4.2 Anticipating changes in monetary policy — 69
  - 4.2.1 Fed watching — 69
  - 4.2.2 ECB watching — 71
- 4.3 Implications for fixed income investors — 73
- Notes — 74
- Recommended reading — 75

5 Human Factors — 77
- 5.1 Group behavior: A demographic approach — 77
- 5.2 The inherently human nature of markets: A psychological approach — 83
  - 5.2.1 Information processing — 84
  - 5.2.2 Attitude and mood: The effect on risk tolerance and judgment — 88
  - 5.2.3 Social psychology: The herding phenomenon — 91
  - 5.2.4 Implications for fixed income investors — 94
  - 5.2.5 Limitations of the psychological approach — 96
- Notes — 96
- Recommended reading — 97
- Appendix: Summary of psychological phenomena — 98

6 Technical Analysis: Applied Social Psychology — 99
- 6.1 Fundamentalists versus technicians — 99
- 6.2 The basic tools of technical analysis — 100
- 6.3 The contrarian approach — 109
- 6.4 The "smart money" approach — 111
- 6.5 Implications for fixed income investors — 112
- 6.6 The limitations of technical analysis — 113
- Notes — 113
- Recommended reading — 114

7 Other Techniques for Short-Term Analysis — 115
- 7.1 Flow analysis — 115

7.2	Supply and demand analysis	118
7.3	Seasonal analysis	120
7.4	Quantitative analysis	121
7.5	The limitations of statistical methods	125
	Notes	126

8 An Integrated Approach to Bond Strategy — 127

8.1	An interdisciplinary model	127
8.2	The appropriate use of tools	130
8.3	Resolving mixed signals	132
8.4	Evaluating downside risk	133
8.5	System checks	133
8.6	A template for constructing a view on which to trade	135
8.7	Limitations of the interdisciplinary approach	137
	Notes	137
	Recommended reading	138

PART III IMPLEMENTING YOUR VIEW — 139

9 Fixed Income Instruments, Investors and Portfolio Management Styles — 141

9.1	The fixed income universe	141
	9.1.1 Government securities	142
	9.1.2 Corporate securities	144
	9.1.3 Structured securities	145
	9.1.4 Fixed income derivatives	146
	9.1.5 Structured products	147
	9.1.6 Country and currency considerations	148
9.2	Investor types	149
9.3	Portfolio management	153
	9.3.1 Passive portfolio management	154
	9.3.2 Structured portfolio management (asset–liability management or ALM)	155
	9.3.3 Active portfolio management	156
	Notes	160
	Recommended reading	161

10 Fixed Income Trading — 163

10.1	Market directional bets	163
10.2	Yield curve bets: Steepeners and flatteners	165
10.3	Yield curve bets: Rising and falling curvature	167
10.4	Spread bets	169
10.5	Volatility bets	171
10.6	Summary	172
	Notes	174
	Appendix: Bullets, barbells, and butterflies	175

11	**Odds and Ends**	**177**
	11.1 Asset allocation	177
	11.2 Individual bond selection	179
	11.3 Leverage	180
	11.4 Risk management	180
	11.5 Strategy management	182
	Notes	183
	Recommended reading	183
12	**Survival Principles for the Financial Battlefield**	**185**
	12.1 Six pearls of wisdom	185
	12.2 Concluding remarks	187
Bibliography		**189**
Index		**195**

Acknowledgments

This book in many ways reflects the journey of my life, which has had the benefit of many teachers and supporters along the way. I am particularly indebted to my parents, and to the late Abner Sachs, Tom Willett, Benedicte Vibe Christensen, and Rachael Wilkie – all of whom had pivotal roles at key junctures. Many dear friends have accompanied me along this journey, no matter where it has led, offering tireless encouragement, humor and hugs. I have also had the privilege of working with an amazing group of supervisors and colleagues throughout my career. Thank you for your wisdom, inspiration, and thoughtfulness.

This project has benefited from the input of many individuals, some of whom preferred to remain anonymous. Mohamed El-Erian, Amer Bisat, and Tsuyoshi Fukui introduced me to a number of the concepts presented here, well before there was any inkling about writing a book. Robert Minikin and Rashique Rahman patiently responded to numerous rounds of endless questions and provided comments on draft material. Karl Massey provided key insights on trading and the significance of the motivations behind the flows. Rob Drijkoningen, Bea Groeger, Robert McAdie and Wilfried Schnedler also took time from their busy schedules to participate in interviews.

Everett Brown, Howard Friend, Darrene Hackler, Tracey Johnson, and Truman Mast provided valuable comments on portions of earlier drafts. Callum Henderson and Orlando Roncesvalles were kind enough to go through the entire manuscript. Frances Phillips and her team at Connaught Communications provided superb editorial support on the full manuscript. Bill Goldy and Glyn Bradney at Reuters and Chris Manuell at IDEAglobal graciously provided the technical charts. Chris Swain, Samantha Hartley and Alex Whyte at Wiley did a fantastic job of transforming this project into a book. I would also like to thank Alan Brown and Peter Smith for their reviews.

Last but not least, I owe my deepest gratitude to my husband, Callum. This project would not have gotten off the ground, nor would it have stayed off the ground, if not for his unwavering encouragement, advice, and patience. Callum is not just my soulmate in life, but his character, dedication, and hard work are a daily inspiration to push for more and gut it out. Thank you.

Biography

The author is a senior fixed income strategist for a leading provider of independent research and market analysis, responsible for European sovereign debt. Ahead of this, Dr. Henderson was deputy head of the International Monetary Fund's Investment Unit, responsible for the management of $11 billion in trust funds. Henderson has also worked as an economist for the US Department of Commerce, IMF and Salomon Smith Barney. She has a B.A. in Foreign Affairs and Economics from the University of Virginia, and a M.A. and Ph.D in Economics from Claremont Graduate University.

Introduction

There are, of course, numerous books on the subject of fixed income, so why write one more? The answer is simple. The vast majority focus solely on fixed income theory; this book, on the other hand, merges theory with the reality of the trading room. It is an attempt to address the needs of practitioners who find themselves frustrated by either the theorists or the alchemists, or both. Whether you are on the buy-side or the sell-side, or whether you are a pension fund or a proprietary trader, this book should provide you with specific insights that help you to do your job better.

The book is targeted at fixed income practitioners: (1) those who *develop* fixed income strategies (economists, analysts, and strategists); (2) those who *implement* strategies (asset managers and traders); and, ultimately, (3) those who *benefit* from the strategies (individuals, corporates, and governments). Hence, the focus is on building a view on interest rates and creating trades that capitalize on that view – all while being mindful of the objectives and risk tolerance of the particular practitioner. That said, non-practitioners may also find this book useful as a starting point to guide more focused studies or as an overview to fixed income investment.

Also mindful of the audience, the style of the book is abbreviated to minimize unnecessary repetition and to manage a vast amount of knowledge in a practical way (i.e. to avoid losing the forest for the trees). Inevitably, such a project is a delicate balancing act between simplification and detail. The aim is to focus on the essential aspects of the theoretical tools – the *critical thinking* – so that there is a clear and practical understanding of the nature of risks and returns in fixed income investment.

The purpose of this book is to bridge the different worlds of theoretical models and practical market experience, while at the same time to offer an interdisciplinary framework for fixed income investing and trading. The building blocks of finance and economics are used as a starting point, upon which other tools – drawing from politics, demography, psychology, and various forms of technical analysis – are incorporated to construct a comprehensive, but also utilitarian, framework. It should be understood that this book is not intended to be a substitute for the vast literature that is referenced within. Instead, the book seeks to extract the applicable "gemstones" from each discipline and combine them in such a way that the whole is more powerful than the sum of its individual parts. For readers seeking more details about the underlying models or empirical research, ample references are provided.

Models, no matter the discipline, are constructed as a necessary simplification of the "real" world. Some simplifications are more problematic than others, depending on the application.

For example, a fundamental assumption of economics is that individuals seek to "maximize utility". However, economics stops short of explaining what utility means for each individual – the explanation of how preferences are formed is left to other disciplines such as politics, sociology and psychology. The theoretical link between economics and politics is long established, but the link with psychology is relatively new.

The "real world" relevance of the gap between economics and psychology can be illustrated by the notorious collapse of Long-Term Capital Management (LTCM) in 1998. LTCM was a hedge fund run by the supreme of the super analysts, including *two Nobel Prize winners* in economics (Robert Merton and Myron Scholes) and *the architect of fixed income arbitrage* (John Meriwether).[1] The strategies employed by LTCM were based on the most sophisticated of financial models but were implemented in a way that failed to appreciate the real world behavioral aspects of market dynamics – greed, fear, and panic. Recognizing the limits of purely financial models, attention has turned toward behavioral influences. In fact, a 2002 Nobel Prize in Economics was awarded to a psychologist – Daniel Kahneman, a pioneer in the discipline of behavioral finance.

Interest rate movements are crucial for fixed income investors. However, economists have yet to develop a model of interest rates that has explanatory power across all time periods and markets. Although models have proven generally useful for explaining long-term trends, market practitioners require guidelines that are more suitable for short-term dynamics. Lacking guidance from economics in the short-term, some investors rely on various types of technical analysis. Others simply rely on "gut" instinct.

The book is divided into three sections, progressing from theory to practice. The first task in constructing a fixed income strategy is to assemble the relevant analytical tools, along with an explicit understanding of their power and limitations. Part I discusses essential concepts taken from finance and economics, which provide the foundation of our interdisciplinary framework. The financial concepts discussed in Chapters 1 and 2 illustrate the relationship between risk and return for a spectrum of fixed income securities. The economic principles discussed in Chapter 3 illustrate the transmission mechanisms at work in the macro-economy which underpin long-term trends in interest rates.

In Part II, we temporarily abandon "the fundamentals" in search of additional analytical tools that can be useful in understanding what drives short-term movements in interest rates. Chapter 4 illustrates the effect of politics on economic outcomes. Chapter 5 examines how the behavioral biases of individuals and groups can lead to systematic errors that produce deviations from fundamental trends. The discipline of technical analysis is introduced in Chapter 6, including qualitative as well as quantitative tools to evaluate trends. Chapter 7 illustrates various other quantitative techniques that can be used to anticipate market movements and value fixed income securities. In Chapter 8, the principle of diversification – a fundamental building block of portfolio theory – is applied to the construction of an interdisciplinary model aimed at anticipating fixed income investment opportunities.

Part III turns theory into practice. The implementation of a fixed income strategy begins with the evaluation of alternative investment instruments and strategies – the subject of Chapter 9. Strategies are activated by taking positions and then managed over the course of the investment horizon. Chapter 10 details how positions (or bets) are established on market direction, the yield curve, spreads, and volatility. Chapter 11 discusses asset allocation, security selection, leverage, and risk management, and Chapter 12, the concluding Chapter, presents six principles of survival for the financial battlefield.

---

[1] Robert C. Merton and Myron Scholes were awarded the Nobel prize in 1997 for their work on option pricing.

I thank you for your interest, and truly hope that my attempt at unraveling the complexities of fixed income investment proves useful to you. All constructive feedback is welcomed at my e-mail address, fistrategy2003@aol.com.

Tamara Mast Henderson
London

Part I
Basic Tools for Establishing a Fixed Income Strategy

The fixed income investment process essentially boils down to setting objectives and managing risks. Part I lays the foundation for constructing a strategy to achieve objectives and manage risks. Within this section, Chapter 1 clarifies the nature of risk and return associated with simple bonds, Chapter 2 tackles more complex fixed income instruments, while Chapter 3 presents key economic relationships that have implications for interest rate behavior – the key source of risk and return in fixed income investment. The point here is not to reiterate every detail of fixed income mathematics or economic theory, but to highlight the key structural mechanisms of finance and economics. Specific nuances are, of course, important to practitioners; however, they are left to other references as the requirements of each investor are quite specific.

1
Fixed Income Basics

Over the years, fixed income investment has become increasingly complex. Irrespective of the specific characteristics of a particular fixed income instrument, it is crucial that practitioners do not lose sight of the risks undertaken – which, after all, have a large bearing on the returns that are generated. Just as essential, is knowing how to measure these risks and being able to differentiate the various components of return. Abstracting from details such as the issuer or structure of a specific security,[1] this chapter sticks to generic, but essential concepts – price, risks to price, and components of return – all with vital implications for strategy. Strategy is, after all, about the management of risk for the purpose of generating an attractive return.

Before diving into the subject, it is first useful to distinguish fixed income from other asset classes. In the investment world, a primary distinction is made between fixed income and equities. Fixed income represents securitized debt instruments, involving the payment of interest in compensation for the use of borrowed funds. In contrast, equities represent shares of ownership, where the payment of dividends to shareholders is at the discretion of management. In the event of bankruptcy, holders of corporate debt have higher priority in the claim on assets of a firm than holders of equity.

1.1 PRICING A BOND

The value of an asset is logically linked to the income stream generated by that asset. Allowing for the time value of money – the fact that we require compensation for postponing consumption – the value *today* of an income stream in the *future* is equivalent to the sum of the discounted cash flows.

For a bond, future cash flows consist of coupon (i.e. interest) payments over the life of the bond and the repayment of principal at maturity. Equation 1.1 illustrates the theoretical price of a bond with a 3-year maturity. The future cash flows received by the bond holder are discounted using the interest rate (r) for the corresponding period ($t = 1, 2,$ and 3).[2] The coupon, term, and face value are fixed, as specified in the bond indenture.

Equation 1.1 Theoretical price of a 3-year bond

$$\text{Bond price} = \frac{\text{Coupon}_1}{(1+r_1)} + \frac{\text{Coupon}_2}{(1+r_2)^2} + \frac{\text{Coupon}_3}{(1+r_3)^3} + \frac{\text{Face value}}{(1+r_3)^3}$$

It is quite evident from Equation 1.1 that the value of the bond is affected by unanticipated changes in interest rates, and that the bond price is inversely related to the change in interest rates. That is, increases in interest rates reduce the value of the bond, while reductions in rates increase the value of the bond.

Moreover, the bond price is affected by the size of the coupon and the term to maturity. Larger coupons enhance price, while longer terms reduce the present value of the bond. Bonds with larger coupons are less sensitive to changes in interest rates, whereas bonds with longer maturities are more sensitive to changes in interest rates. This is best illustrated by example.

Example 1.1 – Coupon size and interest rate sensitivity

If Bond A has a maturity of 3 years, a coupon of 5% and interest rates are expected to be 8% in year 1, 9% in year 2, and 10% in year 3 – the theoretical bond price is 87.73 (based on a par value of 100).[3] If actual interest rates are 100 basis points (bps) higher than expected – 9%, 10%, and 11% respectively over the next 3 years – the price of Bond A would fall to 85.49 – a decrease of 2.61%. Now consider Bond B which has the same 3-year term, but a coupon twice as large. Under the same interest rate scenario, the price of Bond B would fall from 100.32 to 97.87 – a decrease of 2.50%.

Table 1.1 Coupon size and market risk

	Forecast	Actual (+100 bps)
Bond A:	$R_1 = 8\%$	$R_1 = 9\%$
Coupon 5%, $T = 3$	$R_2 = 9\%$	$R_2 = 10\%$
	$R_3 = 10\%$	$R_3 = 11\%$
Price	87.73	85.49 (−2.61%)[4]
Bond B:	$R_1 = 8\%$	$R_1 = 9\%$
Coupon 10%, $T = 3$	$R_2 = 9\%$	$R_2 = 10\%$
	$R_3 = 10\%$	$R_3 = 11\%$
Price	100.32	97.87 (−2.50%)

Example 1.2 – Term and interest rate sensitivity

If Bond C has a maturity of 2 years, a coupon of 5% and interest rates are forecasted at 8% in year 1 and 9% in year 2 – the theoretical bond price is 93.01 (based on a par value of 100). If interest rates actually rise 100 bps to 9% in year 1 and to 10% in year 2, the price of Bond C would fall to 91.36 – a decrease of 1.80% compared to 2.61% for Bond A in Example 1.1. Now consider Bond D which has the same 2-year term, but a larger coupon of 10%. Under the same interest rate scenario, the price of Bond D would fall from 101.84 to 100.08 – a decrease of 1.76% compared to 2.50% for Bond B in Example 1.1.

Taken together, Examples 1.1 and 1.2 demonstrate the tendency for the price of a bond to be "pulled to par" as the bond approaches maturity. That is, the price of a bond valued at a discount to par will rise as it approaches maturity. Conversely, the price of a bond valued at a premium to par will fall as it approaches maturity. Again with the help of Equation 1.1, one can see that the future bond price equals the par value at maturity – as the relevant interest rate at that point in time is zero.

It should now be clear that bonds with smaller coupons and longer maturities are more sensitive to a given change in interest rates. As such, if interest rates are expected to fall we

Table 1.2 Maturity and market risk

	Forecast	Actual (+100 bps)
Bond C: Coupon 5%, $T=2$	$R_1 = 8\%$ $R_2 = 9\%$	$R_1 = 9\%$ $R_2 = 10\%$
Price	93.01	91.36 (−1.80%)
Bond D: Coupon 10%, $T=2$	$R_1 = 8\%$ $R_2 = 9\%$	$R_1 = 9\%$ $R_2 = 10\%$
Price	101.84	100.08 (−1.76%)

would prefer bonds with smaller coupons and longer maturities (i.e. those with the largest price sensitivity) in order to maximize our potential capital gain. Similarly, if interest rates are expected to rise, we would prefer bonds with larger coupons and shorter maturities (i.e. those with the smallest price sensitivity) in order to minimize our potential capital loss.

In cases where one must choose between bonds with mixed characteristics – such as bonds with smaller coupons as well as shorter maturities – a more summary measure of interest rate risk is required. We shall address such considerations in the next section.

1.2 MARKET RISK: THE PRICE–YIELD RELATIONSHIP

> **Yield → Price**

Interest rate risk (also known as market risk) is the risk that interest rates will rise, thereby decreasing the value of a bond. Graphically, market risk is represented by the slope of the price–yield relationship. As we saw in the previous section, the slope is negative – that is, the price of a bond is inversely related to movements in interest rates. In general, the relationship between price and yield is curvilinear (convex) as opposed to linear. In other words, the sensitivity of the bond price to changes in interest rates varies depending on the level of interest rates.

Figure 1.1 illustrates the price–yield relationship for two bonds with the same 5% coupon rate, but different maturities (3 years versus 30 years). Note that the bond with the 3-year maturity is more linear, while the bond with the 30-year maturity is more convex. Generally, bonds with longer maturities (beyond 10 years) are more convex, while short-term bonds exhibit little convexity.

Figure 1.2 illustrates the price–yield relationship for two bonds with the same 10-year maturity, but different coupons (10% versus 5%). The bond with the larger coupon is more convex than the bond with the smaller coupon. Generally, bonds with higher coupons have greater convexity.

The price–yield relationship is curvilinear because the coupons paid to the bond holder over the life of the bond are reinvested, earning interest on interest. Intuitively, the magnitude of the compounded interest depends positively on the size of the coupons and the period of time for which the coupons are reinvested.

Figures 1.1 and 1.2 also illustrate how convexity is larger at very low yields and at very high yields. As such, convexity varies depending on the magnitude of change in interest rates.

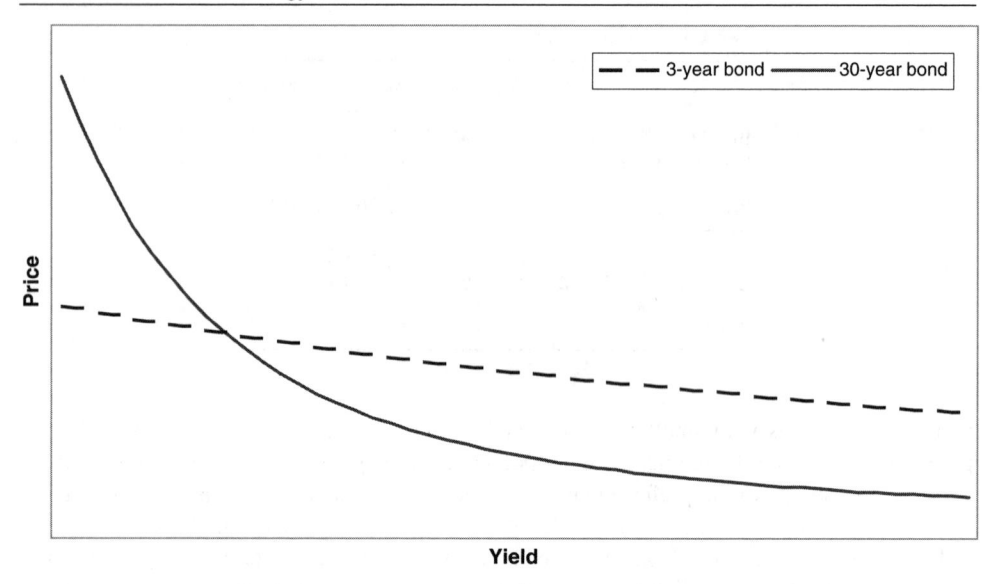

Figure 1.1 The price–yield relationship for bonds with different maturities

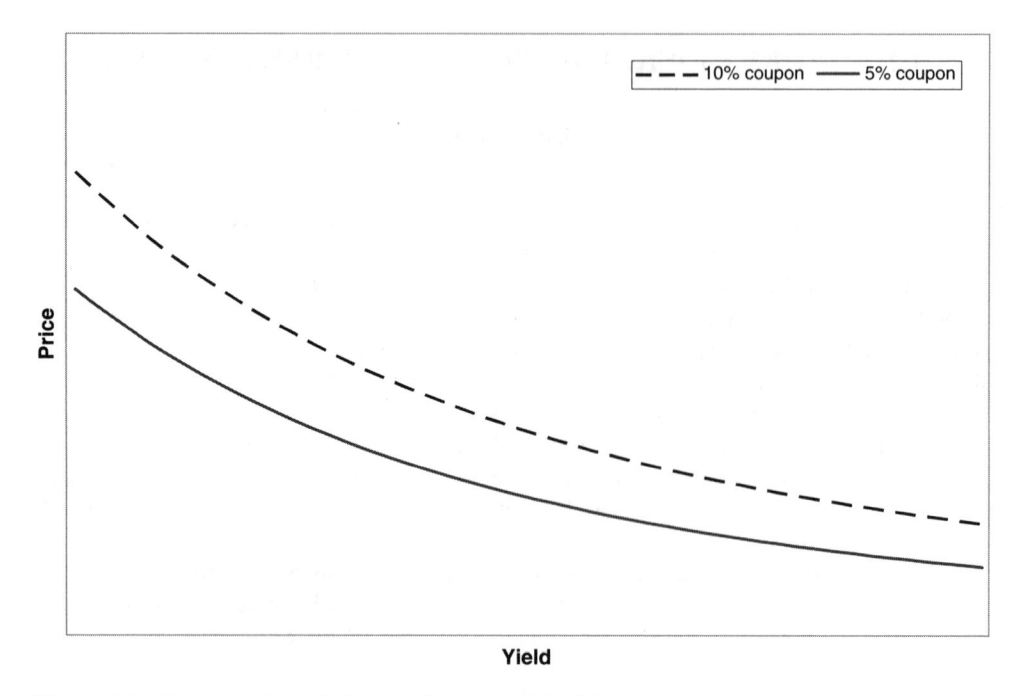

Figure 1.2 The price–yield relationship for bonds with different coupons

By implication, highly convex bonds are more valuable in volatile interest rate environments. Like anything of value, the market charges for convexity in the form of a higher price and lower yield. So, ultimately, the benefit of convexity depends on how much yields actually change.[5]

The Measurement of Market Risk

Duration is a summary measure of maturity, coupon, and yield effects that is used to approximate interest rate risk. A bond with a larger coupon and yield has lower duration, while a bond with a longer maturity has higher duration. Bonds with lower duration are less sensitive to changes in yield, while bonds with higher duration are more sensitive to changes in yield.[6]

There are a number of ways to represent duration.[7] For intuitive as well as practical reasons, the focus here is on modified duration – defined as the percentage change in bond price for a 1% (100 bps) change in yield. In mathematical terms, modified duration is the first derivative of the price–yield relationship.

Equation 1.2 shows an approximation of modified duration calculated as the average impact $((P^- - P^+) \div 2)$ from a given change in yield (ΔY) on the initial value of the bond (P_0). The price that results from an increase in yield the size of ΔY, (P^+), and the price that results from a decrease in yield the size of ΔY, (P^-), are calculated using a valuation model based on a given change in interest rates (e.g. if the given change in interest rates is 100 bps, $\Delta Y = 0.01$). Even though price and yield have a negative relationship, in practice duration is represented as a positive number.

Equation 1.2 An approximation for modified duration

$$\text{Modified duration} \cong (P^- - P^+) \div (2P_0(\Delta Y))$$

Note that duration remains constant for different levels of interest rates. In other words, duration assumes a linear relationship between interest rates and bond prices. Since the actual price–yield relationship is curvilinear (i.e. interest rate risk varies depending on the level of interest rates), duration is only an *approximation* of the true interest rate risk of a bond (Figure 1.3). As such, duration is not an appropriate measure of market risk for large changes in yield.

Because duration is a linear approximation of the convex relationship between price and yield, duration overstates the fall in the bond price when interest rates rise. Similarly, duration understates the rise in the bond price when interest rates fall. In other words, convexity leads to higher profits and smaller losses.[8] For large movements in yields, the underestimation of profits and the overestimation of losses is the greatest. Hence, convexity is highly valued when interest rate volatility is high. Conversely, when there is no volatility, convexity has no value.

Particularly in volatile interest rate environments, duration is an inadequate measure of interest rate risk. The adjustment to account for convexity is shown in Equation 1.3. As before, P_0 is the initial value of the bond and ΔY represents a 100 bps change in yield. The price that results from a 100 bps increase in yield (P^+) and the price that results from a 100 bps decrease in yield (P^-) are calculated using a valuation model. In mathematical terms, convexity is the second derivative of the price–yield relationship. That is, the change in duration for a given change in yield.

Equation 1.3 An approximation for convexity

$$\text{Convexity} \cong (P^- + P^+ - 2P_0) \div (P_0(\Delta Y)^2)$$

Equation 1.4 presents a close approximation of the true interest rate risk, consisting of both duration and convexity components. Note that there is a sign change as interest rates and bond

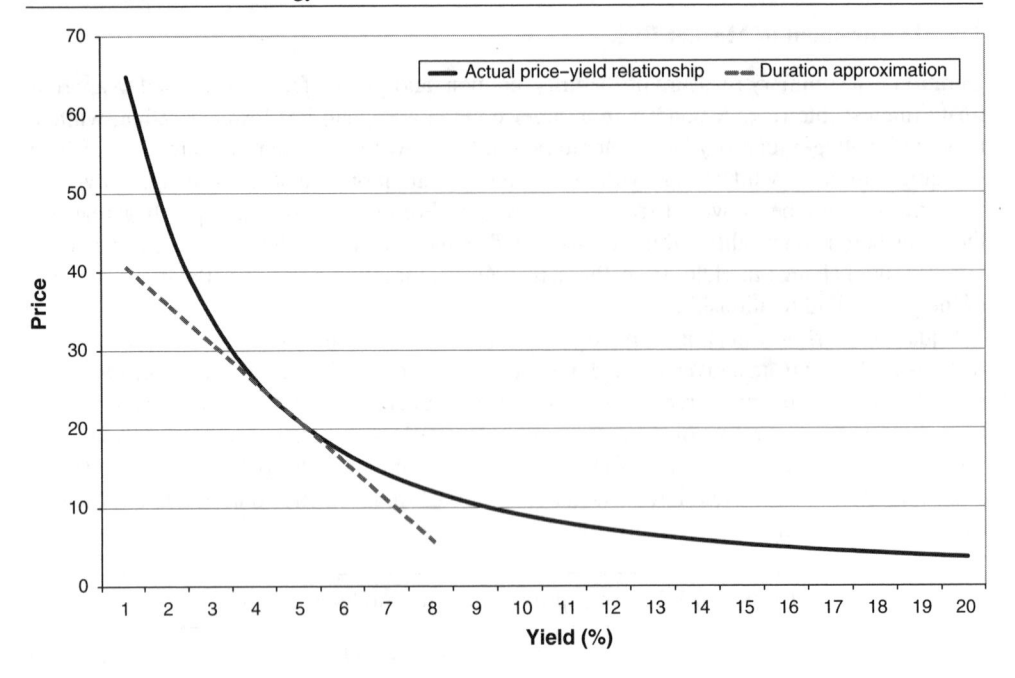

Figure 1.3 Duration versus convexity

prices have an inverse relationship. In a stable interest rate environment, the convexity effect (shown in Equation 1.5) can be removed.

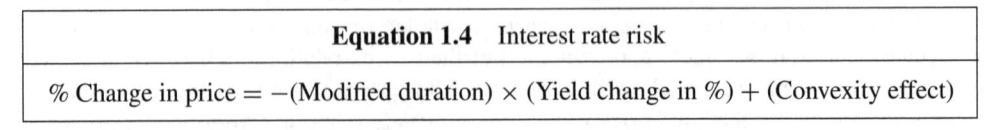

Equation 1.4 Interest rate risk

% Change in price = $-$(Modified duration) $\times$ (Yield change in %) + (Convexity effect)

Equation 1.5 The convexity effect

% Change in price due to convexity alone = $\frac{1}{2} \times$ Convexity $\times$ (Yield change in %)^2

Implications for Strategy

Duration strategies attempt to capitalize on expected increases/decreases in interest rates, while convexity strategies are based on changes in volatility. A position in a long-term bond is long duration and long convexity (i.e. long volatility).

- Duration approximates interest rate sensitivity. Hence, increase duration if interest rates are expected to fall, and reduce duration when interest rates are expected to rise. Longer duration bonds have lower coupons and longer maturities.
- Convexity is highly valued during periods of highly volatile interest rates. Hence, shift to bonds with higher convexity if interest rate volatility is expected to rise, and shift to bonds with lower convexity when interest rate volatility is expected to fall. Highly convex bonds tend to have maturities beyond 10 years.

- When uncertain about the direction of interest rate movements (or you agree with market expectations), maintain a neutral duration position relative to the targeted benchmark. The market risk of bonds with different durations can be equalized by adjusting the weights of the bonds in the overall portfolio.[9]

Even if two portfolios have the same degree of market risk (i.e. they are "duration neutral"), their relative performance may differ considerably. The key is the spacing of the maturity of the bonds held in the two portfolios and what happens to the yield curve. In other words, the difference in performance will depend upon the exposure to yield curve risk.

1.3 YIELD CURVE RISK: THE YIELD–MATURITY RELATIONSHIP

$$\text{Maturity} \rightarrow \text{Yield} \rightarrow \text{Price}$$

The yield curve – also known as the term structure of interest rates – illustrates the relationship between the yield and maturity of bonds with the same credit quality.[10] There are four classic yield curve shapes:

- *Rising (normal):* Yields rise continuously, with some reduction in the rate of increase at longer maturities.
- *Falling (inverted):* Yields decline over the entire maturity range.
- *Flat:* Yields are unaffected by maturity.
- *Humped:* Yields initially rise, but then peak and decline.

The shape of the yield curve has important implications for the performance of a bond portfolio. Yield curve risk is the risk that an unanticipated shift in the curve will reduce the value of the bond portfolio. Exposure to yield curve risk depends on the spacing of the maturity of bonds within a portfolio. Before considering different types of yield curve shifts and their effect on the performance of a bond portfolio, it is useful to see how the shape of the yield curve can affect the performance of a single bond.

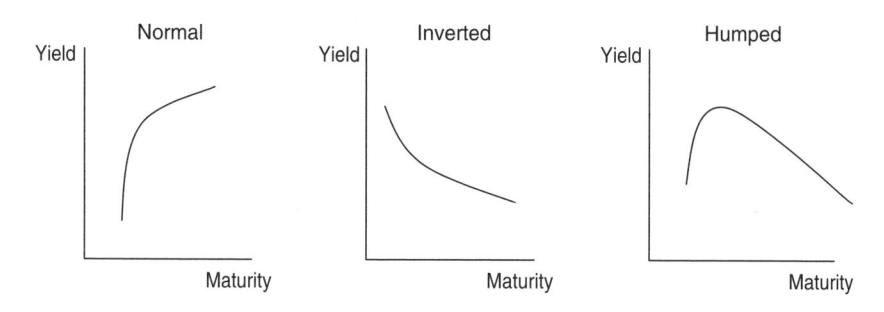

Figure 1.4 Classic yield curve shapes

The examples in Section 1.1 assumed that the yield curve had a normal rising shape and that the unforeseen rise in interest rates resulted in a parallel shift in the yield curve. Table 1.3 summarizes the effect of a 100 bps increase in interest rates on the price of Bond A using different assumptions for the shape of the yield curve.

Table 1.3 Performance and yield curve shape[11]

Bond A	Forecast	Actual (+100 bps)
Rising yield curve Coupon 5%, $T=3$	$R_1 = 8\%$ $R_2 = 9\%$ $R_3 = 10\%$	$R_1 = 9\%$ $R_2 = 10\%$ $R_3 = 11\%$
Price	87.73	85.49 (−2.61%)
Flat yield curve Coupon 5%, $T=3$	$R_1 = 8\%$ $R_2 = 8\%$ $R_3 = 8\%$	$R_1 = 9\%$ $R_2 = 9\%$ $R_3 = 9\%$
Price	92.27	89.87 (−2.66%)
Falling yield curve Coupon 5%, $T=3$	$R_1 = 8\%$ $R_2 = 7\%$ $R_3 = 6\%$	$R_1 = 9\%$ $R_2 = 8\%$ $R_3 = 7\%$
Price	97.16	94.59 (−2.72%)

A parallel shift of the yield curve in a rising yield curve environment produces a 2.61% decline in the value of Bond A, while the same shift in a falling yield curve environment produces a 2.72% decline in value. The pure market risk associated with a 100 bps rate increase is 2.66% – that associated with a parallel shift of a flat yield curve. The pure yield curve risk of the bond is derived by netting out the market risk – in this case, +5 bps with a rising yield curve and −6 bps with a falling yield curve.

Thus far, we have only considered parallel shifts in the yield curve – that is, when yields across the entire curve move by the same magnitude. In most cases, however, yield curve shifts are non-parallel – that is, movements in short-, intermediate- and long-term rates are not in sync. Non-parallel shifts are characterized by either twists (i.e. steepening or flattening) or butterfly movements. In a study of yield curve shifts during the period 1979–1990, Jones (1991) found that the two most common types of movements were: (1) a downward shift combined with steepening; and (2) an upward shift combined with flattening.

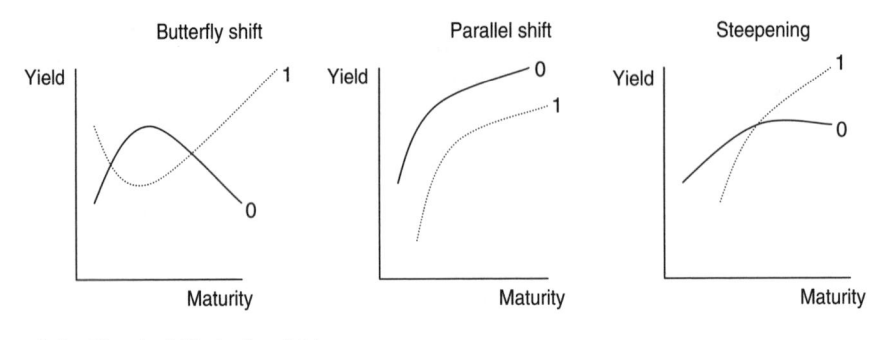

Figure 1.5 Classic shifts in the yield curve

Curve flattening/steepening means that the spread between the yields at the longer and shorter ends of the curve has decreased/increased. A standard measure of steepness is the spread between the 10- and 2-year yields. However, other spreads are also used (2s/30s, 10s/30s, or 2s/5s), depending on the application. The effect on performance of an unanticipated steepening

Table 1.4 Performance with steepening

Bond A	Forecast	Actual (+100 bps, 1s/3s spread)
Base case: Parallel shift Coupon 5%, $T = 3$	$R_1 = 8\%$ $R_2 = 8\%$ $R_3 = 8\%$	$R_1 = 9\%$ $R_2 = 9\%$ $R_3 = 9\%$
Price	92.27	89.87 (−2.66%)
Steepening scenario 1 Coupon 5%, $T = 3$	$R_1 = 8\%$ $R_2 = 8\%$ $R_3 = 8\%$	$R_1 = 8\%$ $R_2 = 8\%$ $R_3 = 9\%$
Price	92.27	90.00 (−2.53%)
Steepening scenario 2 Coupon 5%, $T = 3$	$R_1 = 8\%$ $R_2 = 8\%$ $R_3 = 8\%$	$R_1 = 8\%$ $R_2 = 9\%$ $R_3 = 9\%$
Price	92.27	89.92 (−2.62%)

Table 1.5 Performance with butterfly shifts

Bond A	Forecast	Actual (0 bps avg change)
Positive butterfly shift Coupon 5%, $T = 3$	$R_1 = 8\%$ $R_2 = 8\%$ $R_3 = 8\%$	$R_1 = 9\%$ $R_2 = 6\%$ $R_3 = 9\%$
Price	92.27	90.12 (−2.39%)
Negative butterfly shift Coupon 5%, $T = 3$	$R_1 = 8\%$ $R_2 = 8\%$ $R_3 = 8\%$	$R_1 = 7\%$ $R_2 = 10\%$ $R_3 = 7\%$
Price	92.27	94.52 (+2.38%)

or flattening in the curve will also depend on the behavior of interim interest rates, and is best illustrated by an example.

Let's return again to Bond A, which has a 3-year maturity and 5% coupon. In this example, curve steepening can occur in two ways, as the yield shift may occur in period 2 or period 3. Table 1.4 shows the effect of a 100 bps of steepening in our short yield curve. For Bond A, curve steepening improves performance by 4–13 bps, depending on the particular steepening scenario. In this case, the yield curve effect offsets some of the exposure to market risk.

Butterfly shifts in the yield curve may be positive or negative. A positive butterfly shift occurs when intermediate rates fall while the rates at the two ends of the yield curve rise. A negative butterfly shift occurs when intermediate rates rise while the rates at the two ends fall.

The effect of butterfly shifts on the performance of Bond A is illustrated in Table 1.5. The butterfly shifts have been selected such that, on an average basis, there is no market bias. Nevertheless, the positive butterfly shift selected in the example worsens the performance of Bond A by 239 bps, while the selected negative butterfly shift *improves* performance by 238 bps. In this case, the positive butterfly shift has the potential to almost double the losses associated with a 100 bps increase in interest rates (−239 versus −266). On the other hand, the negative butterfly shift has the potential to neutralize all but 28 bps ($-28 = +238 - 266$) of the risk from a 100 bps increase in interest rates.

These specific examples demonstrate the powerful influence that different yield curve shifts can have on the performance of a single bond.[12] The yield curve has similar implications for a portfolio of bonds. Just as a single bond will perform quite differently depending on how the yield curve shifts, two bond portfolios can perform quite differently. The relative performance of bond portfolios will depend on the maturity spacing of the bonds held and on the type of yield curve shift.

The maturity spacing of bonds within a portfolio affects the portfolio's sensitivity to yield curve risk. In the case of a portfolio that consists entirely of securities maturing in one year, over a 1-year investment horizon the value of this portfolio is not sensitive to shifts in the yield curve because all the securities will have matured at the end of the horizon.

In sharp contrast, a portfolio that consists entirely of securities maturing in 15 years will be highly exposed to yield curve risk because at the end of the 1-year investment horizon, the value of the portfolio will depend on the yield offered on 14-year securities. Intuitively, a portfolio that is equally divided between 1- and 15-year securities will have half the sensitivity to yield curve movements as the portfolio consisting entirely of 15-year securities.

Even if two portfolios have the same exposure to market risk, performance can be quite different depending on the change in the yield curve. For example, consider two portfolios with the same duration (Table 1.6). The first portfolio – the bullet portfolio – consists of a single security that pays a yield of 8%. The second portfolio – the barbell portfolio – consists of two equally weighted securities paying yields of 2% and 10%, respectively.

Because the two portfolios have different convexity, they will perform differently even if there is a parallel shift in the yield curve. Even though the yield of the bullet portfolio is larger than the yield of the barbell portfolio, the barbell portfolio has the potential to deliver better performance when yields change because it has larger convexity. A barbell portfolio is more convex than a duration-matched bullet portfolio (i.e. it has a convexity advantage) because the barbell has a wider dispersion of cash flows.[13]

Just as it is not enough to know the relative yield, duration, and convexity when assessing whether to buy a bond, it is not enough to know the relative yield, duration, and convexity when assessing whether to buy a bullet or barbell. Whether for a bond or a portfolio of bonds, the answer depends on the potential magnitude of the shift in the yield curve and on the potential change in the shape of the curve.

Table 1.6 Portfolio performance

	Security				Portfolio		
	Yield	Duration	Convexity		Yield	Duration	Convexity
Bond 1	8%	5	1	Bullet	8%	5	1
Bond 2	2%	1	0	Barbell	6%	5	1.5[14]
Bond 3	10%	9	3				

The Measurement of Yield Curve Risk

In contrast to market risk (which is associated with parallel shifts in the yield curve), yield curve risk is associated with non-parallel shifts – that is, changes in the shape of the yield curve.

Bond holdings distributed along the yield curve (in contrast to the distribution of a benchmark portfolio) are especially important when yield curve shapes are frequently variable or when changes in shape are of substantial magnitude. Even in the analysis of returns for a single point on the curve, no dimension is more important than the maturity dimension, particularly in a volatile interest rate environment.

There are three primary techniques used to measure yield curve risk: (1) spot duration (i.e. modified duration); (2) partial or key rate duration (i.e. "bucket" duration); and (3) directional duration (i.e. weighted average duration). *Modified duration*, which is essentially an average of all the partial durations along the curve, only immunizes a portfolio against parallel shifts in the yield curve. We also know from Section 1.2 that duration-neutral portfolios do not protect against large shifts in the yield curve.[15]

The sensitivity of a portfolio to non-parallel shifts in the yield curve can be quantified by calculating a set of *partial* or key *rate durations*[16] for specific points on the yield curve. Partial duration is defined as the percentage change in price for a 100 bps yield movement in a particular maturity segment while the remainder of the yield curve remains constant. Although the use of partial duration immunizes a portfolio against non-parallel shifts in the curve, it is difficult to calculate and costly to implement.

Directional duration immunizes much – but not all – of a portfolio against non-parallel movements in the yield curve. Intuitively, directional duration combines the concepts of partial rate and modified duration. Although directional duration does not fully immunize against yield curve risk, it is not as difficult or as costly as partial duration to implement.

Implications for Strategy

Yield curve strategies involve taking positions in bonds of varying maturities in order to capitalize on expected changes in the shape of the yield curve.

- If the yield curve is expected to flatten, longer duration strategies should outperform shorter duration strategies.
- If the yield curve is expected to steepen, shorter duration strategies should outperform longer duration strategies.
- Longer duration bonds take advantage of a positively sloped yield curve.

1.4 BEYOND THEORETICAL VALUE: OTHER SOURCES OF RISK

Thus far, we have focused solely on interest rate risk – market as well as yield curve risk – using as our point of reference a bond valuation model based on discounted cash flows. There are, however, a number of other factors which also affect the valuation bonds.

Credit Risk (also known as Default, Downgrade, or Spread Risk)

This is relevant for all bonds, except US Treasuries which are considered free of credit risk. This is the risk that the issuer fails to pay coupons and/or principal as promised (i.e. defaults), receives a credit downgrade, or that the credit spread widens. Credit risk is assessed using credit ratings and in-house analysis. Higher interest rates generally lead to wider credit spreads. Credit risk can be hedged using credit default swaps or other credit derivatives.

Event Risk

This is relevant for all bonds, and is the risk that a one-time event affects the ability of the issuer to repay, reducing the value of the bond. Examples of events affecting corporate bonds include natural disasters, industrial accidents, takeovers, or corporate restructurings. For sovereign government debt these are extreme flight-to-quality episodes, such as war, dramatic economic shocks or changes in government policy. These "events" are accompanied by a sharp widening of credit spreads and an evaporation of liquidity as many market participants seek to liquidate positions all at once.

Exchange Rate Risk

This is relevant for foreign currency denominated bonds, and is the risk that the value of the bond cash flows in local currency terms will fall (e.g. that the foreign currency will depreciate against the local currency).

Inflation Risk

This is relevant for all bonds, except inflation-linked bonds (such as US TIPS or French OATei) and adjustable (or floating) rate bonds. This is the risk that unanticipated inflation will erode the value of the bond cash flows (coupons and principal repayment).

Liquidity Risk

This is relevant for all bonds, except US Treasuries and those securities held until maturity; it is also relevant for positions that are large relative to a particular investment pool or market segment. It is the risk that an investor may find it difficult to unwind a position – either because of higher-than-normal bid–ask spreads or because closing the position affects the market price of the asset. Another form of liquidity risk is the inability of leveraged investors to meet margin calls (or the risk of higher margin haircuts) when brokers withdraw financing (usually at particularly difficult times). For example, extreme financial market volatility could precipitate a flight-to-quality, causing non-benchmark bond prices to fall rapidly, liquidity to dry up, and bid–ask spreads to widen dramatically. At such a time, prime brokers may withdraw financing, which might necessitate the liquidation of the portfolio. The primary measure of liquidity risk is the size of the bid–ask spread. Illiquid bonds have wide bid–ask spreads. Liquidity is related to risk tolerance.[17]

Political and Legal Risk

This risk is relevant for all bonds. It is the risk that political, legal, or regulatory actions will adversely affect the value of the bond. Examples include unanticipated taxes or regulations as well as a new government that adversely affects the willingness to repay debt. Changes in taxes or regulations can also cause a stable relationship between two instruments to be disrupted.

Reinvestment Risk

This risk is relevant for all, except zero coupon bonds. It is the risk that interest rates fall, causing an investor to earn lower-than-expected "interest-on-interest" on coupon payments paid over the investment horizon. Reinvestment risk offsets market risk (which is the risk that interest rates increase). A strategy based on offsetting reinvestment and market risk is called *immunization*. Reinvestment risk is greater for amortizing securities with monthly payments. It is also greater for longer dated bonds with high coupons. In high interest rate environments, the interest-on-interest component for long bonds may be as high as 80% of the bond's potential total dollar return (Fabozzi, 1997).

1.5 SOURCES OF RETURN

Just as it is important to understand the nature of the risks associated with fixed income securities, it is essential to keep in mind the components of expected return. From our valuation model in Equation 1.1, we know that a fixed income security has three sources of return:

1. Interest payments (coupon income)
2. Income from the reinvestment of coupon income
3. Capital gain/loss from the price change in the bond.

Unless the issuer of the bond defaults, coupon income is fixed over the life of the investment (hence the term, "fixed income"). The remaining two sources of return are uncertain, or risky, as they are affected by changes in interest rates, which at any given time for "risk-free" government securities[18] reflect the overall level in market rates (i.e. market or duration risk), the remaining maturity of the security (i.e. yield curve risk), and the magnitude of interest rate changes (i.e. volatility risk). For an investor who plans to hold a bond to maturity, however, capital gains/losses are irrelevant.

Even if, on average, the overall level of interest rates were to remain unchanged over the investment horizon, a bond's price may rise or fall depending on the value of convexity and the "roll" – both of which are affected by changes in the shape of the yield curve. For corporate or foreign government bonds, there are other factors that affect return – chiefly, credit and currency risk. For bonds priced off of the fitted curve, there is also a richening/cheapening effect.[19] The relative importance of the sources of return will depend on the circumstances.

The *roll*, or roll-down return, refers to the capital gain associated with a falling yield that is typical of a bond approaching maturity. In normal conditions, the yield curve is positively sloped. Hence, as time passes and a bond's maturity shortens, the yield typically decreases (i.e. it "rolls down the curve").[20] The steeper the curve, the greater is the rolling yield advantage – particularly for bonds with longer maturities.

Another potential source of return stems from the carry of a trade. *Carry* is the net financing cost of a trade – that is, the difference between the coupon rate earned on a bond and the interest paid to finance the position (often the repo rate). A position earns positive/negative carry on long bond positions when the coupon is greater/less than the repo rate.[21] For example, borrowing short to invest long in a positively sloped yield curve environment would incur positive carry gains.

Positive carry provides a cushion against losses if bond prices fall. Negative carry means that the position may lose money even if bond prices rise. When spreads are compressed there is little value in carry trades. Market expectations about carry can affect the slope of the yield curve – steepening when carry is expected to be high and flattening when carry is expected to be low.

An upward sloping yield curve has positive carry and a roll-down return advantage – both of which cushion the downside risk from extending duration if interest rates should happen to rise. When the yield curve is very steep and the positive carry is large, duration extensions are cheap as these trades only lose money if the capital loss associated with an increase in interest rates offsets the initial yield advantage.

The break-even yield change required to offset the carry and roll advantage is illustrated in Equation 1.6 for the case of a 3-year bond financed by a 1-year bond, where f_{13} is the 2-year spot rate 1 year forward and s_1, s_2, and s_3 are the spot interest rates. This trade only loses money if the spot rate in 1 year's time (s_2) exceeds the 2-year spot rate 1 year forward (f_{13}).

Equation 1.6 Break-even yield change

B/E yield change = Positive carry ($f_{13} - s_3$) + Roll-down yield advantage ($s_3 - s_2$)

Often yield curves are positively sloped, but concave – meaning that the rise in the slope tends to lessen as maturity is extended. In such a case, the increase in the expected total return as one extends along the curve reaches an inflection point and begins to diminish.[22] The reason is that the roll-down advantage diminishes significantly beyond the inflection point.

1.6 SUMMARY

Table 1.7 summarizes the sources of return and risk associated with a generic fixed income security. In Chapter 2, we move on to consider more complex structures.

Table 1.7 Sources of return and risk

Sources of return[23]	Return relationship	Sources of risk
Coupon income	Higher for longer term bonds	Credit, Inflation, FX risks
Roll-down return	Higher for longer term bonds	Yield curve risk
Value of convexity	Higher for longer term bonds	Volatility risk
Duration impact	Depends on market rate view	Market risk
Rich/cheap effect[24]	Depends on mispricing	Model risk
Carry	Depends on trade financing	Yield curve, Liquidity risks

NOTES

1. These complexities are taken up in Chapter 2 and Chapter 9.
2. There are three equivalent ways of representing the interest rate over time: (1) spot rates (from yields on zero coupon bonds); (2) discount factors (from STRIPs); and (3) forward rates (from FRAs).
3. Bond prices are specified in relation to a par value of 100 – that is, a notional face value that equals 100.
4. Calculations may differ due to rounding.
5. Ilmanen (1995a) demonstrates that volatility and the value of convexity have varied over time.
6. Note that in the case of coupon size, we have a divergence between duration and convexity. On the one hand, bonds with larger coupons have lower duration. On the other hand, bonds with larger coupons are more convex.
7. Other measures are Macaulay duration (which is defined in terms of years) and dollar duration (which is defined in terms of the dollar price of a bond). The dollar value of a basis point (DV01) is the change in the dollar price of a bond for a 1 bp change in yield. Similarly, the price value of a

basis point (PVBP) is the change in price for a 1 bp change in yield. Portfolio duration is calculated by taking a weighted average of the modified durations for each of the bonds in the portfolio.
8. This is a particular type of convexity (i.e. positive) which is associated with bonds that have certain cash flows. In Chapter 2, we discuss bonds with embedded options which often exhibit negative convexity.
9. In later chapters we will discuss how to anticipate changes in interest rates and how to take different duration positions.
10. The term structure has different interpretations which are examined in more detail in Chapter 3.
11. Note that different bonds have different sensitivities.
12. The intuition for two bonds can be applied to two bond portfolios.
13. The convexity increase associated with a wider dispersion of cash flows for a portfolio of given duration is intuitively analogous to the convexity increase associated with bonds of longer maturities. With a wider dispersion of cash flows, a given increase in yield reduces the present value of the longer cash flow more than it lowers the present value of the shorter cash flow. An excellent reference on convexity and the yield curve is Ilmanen (2000).
14. The convexity of a barbell is equal to the weighted average of the component bond convexities.
15. Despite all its deficiencies, Gibson (1997) finds that duration accounts for 92% of bond price variance on average.
16. Key rate duration is the sensitivity of a portfolio's value to a yield change in just one maturity, assuming that interest rates for other maturities do not change. Key rate duration is only calculated for key – not all – maturities. For further information on partial duration, see Robert R. Reitano, "Non-parallel Yield Curve Shifts and Immunization." *Journal of Portfolio Management* (Spring 1992).
17. Supply is not the same as liquidity. For example, the JGB market is the largest in the world but it is not the most liquid in that JGBs can be traded only during Japan's trading hours. The same is true for UK Gilts. On the other hand, 24 hours a day and anywhere in the world someone will make a market in US Treasuries.
18. Government bonds are not risk free, but have inflation and tax risk.
19. This concept is covered in more detail in Chapter 7.
20. For example, a 20-year bond earning 8% becomes a 19-year bond earning 7.5% after a year passes.
21. For short bond positions, a position earns negative carry when the coupon rate exceeds the repo rate, and earns positive carry when coupon rate is less than the repo rate.
22. This effect on expected return assumes an unchanged yield curve. In practice, the total return of a portfolio consists of only the coupon income and the capital gain/loss on the bond over the relevant time horizon.
23. Source list is adapted from Ilmanen (1995b). Roll down return is calculated for an unchanged yield curve. Duration impact is equal to the product of duration and expected yield change. The longer the bond's duration and the shorter the investment horizon, the greater is the relative importance of the duration impact.
24. The rich/cheap effect is relevant for individual security selection as well as asset allocation among bond sectors.

RECOMMENDED READING

Fabozzi, F.J. (1997). *Fixed Income Mathematics: Analytical and Statistical Techniques* (3rd edn). New York: McGraw-Hill.

Jagadeesh, N. and Tuckman, B. (2000). *Advanced Fixed-Income Valuation Tools*. New York: John Wiley & Sons.

2
Fixed Income Securities: Beyond the Basics

In Chapter 1 we abstracted from some of the complexities associated with particular issuers and structures of fixed income securities. In this chapter, the focus turns to credit risk, bonds with embedded options, and interest rate derivatives. No matter the complexities of a specific instrument, it is important not to lose sight of the pricing mechanism – as this has crucial implications for strategy.

Within the universe[1] of fixed income, the primary distinction between securities is made on the basis of issuer (i.e. credit quality). The major issuers are governments (supranational, national, and municipal) and corporations (high grade and high yield). There are also quasi-government issuers, such as KfW in Germany and Fannie Mae in the US. At one end of the credit quality spectrum are US Treasuries, which are backed by the full faith and credit of the US government. As such, Treasuries are considered free from default risk. At the other end of the credit quality spectrum is high yield corporate debt (i.e. junk bonds). In addition to market and yield curve risk discussed in Chapter 1, non-Treasury bonds are exposed to spread risk.

Fixed income securities can also be distinguished by their structure. In Chapter 1 we examined the properties of "straight" bonds – those with certain cash flows. Many bonds, however, have uncertain cash flows due to an option embedded in the indenture. For example, corporate bonds often have a call option which allows the issuer to retire part (or all) of the debt before maturity (i.e. callable bonds). Similarly, mortgage-backed securities (MBS) have uncertain cash flows because borrowers are allowed to prepay part (or all) of their mortgages in advance. Other bonds have a put option which allows bond holders to redeem the bond at par before maturity (i.e. putable bonds). The value of bonds with embedded options is particularly sensitive to changes in interest rate volatility.

Finally, derivatives are securities whose value is linked to another asset. Interest rate derivatives – including bond futures, options on bond futures, and interest rate swaps – can be used in a cost-effective way to speculate on future movements in interest rates (i.e. take on interest rate exposure), create synthetic securities that enhance yield, or manage (i.e. hedge) the interest rate risk of an existing bond portfolio without having to purchase/sell a bond. It is quite easy to become consumed by the complexities of derivatives and lose sight of the basic risk/return mechanism. As such, our focus is on the essentials – pricing, uses, and strategy implications.

2.1 SPREAD RISK: EVALUATING BONDS OF DIFFERENT QUALITY

Thus far, our analysis has been confined to comparisons of bonds with the same credit quality (i.e. a single yield curve). In this section, we evaluate bonds with different levels of credit risk. The primary measure of credit risk is the yield spread (also called the credit spread), which is the yield difference between a "risky" and "risk-free" bond of comparable maturity.[2] A common frame of reference for comparing bonds across sectors is the risk-free US Treasury. As such, non-Treasury securities are often referred to as "spread products".

Pricing

The yield of non-Treasury securities has two components: (1) the risk associated with Treasuries (e.g. the market risk); and (2) the additional risk of not holding Treasuries (e.g. the risk premium). When the risk premium rises, the price of the spread product falls. Conversely, when the yield spread demanded by the market falls (i.e. the spread narrows), the price of the "risky" bond rises. In addition to the returns generated from changes in the spread, investors in spread products can benefit from credit spread carry – that is, holding bonds that pay a higher yield.

The economic cycle is the main determinant of the overall environment for spread products. Spreads widen during recession and narrow during periods of economic expansion. Investor appetite for risk also affects the overall environment for spread products. For specific bonds, the yield spread is also affected by[3]:

- Perceived credit risk
- Value of embedded options
- Liquidity of the instrument
- Tax factors
- Temporary supply and demand.

As such, the spread captures a number of factors beyond credit risk. For example, the yield spread between US Agencies and Treasuries reflects differences in liquidity as well as perceived credit risk. Yield spreads within the corporate bond market for the same maturity are attributable to differences in credit ratings, liquidity, as well as corporate sector.[4]

There is a term structure of credit spreads, known as "the spread curve". Analytically, the spread curve is comparable to the yield curve, except that there is an extra layer of risk. Generally, the spread curve is upward sloping (similar to the normal position of the Treasury curve), such that spreads are wider at longer maturities. The term structure tends to be steeper for issuers with lower credit ratings than for those with higher credit ratings. The long-end of the spread curve has a downward bias because longer maturity bonds have greater spread convexity.[5]

Risk Measurement

Investors in spread products are subject to the risk that the spread over Treasuries moves adversely as well as the risk that the Treasury yield moves adversely. Hence, the risk associated with spread products has two components: (1) spread duration and (2) Treasury duration. *Spread duration* quantifies the price sensitivity of the bond to a 100 bps change in the yield spread. Likewise, *Treasury duration* measures the price sensitivity of the bond to a 100 bps change in the Treasury yield. Note that the spread (the risk premium) and the yield (the Treasury risk) will not always move in the same direction (Example 2.1). Together, spread duration and incremental rolling yield quantify the risk–reward trade-off of increasing exposure to a different bond sector.

Example 2.1
Consider a bond sector with Treasury duration of 2.4 and spread duration of 3.4. From Chapter 1, we know that if interest rates rise by 10 bps, the market value of the sector is expected to fall by 0.24% (=2.4 × 0.10). Analogously, if the spread for the sector narrows by 10 bps, the market value of the sector is expected to rise by 0.34% (=3.4 × 0.10). Overall, an increase in interest rates of 10 bps, combined with a 10 bps narrowing in spread, would be expected to generate an increase of 0.10% (=0.34% − 0.24%) in market value.[6]

Spread duration in combination with spread convexity approximate the sensitivity of a bond's price to changes in the spread (Equation 2.1). For fixed rate bonds with certain cash flows, spread duration is calculated in the same manner as Treasury duration.[7] Spread convexity – which measures the change in spread duration as spreads change – can be calculated using Equation 1.3 in Chapter 1, substituting the spread change for ΔY. The calculation of spread duration and spread convexity requires a valuation model which accounts for the risk premium – a topic discussed in Chapter 3.

Equation 2.1   Spread risk approximation

Price change = −(Spread duration) × (Spread change)
             + ½(Spread convexity) × (Spread change)²

For emerging market sovereign bonds – typically of long duration and high spread volatility – spread convexity plays a more important role than interest rate convexity in the management of US corporate bond portfolios (Loucks et al., 2002). For Eurobonds within the same country, most of the spread can be explained by spread duration, spread convexity, and the implied probability of default.

Implications for Strategy

Spread strategies attempt to capitalize on expected changes in the risk premium. For example, when the prevailing spread between two bonds or bond sectors is out of line with their historical spread (i.e. out of line with the spread implied by your valuation model) and the yield spread is expected to realign by the end of the investment horizon, a spread strategy is implemented.

When assessing spread strategies, it is critical to compare positions that have the same duration. Failure to do so will mean that the outcome of the spread strategy will be affected by both the change in the yield spread and the change in yield level.

- A narrowing of the spread boosts performance (because yields fall and bond prices rise).
- A widening of the spread undermines performance (because yields rise and bond prices fall).

2.2 VOLATILITY RISK: EVALUATING BONDS WITH EMBEDDED OPTIONS

In Chapter 1 we saw how interest rate volatility and the value of convexity are positively related for "straight" (option-free) bonds – those with certain cash flows. However, many bonds have provisions that make their cash flows uncertain. For bonds with embedded options,

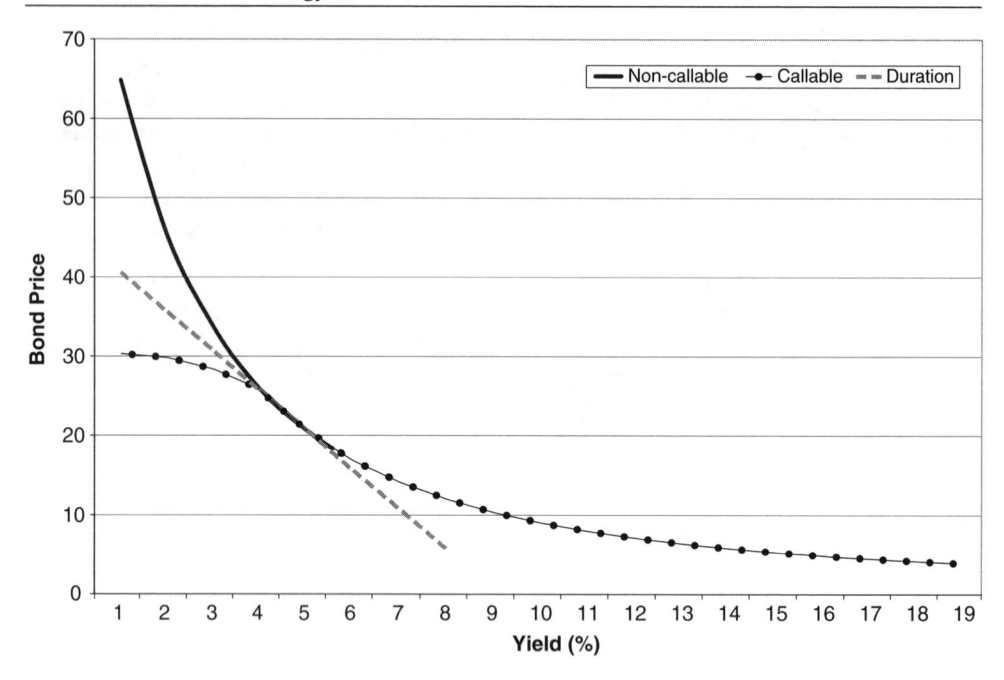

Figure 2.1 Convexity: callable versus straight bonds

the relationship between volatility and convexity depends on the nature of the particular option. In this section, we consider bonds with call and put provisions, as well as mortgage-backed securities.

Pricing Callable Bonds and Mortgage-Backed Securities

Callable bonds give the issuer the right to retire the bond ahead of maturity. Similarly, borrowers are allowed to prepay their mortgages. These call and prepayment options pose two disadvantages to the holders of callable bonds and mortgage-backed securities (MBS). First, there is exposure to reinvestment risk. Because the issuer will call the bond (and the borrower will prepay the mortgage) only when the market rate falls below the coupon/mortgage rate, the expected total return is diminished. Second, the potential for capital gain is restricted as callable bonds and MBS trade at a price below that of a comparable option-free bond. The reason is that the call/prepayment provision benefits the borrower instead of the investor, which reduces the value of the security.

Equation 2.2 Callable bond price

Price of callable bond = Price of comparable option-free bond − Call option value

---

For securities with call or prepayment options, the relationship between price and yield is negatively convex (Figure 2.1). That is, as interest rates fall, prepayments are expected to rise – thereby reducing the value of the bond. In contrast, the price of an option-free bond will always

Fixed Income Securities: Beyond the Basics   23

increase at an increasing rate as interest rates fall. Intuitively, the duration of a callable bond is equal to the duration of a comparable option-free bond less the duration of the call option.

> **Callable bonds are more negatively convex than option-free bonds.**

In a highly volatile interest rate environment, the value of a call provision increases, reducing the value of the bond. Hence, bonds with call options will underperform a comparable option-free bond when volatility is high. Conversely, when volatility is low, bonds with call options outperform. In the language of the practitioner, bonds with call options are "long the bond" and "short the call option". Hence, a callable bond is short volatility and convexity (e.g. sells volatility). The compensation required for selling volatility and convexity is the value of the call option.[8]

Pricing Putable Bonds

Putable bonds give the bond holder the right to redeem the bond ahead of maturity. The put provision benefits the bond investor instead of the borrower – which increases the value of the bond. The put provision effectively caps the interest rate risk borne by the bond holder, as the bond holder can "put" the bond to the issuer if the market rate rises sharply. Hence, the expected return is enhanced by the put option.

> **Equation 2.3   Putable bond price**
>
> Price of putable bond = Price of comparable option-free bond + Put option value

For bonds with put options, the relationship between price and yield is positively convex (Figure 2.2). Greater volatility increases the value of a put option and the value of a putable bond – as the value of the option (to "put the bond to the issuer") benefits the investor. When compared to option-free bonds, putable bonds have greater positive convexity. As interest rates rise, redemptions are expected to rise – thereby increasing the value of the bond. Bonds with put options will outperform/underperform a comparable option-free bond when volatility is higher/lower than expected. Bonds with put options are long volatility and convexity. The premium paid to compensate the issuer for selling volatility and convexity is the value of the put option.

> **Putables are more positively convex than straight bonds.**

Callable versus Non-callable Bonds

Figures 2.1 and 2.2 illustrate how bonds (or bond portfolios) with negative convexity are adversely affected by volatility, while bonds with positive convexity benefit from volatility. The relationship between volatility and bond value for different bond structures is summarized in Table 2.1. Forecasts for high volatility relative to market expectations imply that an embedded call/put option is of greater value, thereby reducing/increasing the value of the bond.

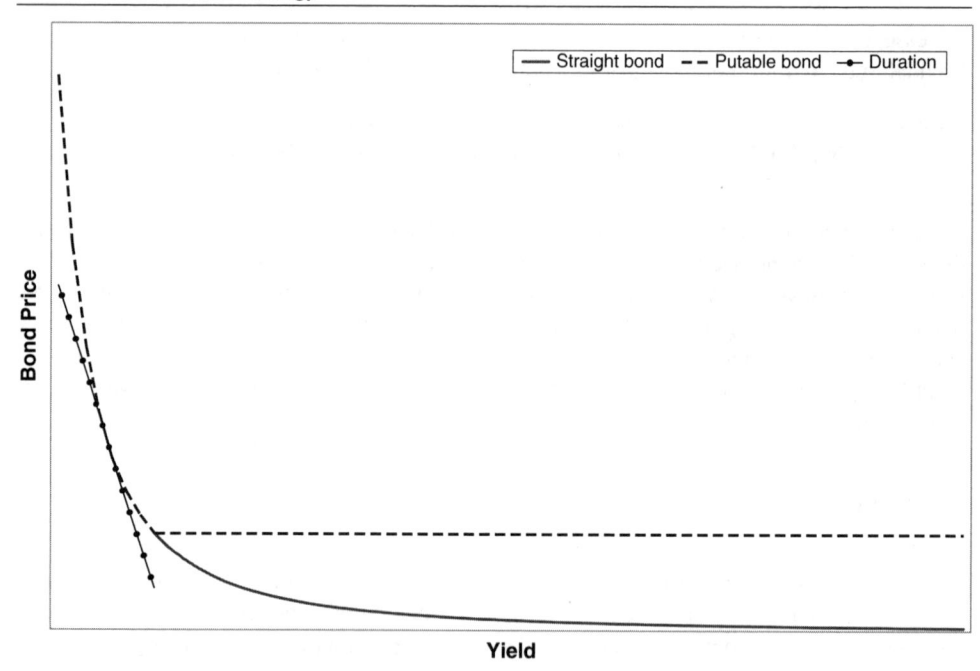

Figure 2.2 Convexity: putable versus straight bonds

Table 2.1 Convexity, volatility, and bond value

Bond structure	Convexity	Impact of volatility on bond value
Putable bonds	Positive	Increase
Straight bonds	Positive	Increase
Callable bonds	Negative	Decrease
Mortgage-backed securities	Negative	Decrease

Bonds with call provisions offer a higher yield relative to comparable non-callable bonds to compensate the investor for taking on call risk. The change in the yield spread between callable and non-callable bonds depends on the direction of change in interest rates as well as the volatility of interest rates. Callable bonds do well in rising rate environments[9] and in decreasing volatility environments. An increase in the level of interest rates will narrow the spread between callable and non-callable bonds as higher interest rates reduce the prospect that the issuer will exercise the call option – thereby reducing the value of the call option and increasing the value of the callable bond. A decrease in interest rate volatility reduces the value of the embedded call option which increases the callable price and thus reduces the spread with non-callable bonds.

> **Callable bonds outperform non-callable bonds when interest rates rise or volatility falls**

Similarly, non-callable bonds outperform callable bonds in a decreasing rate environment and increasing volatility environment.[10] An expected drop in the level of interest rates will widen the spread between callable and non-callable bonds as the prospect that the issuer will call the bond increases. An increase in interest rate volatility also increases the value of the embedded call option, which reduces the callable price and increases the spread with non-callable bonds.

Convex portfolios have a high percentage of non-callable bonds. Conversely, portfolios with little convexity hold many callable bonds. A more convex portfolio yields less than a non-convex one and is much more sensitive to changes in interest rates and changes in volatility.

Accounting for Volatility Risk

Bonds with embedded options have uncertain maturities, which complicates bond valuation and the assessment of the risk–reward trade-off. In other words, will a 10-year bond with 3 years of call protection behave more like a 3-, 7-, or 10-year bond? The answer depends on interest rate volatility.

In contrast to the nominal yield spread that is used to make comparisons across straight bonds, bonds with embedded options are evaluated using the option-adjusted spread (OAS). The OAS is stripped of option risk, leaving a premium for credit and liquidity risk that is comparable to the yield spread of option-free bonds (Equation 2.4). Just like other spread products, bonds with embedded options are subject to spread risk, which is measured by spread duration.

Equation 2.4 OAS for callable bonds

OAS = Yield spread (against similar maturity risk-free bond) − Call option value

---

The OAS will change whenever the market reassesses the risk premium and in response to supply and demand conditions. The calculation of OAS requires a valuation model and is highly sensitive to the assumptions made about volatility and the shape of the yield curve. As such, OAS introduces model risk.[11]

While OAS allows for the proper evaluation of bonds with embedded options, effective duration (as opposed to modified duration[12]) provides the proper measure of market risk. *Effective duration* quantifies the price sensitivity of an option-embedded bond to a parallel shift in the yield curve while taking into consideration the uncertain timing of cash flows and holding the OAS constant. Intuitively, effective duration is the slope of the price–yield relationship for a bond with an embedded option.

Equation 2.5 is a repetition of Equation 1.2 in Chapter 1. In this case, however, P^+ and P^- are based on a valuation model that accounts for interest rate volatility and the uncertain timing of cash flows. P^+ and P^- are constant OAS prices – that is, they represent the pure effect from the shift in the yield curve.

Equation 2.5 Effective duration

Effective duration = $(P^- - P^+) \div (2P_0(\text{Yield curve shift}))$

Analogously, *effective convexity* can be calculated using Equation 1.3 in Chapter 1. Intuitively, effective convexity is the change in the slope of the price–yield relationship for a bond with an embedded option. It is essentially an adjustment for the inaccuracy in the effective duration measure.

Together OAS and effective duration are used to assess the risk–return trade-off for bonds with embedded options. (In contrast, the nominal yield spread and key rate duration are used in the risk–return assessment for straight bonds.) This is best illustrated by an example.

Example 2.2

Consider a MBS with effective duration of 2.5 and spread duration of 3.5. If interest rates rise by 10 bps we expect the market value of the MBS to fall by 25 bps (2.5 × 10 bps). If the mortgage OAS narrows by 10 bps we expect the market value of the MBS to rise by 35 bps (3.5 × 10 bps). Overall, an increase in interest rates of 10 bps combined with a 10 bps narrowing in the OAS would be expected to generate a 10 bps (35 − 25) increase in market value.[13]

In summary, interest rate volatility has crucial implications for the value of bonds with embedded options (Table 2.2). As most corporate bonds have embedded options and mortgage securities have prepayment provisions, these asset classes are particularly affected by volatility risk.

Generally interest rate volatility is a declining function of maturity.[14] That is, shorter securities are expected to be more volatile in terms of yield than longer bonds. Given the importance of volatility for the value (and risk) associated with bonds with embedded options, the selection of volatility along the yield curve has important implications for expected return.

Table 2.2 Risk and return implications for bonds with embedded options

Risk	Description	Measurement	Value
Volatility risk	For the bond holder, volatility risk includes call risk, prepayment risk and model risk.	Historical volatility or model-based implied volatilities from current option prices.	Low/falling volatility reduces the value of an embedded option.
Call risk (callable bonds)	The risk of early termination of bond, requiring reinvestment in unfavorable environment of declining yields.	The magnitude of call risk depends on the parameters of the call provision and market conditions.	Reduced call risk enhances return.
Prepayment risk (MBS)	The risk that homeowners prepay all or part of their mortgage when interest rates decline, requiring reinvestment in unfavorable environment.	Prepayment risk is measured using prepayment duration[15] and is directly linked to the level, direction, and volatility of interest rates.	Prepayments enhance returns if the MBS is purchased at a discount.
Model risk[16]	The risk that a valuation model is either mis-specified or applied incorrectly.	Periods of instability enhance model risk.	—

Fixed Income Securities: Beyond the Basics

Implications for Strategy

Investors in bonds with embedded options position portfolios to take advantage of expected changes in the OAS over the investment horizon. Changes in interest rate volatility affect the value of the embedded option and, hence, the OAS.

- If you expect the OAS on a callable bond to narrow relative to a comparable non-callable bond, buy the callable bond. Alternatively, if you expect the OAS on a callable bond to widen relative to a comparable non-callable bond, buy the non-callable bond.
- If volatility is expected to be high (that is, exceed the market's expectation of volatility), invest in non-callable bonds (i.e. buy volatility). An increase in volatility increases the value of the call provision and reduces the price of callable bonds.
- If volatility is low and is expected to increase (in contrast with market expectations), consider buying bonds with put provisions. In an environment of low volatility, bonds with put provisions are often priced way above par – or, so far out-of-the-money that a very low likelihood of put exercise exists.
- If volatility is expected to be low, invest in callable bonds (i.e. sell volatility). A decrease in volatility reduces the value of the put provision and reduces the price of putable bonds. As volatility decreases, the price of callables or MBS will increase in value. If forecasted volatility is less than the market's expectation of volatility, then sell volatility (i.e. buy callables).

2.3 INTEREST RATE DERIVATIVES

Derivatives can be used to take on additional risk or to hedge existing risk. Interest rate risk can be hedged using bond futures, options on bond futures, and interest rate swaps.

2.3.1 Futures

A futures contract represents an obligation to buy (or sell) an asset at a specific price on a specific date in the future. The seller of a bond futures contract has the obligation to deliver to the buyer of the futures contract at the settlement date the underlying bond with a prespecified period remaining to maturity and face value. The bond may be newly issued or seasoned. The specific bonds that the seller can deliver are published by the futures exchange prior to the initial trading of the futures contract. In selecting the issue to be delivered, the seller of the futures contract will select from all the deliverable issues the one that is the cheapest to deliver. As such, the buyer of the bond futures contract can never be sure exactly which bond will be delivered.

The Pricing of Bond Futures

The theoretical price of a bond future is equal to the cash price of the underlying bond plus the cost of carry. However, the actual price is lower than the theoretical price because of the delivery options afforded to the seller of the futures contract. The price of a futures contract moves with the price of the underlying asset. The buyer/seller of the futures contract realizes a profit if the futures price increases/decreases. Hence, the price of a bond future moves in the opposite direction of interest rates. When interest rates rise, the futures price will fall, and vice versa. The expected return on a futures contract is the expected return on the deliverable bond, less the cost of financing.

Uses of Bond Futures

The risk associated with a bond future depends on its use. Bond futures contracts have four uses:

1. To speculate on the movement of interest rates
2. To control the interest rate risk of a portfolio (i.e. manage duration)
3. To create synthetic securities to enhance yield
4. To hedge price risk incurred from normal business operations.

Since investors in futures often finance their positions, there is also the added risk associated with using leverage.

An investor that wants to speculate that interest rates will rise/fall can sell/buy bond futures. Using bond futures instead of the cash security (going short or long on the bond itself) has three advantages: (1) lower transactions costs; (2) lower margin requirements (making leverage easier); and (3) the relative ease of selling short in the futures market as opposed to the cash market.

An investor adjusts interest rate risk by altering the interest rate sensitivity of a bond portfolio. Instead of purchasing or selling a bond in the cash market to modify duration, an investor can alternatively use bond futures contracts, which are more cost-efficient. Duration is extended/shortened by purchasing/selling the appropriate number and type of bond futures. Futures have the added advantage that an investor can use them to extend the duration of a portfolio beyond what is available in the cash market.

Bond futures can be used to create synthetic securities for the purpose of enhancing yield. A synthetic security is created by taking a position in the futures contract together with the deliverable instrument. For example, an investor who holds a 10-year Treasury note can synthetically create a risk-free 6-month Treasury bill by selling a Treasury future requiring delivery of that 10-year note in 6 months. The maturity has effectively been shortened to 6 months and the position is risk-free because the investor has locked in the price to be received 6 months from now – the futures price. The return one would expect to earn on this synthetic 6-month T-bill would be the yield on the 6-month T-bill. If the yield on the synthetic position is greater than the yield in the cash market, the investor can realize an enhanced yield by creating the synthetic short-term security.

Bond futures can also be used to hedge an existing position in the cash market. A perfect hedge would be constructed such that any capital loss realized from one position (either the cash position or the future) would be completely offset by the capital gain from the other position.[17] An unhedged position is exposed to price risk – the risk that the cash market price will move adversely. In contrast, a hedged position is exposed to basis risk.[18]

Implications for Strategy

A *short hedge* is used to protect against a decline in the cash price of a bond. To execute a short hedge, futures contracts are sold. By establishing a short hedge, the hedger has fixed the future cash price and transferred the price risk of ownership to the buyer of the futures contract. An investor concerned that interest rates will rise might use a short hedge when a substantial cash payout is required in the near future, locking in a price for the bond liquidation.

A *long hedge* is used to protect against an increase in the cash price of the bond. To execute a long hedge, futures contracts are bought – locking in the purchase price of a bond. An investor concerned that interest rates will fall might use a long hedge when substantial cash inflows are expected or when a bond is maturing in the near future, locking in a rate for the proceeds to be reinvested.

2.3.2 Options

An option provides the right – but not the obligation – to buy or sell an asset at a future date (or any time ahead of that date) at a prespecified price (the strike price).[19] Unlike a futures contract which involves an *obligation*, the buyer of an option has the *right* but not the obligation to perform. As such, options do not provide a symmetric risk–reward for the buyer and seller – as is the case with a futures contract.

The writer of the option (the seller) grants the buyer of the option an entitlement in exchange for the option price. In the case of a call/put option, the buyer has the right to buy/sell to the option writer a designated instrument at a specified price within/at a specified period of time. The buyer of the option is long the option and the seller is short the option.

The maximum amount that an option buyer can lose is the option price, and the maximum profit that the option writer can realize is the option price. The option buyer has unlimited upside return potential, while the option writer has unlimited downside risk.

There are two ways the buyer of a call option may close a position taken in an option. First, the investor may exercise the option (which gives him or her a position in the underlying asset) and then sell the underlying asset at the current price. Alternatively, the investor may sell a corresponding option.

The Pricing of Options on Bond Futures

An option has intrinsic value as well as time value. The intrinsic value of a call option is equal to the current market price of the bond less the strike price. The intrinsic value of a put option, on the other hand, is equal to the strike price less the bond price. An option is "in-the-money" when the intrinsic value is greater than zero. The time value of an option is the amount that the option price exceeds the intrinsic value. Time value – which represents the opportunity for the intrinsic value to increase further – decays as the period to expiry shortens. It is the time value of an option that is most difficult to price. The assumptions underpinning the classic Black–Scholes option-pricing model make it suitable only for European-style options on bond futures. According to the Black–Scholes model, the theoretical price of an option depends on:

1. The current market price of the underlying asset
2. The strike price of the option
3. The risk-free interest rate corresponding to the remaining life of the option
4. The time to expiration of the option
5. The interest rate volatility over the life of the option.

All but the last of these specifications is observable. Although volatility is not observable, the market's belief about future volatility (i.e. implied volatility) can be inferred using the option price observed in the market plus the four known variables. In theory, the implied volatility of all Treasury (or other) index options should be the same.[20] At-the-money call options are the most common measure of implied volatility.

A popular methodology to assess whether an option is fairly valued is to assume that the option is priced correctly and then, using the Black–Scholes option-pricing model, estimate the volatility implied by the model. For example, if the implied volatility is 10% when the investor expects interest rate volatility to be 8% over the life of the option, the option is considered undervalued. Hence, trading and investing in options involves buying and selling volatility.

There are four problematic assumptions with the Black–Scholes model which limit its usefulness in the pricing of options on bond instruments:

1. The assumed probability distribution permits bond prices to be higher than the maximum bond value (implying negative interest rates)
2. The short-term interest rate is assumed constant over the life of the option
3. Price volatility remains fixed over the life of the option
4. The model only applies to European-style options.

A better methodology for valuing options on bond instruments would take into account the yield curve as well as different volatility assumptions along the curve. The most popular model employed by dealer firms is the Black–Derman–Toy model (Black et al., 1990).

Uses of Options on Bond Futures

Options on bond futures have four uses:

1. To speculate on the movement of interest rates (using naked option positions)
2. To create synthetic securities to enhance yield (using option combinations)
3. To hedge price risk (using covered option positions)
4. To profit from interest rate volatility.

Interest Rate Speculation: Naked Option Positions

- *Long call strategy* – Buy a call option on a debt instrument in anticipation of an increase in the price of bonds (decrease in interest rates). The potential profit for the buyer of the call option will be less than the profit for the buyer of the underlying instrument by the amount of the option price. On the other hand, the potential loss for the buyer of the call option will be no more than the cost of the option, whereas the loss for the buyer of the underlying instrument could lose the entire value of the investment. In other words, there are one-to-one losses and gains to the holder of the underlying; whereas the loss for the holder of the option is limited to the price of the option and the upside potential is reduced by the cost of the option.
- *Short call strategy* – Sell a call option on a debt instrument in anticipation of a decrease in the price of bonds (increase in interest rates). There are one-to-one losses and gains to the holder of the underlying. Whereas the maximum profit for the holder of the option is limited to the price of the option and the maximum loss is limited by how high the price of the bond can increase (how far the market yield can fall) less the price earned from the sale of the option.
- *Long put strategy* – Buy a put option on a debt instrument in anticipation of a decrease in the price of bonds (increase in interest rates). Both a long put and a short bond position realize profits if interest rates rise. The investor with the short bond participates in all the upside potential and all the downside risk. The investor with the long put limits the downside risk to the price of the option while still participating in the upside potential reduced by the cost of the option.

- *Short put strategy* – Sell a put option on a debt instrument in anticipation of an increase in the price of bonds (decrease in interest rates). The maximum loss of a short put is limited only by how low the price of the bond can fall, less the option price received for writing the option. The maximum gain is the price earned from writing the option.

Yield Enhancement: Synthetic Positions

Synthetic option positions can be created by combining a position in a bond with a position in an option. Alternatively, synthetic bond positions can be created by combining positions in two types of options. Table 2.3 provides a summary.

Table 2.3 Summary of synthetic positions

Synthetic position	Instrument combinations
Long call	Long bond + Long put
Short call	Short bond + Short put
Long put	Short bond + Long call
Short put	Long bond + Short call
Long bond	Long call + Short put
Short bond	Long put + Short call

Hedging Price Risk: Covered Option Positions

Options can be used to offset an unfavorable price (interest rate) movement in a bond portfolio (e.g. hedge an existing cash position in a bond). The choice of hedging instrument depends on the investors' expectations of interest rates. A covered call can be used to hedge a long bond position against the possibility of interest rate hikes. Alternatively, a protective put can be used by an asset manager who is required to hold long bond positions but expects rate hikes. The difference is the intensity of the rate hike expectation.

- *Covered call* – Sell an out-of-the-money call option on an existing bond portfolio based on the belief that the market will not trade much higher or much lower than its present level. Selling the call brings option premium income that provides partial protection if interest rates increase. If interest rates fall, total return is limited by the obligation of the call option (this liability increases as rates fall). In other words, the covered call is the synthetic equivalent of a short put option. Hence, there is limited upside potential with a covered call. Note that this position becomes a costly bet when volatility increases.
- *Protective put* – Hedge long-term bonds with a long put to protect against a possible increase in interest rates by buying an out-of-the-money put option. The protective put is the synthetic equivalent of a long call option. The success of the strategy will depend on whether the cheapest-to-deliver issue changes and the yield spread between the hedged bonds and the cheapest-to-deliver issue. Unlike hedging with futures, the options hedge protects the investor if rates rise but allows the investor to profit if rates fall.

Trading Volatility

Buying volatility means taking positions that will profit from large price movements – either up or down. Selling volatility means taking positions that profit in situations where the price is stable. Trading volatility can be achieved a number of ways – with or without the use of options. For example, volatility is bought/sold by taking a short/long position in an option. One might also buy/sell volatility through the simultaneous purchase/sale of call and put options (also known as a straddle or strangle), where the options are based on the same security and have the same strike price and expiration.

Implications for Strategy

The strategy implications of the different uses of options are summarized in Table 2.4.

Table 2.4 Option strategies

Use	Strategy	Forecast
Speculation	Long call option	Increase in price of underlying (very bullish); increase in price volatility of underlying
Speculation	Short call option	Decrease in price of underlying (slightly bearish); or price increase will be insufficient to exercise the option
Speculation	Long put option	Decrease in price of underlying (very bearish)
Speculation	Short put option	Increase in price of underlying (slightly bullish); or price decrease will be insufficient to exercise the option
Hedging	Covered call (long bond + short call option)	Hedge long bond position against rate increase, leaving no upside potential from rate decrease; low volatility
Hedging	Protective put (long bond + long put option)	Hedge long bond position against sharp increase in interest rates, leaving some upside potential; high volatility
Trading volatility	Long straddle (long call + long put)	Increase in volatility – expect major price move but uncertain of direction (e.g. buy volatility)
Trading volatility	Short straddle (short call + short put)	Decrease in volatility – expect price stability (e.g. sell volatility)

2.3.3 Swaps

In an interest rate swap two parties agree to exchange periodic interest payments. The most common arrangement is the "plain vanilla" swap, where one party agrees to pay the other party fixed interest payments (at a spread over Treasuries or another benchmark government yield) in return for floating payments based on a reference rate (usually the 6-month London Interbank Offered Rate – LIBOR).[21] The timing of the cash flows for the fixed and floating payments is generally not the same. The fixed rate payer (i.e. the payer of fixed) is long the swap and benefits if interest rates rise. Conversely, the floating rate payer (i.e. the receiver of fixed) is short the swap and benefits if interest rates fall.

The Pricing of Interest Rate Swaps

A swap can be viewed either as a package of cash flows (from buying/selling cash market instruments) or as a package of forwards or futures contracts. As a package of cash market instruments, the theoretical price of a swap is the interest rate that makes the present value of the fixed payments equal to the present value of the floating payments (Equation 2.6). After the swap transaction, the value of the swap is the difference between the present values of the cash flows of the two legs of the swap, which changes as interest rates change.

Equation 2.6 Swap rate

Swap rate = PV (Floating payments) − PV (Fixed payments)

Alternatively, a swap can be viewed as a package of forward contracts. As such, the swap rate will depend on the price of a package of forward contracts (Example 2.3). An interest rate swap is different from a package of forwards in that swap maturities can be longer (15+ years) and a swap is more efficient (e.g. one swap transaction versus many forward transactions).

Example 2.3
Consider a swap agreement where a fixed rate of 10% is paid on $50 million par in exchange for 6-month LIBOR. This is effectively a 6-month forward contract to pay $2.5 million (2.5 = 50 × 0.10 × 1/2) for 6-month LIBOR. The payer of the fixed rate is effectively long a 6-month forward contract on 6-month LIBOR, while the floating rate payer is effectively short the forward contract. Hence, the swap rate is 6-month forward LIBOR.

The swap rate reflects the cost of capital for banks. As such, the swap rate provides a benchmark for the pricing of new issues and outstanding debt in the corporate bond markets. When swaps are cheap,[22] corporations will issue fixed rate bonds and swap them into floating rates. If a swap rate is lower/higher than a corresponding bond yield then the asset swap package will produce a return above/below LIBOR (McDougall, 1999).

Buy fixed rate paper and swap it into floating rates if swaps are historically cheap and the reason is temporary.

Swap Spreads

The swap spread is the interest rate differential between the swap rate and the government benchmark yield of the same maturity (Equation 2.7). Intuitively, the swap spread reflects the risk premium associated with investing in more risky bank debt – for example, the difference between the 3-month LIBOR and the 3-month T-bill yield.

Equation 2.7 Swap spread

Swap spread = Swap rate − Government benchmark yield

A key determinant of the swap spread for maturities through 5 years is the cost of hedging in the Eurodollar CD futures market (Example 2.4). The Eurodollar CD futures contract is a swap where a fixed dollar payment (the futures price) is exchanged for 3-month LIBOR. There are Eurodollar CD futures contracts that have maturities every 3 months for 5 years.

Example 2.4
Consider a financial institution that has fixed rate assets and floating rate liabilities both with a maturity of 3 years. The interest rate on the liabilities resets every 3 months based on 3-month LIBOR. This institution can hedge its mismatched asset/liability position by buying a 3-year strip of Eurodollar CD futures contracts. By doing so, the institution pays a fixed amount (the futures price) and receives LIBOR over the 3-year period. Alternatively, the institution can enter into a 3-year swap where it pays fixed and receives 3-month LIBOR. The institution will choose the vehicle that has the lowest hedging cost. Hence, swap rates are influenced by the Eurodollar CD futures market (McDougall, 1999).

For swaps with maturities of longer than 5 years, a key determinant of the swap spread is the credit spread in the corporate bond market – with boundary conditions for swap spreads being the prices of fixed- and floating-rate corporate bonds. Within this boundary, the swap spread is largely driven by technical supply and demand factors.[23] A reduction/increase in Treasury issuance, for example, tends to widen/narrow the swap spread. Swap spreads are also viewed as a barometer of investor appetite for risk. As such, a growing appetite for risk tends to be associated with a narrowing in the spread. Even though swaps involve negligible credit risk, swap spreads vary closely with credit/liquidity spreads because swap rates are tied to LIBOR – the rate that banks lend to each other.

Uses of Interest Rate Swaps

Interest rate swaps can be used for arbitrage, hedging, and speculation – including:

1. To enhance returns (or lock in profits) for bond holders (via asset swaps)
2. To reduce funding costs (or lock in debt cost) for issuers (via liability swaps)
3. To alter the mix of floating and fixed rate debt to better match the cash flow character of assets and liabilities.

Investors can use asset swaps to enhance returns by exploiting differences in credit risk.[24] An asset swap involves the purchase of a fixed rate bond and a simultaneous swap of the bond's fixed rate flows for floating rate income at a positive spread to financing costs (Figure 2.3). After the swap, the investor effectively holds a fixed rate bond that behaves like a floating rate note, while at the same time locking in a profit. When the bond is a default-free government benchmark (such as Treasuries), the asset swap is a relatively risk-free arbitrage if the bond is held to maturity. As swaps are not conducted via an exchange, there is the added consideration of counterparty risk. Hence, any savings realized from a swap must be weighed against the additional credit risk.

Similarly, issuers can use liability swaps to lower funding costs (Figure 2.4). The ability of different borrowers to raise funds at different rates presents credit arbitrage opportunities – essentially exploiting a comparative advantage in one market to compensate for a comparative disadvantage in another. Even though a high credit-rated issuer can borrow at a lower cost in both fixed and floating rate markets, it will have a comparative advantage relative to a lower credit-rated issuer in either the fixed or floating rate market, and a comparative disadvantage in the other. In such a case, each borrower would benefit from issuing securities in the market in which it has a comparative advantage and then swapping obligations for the desired type of financing.

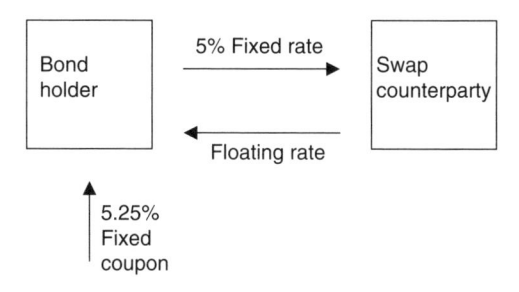

Figure 2.3 An asset swap with return enhancement

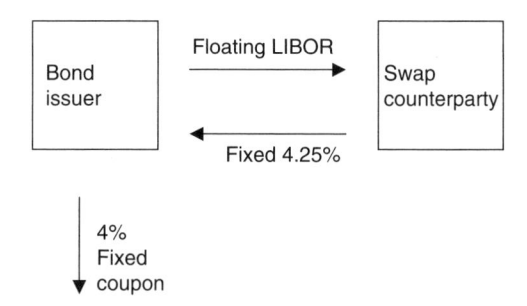

Figure 2.4 A liability swap that reduces funding costs

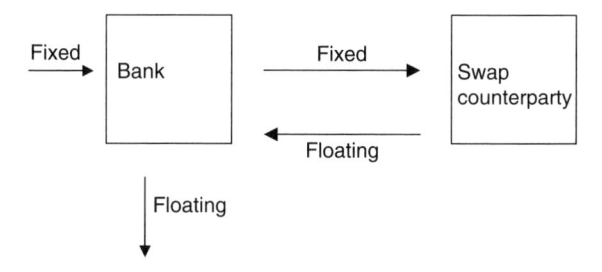

Figure 2.5 A swap that neutralizes interest rate risk

Credit arbitrage opportunities exist because there is no universal price for credit. Moreover, investors who buy fixed rate bonds (such as pension funds, insurance companies, asset managers, banks, and individuals) have a different perspective on the price of credit from the banks which make loans to companies in the syndicated loan market. Differences in regulations and tax treatment also create opportunities. For example, insurance companies in many countries may only invest in domestic instruments. Note that credit arbitrage opportunities diminish as more exploit swaps.

Investors can use interest rate swaps to alter the nature of cash flows – from fixed to floating, or vice versa – as a tool for asset/liability management. For example, a bank borrowing at the short end of the curve on a floating rate basis and lending on a fixed rate basis at the long end of the curve in a normal yield curve environment is exposed to tremendous interest rate risk by this asset–liability mismatch. A bank can eliminate its interest rate risk by engaging in a swap (Figure 2.5). After the swap, the bank's profits and losses solely reflect the pricing of credit risk (from the customer to whom the bank has given the fixed loan and from the swap). Bank customers also benefit as their ability to borrow at fixed rates is no longer conditional on finding a bank that is willing to speculate on interest rates on its behalf.

For a bank, a swap is preferable to hedging with a floating rate note (FRN) as the swap involves no transfer of principal and the additional credit risk is limited to the difference between the floating and fixed payments. In addition, it is easier to match deposit payment dates with a swap than a FRN. For hedges that need to be effective up to a year, futures/forwards may be more liquid than short-term swaps. For longer terms, however, swaps may have the liquidity advantage.

As we have seen in Chapters 1 and 2, equal yield movements will produce a different price response, depending on an individual bond's maturity, coupon, and structure. In Chapter 3, we will see how macroeconomic forces generate movements in interest rates, the yield curve, spreads, and volatility.

NOTES

1. The universe of fixed income securities is discussed in more detail in Chapter 8.
2. Other spread measures include the relative yield spread (which is the ratio of the yield spread to the risk-free yield), and the yield ratio (which is the ratio of risky and risk-free yields). Both of these measures tend to be more stable than the yield spread.
3. The determinants of yield spreads are discussed in more detail in Chapter 3.
4. Different corporate sectors have different exposure to the business cycle.
5. Analogous to interest rate convexity, high spread convexity adds value to a bond.
6. Adapted from Klaffky et al. (1997).
7. This is not the case for spread products with uncertain cash flows (such as floaters or callable bonds). The calculation for bonds with uncertain cash flows is discussed in Section 2.2.
8. The value of an option depends heavily on the assumed level of volatility and in this respect there is little agreement. Option value is discussed further in Section 2.3.
9. Assuming constant conditions in credit, volatility, and yield curve shape. See Dialynas (1997).
10. In extreme cases, non-callable US government bonds perform best because of their liquidity and creditworthiness.
11. Models estimate prepayment behavior (in the case of MBS), interest rate volatility (in the case of callable corporate bonds and MBS), and the sensitivity of the bond price to changes in interest rates. The practice in the corporate bond market is to add the nominal corporate spread to the nearest maturity US Treasury benchmark.
12. Modified duration is inappropriate for bonds with embedded options because it fails to account for the fact that yield changes can affect the timing of cash flows.
13. Adapted from Klaffky et al. (1997).
14. This is discussed further in Chapter 3.
15. For the calculation of prepayment duration, see Klaffky et al. (1997).
16. Complex quantitative models are generally used to forecast shifts in yield curves, interest rate volatility, credit spreads, and the cash flows associated with different option features. The valuation of bonds with uncertain cash flows requires making assumptions about interest rate volatility.
17. Modified duration is frequently used to estimate the required hedge. For example, to hedge a bond position with a duration of 5 bps, you need an offsetting position in a future with the same sensitivity to interest rate risk.
18. The difference between the cash price and the futures price is the basis. Basis risk is the risk that the basis will change in an unpredictable way. Typically the bond to be hedged is not identical to the bond underlying the futures contract.
19. American-style options allow the option to be exercised at any point in time through expiry, whereas European-style options can only be exercised at expiry.
20. Canina and Figlewski (1993) argue that implied volatility is neither a good predictor of future volatility nor a good reflection of past volatility.

21. LIBOR is essentially the global cost of bank borrowing.
22. The cheapness/richness of swaps is usually due to technical reasons, but could also be the result of general trends (e.g. asset/liability management of corporations in the swap market).
23. For more information, see Ellen Evans and Gioia Parente Bales, "What Drives Interest Rate Swap Spreads?" Chapter 13 in Carl R. Beidleman (ed.), *Interest Rate Swaps* (Homewood, IL: Richard D. Irwin, 1991).
24. The use of a swap to alter the cash flow character of assets is an *asset* swap, while the use of a swap to alter the cash flow character of liabilities is a *liability* swap. The term "swap" generally refers to liability swaps (the swapping of debt), while the term "asset swap" denotes swapping investments.

RECOMMENDED READING

Fabozzi, F.J. (ed.) (1997). *Managing Fixed Income Portfolios*. New Hope, Pennsylvania: Frank J. Fabozzi Associates.

Fabozzi, F.J. (2000). *Bond Markets, Analysis and Strategies* (4th edn). Upper Saddle River, New Jersey: Prentice-Hall.

Lau, F. (1997). *Derivatives in Plain Words*. Hong Kong: The Hong Kong Monetary Authority.

3
Economic Fundamentals

As we have seen from Chapters 1 and 2, interest rate changes are a primary risk factor for fixed income investment. Moreover, fixed income strategy requires an independent view to be formed on market direction (e.g. duration), the yield curve, spreads, and volatility. Accordingly, this chapter discusses key interest rate models from economic theory. Before launching into these specific applications, a few essential economic concepts are reviewed.

3.1 THE BUILDING BLOCKS OF ECONOMIC ANALYSIS

For investors in fixed income, the key transmission mechanisms in economics are associated with the law of supply and demand, and the business cycle. Both concepts are crucial for anticipating movements in interest rates. First, however, investors should understand when it is important to think like an economist.

Thinking Like an Economist

The essence of economics is about choosing between alternatives. If choice is not involved, economics is irrelevant. Choice requires scarcity – or rather, constraints.[1] For example, we are constrained by our income and by time. We only earn so much, so we can only spend so much, even with the help of credit cards. There are only 24 hours in a day, and, if we are lucky enough, only 80 or 90 years in a lifetime. Hence, we must choose what to buy and what not to buy; how to spend our time and how not to spend our time.

Economists assume that we try to make the best choices. That is, we try to make the best of what we have. For example, consumers try to maximize their well-being ("utility" in the language of economists) subject to the constraint of what their income can purchase. Firms try to maximize their profits subject to the constraint of the costs of production. Mathematically, these are constrained optimization scenarios.

Never lose sight of the alternatives

Blindly following the output of a constrained optimization problem can get you into trouble. Mathematically, profits are maximized when firms produce a level of output such that the incremental revenue derived from the output equals the incremental cost of producing the output – that is, when marginal revenue equals marginal cost. However, if the optimal level of output, X, is associated with zero or negative profits, firms won't produce any output at all. The key is not to lose sight of the alternatives. In this case the basic alternative of: (1) producing X and earning zero profits; or (2) producing zero and earning zero profits. The latter is preferred since it entails lower production costs.

Fixed Income Strategy

In short, if you are making choices, you are thinking like an economist. If you remain focused on the nature of alternatives when doing your analysis, you will be thinking like a highly skilled economist.

The Law of Supply and Demand

Supply and demand are determined independently by producers and consumers, each faced with a constrained optimization problem. Supply is represented by the choice made by producers, while demand is represented by the choice made by consumers. The quantity supplied by a firm is that which maximizes profits subject to the constraint of rising production costs (e.g. the firm produces the quantity, q_s, where the incremental revenue earned from the item equals its incremental cost). Profits and incremental revenue are a function of consumer demand. The quantity demanded by a consumer is that which maximizes the individual's well-being, or "utility", subject to a spending limit or budget constraint (e.g. the consumer consumes the quantity, q_d, where the incremental benefit of the item equals its incremental cost). Incremental cost is a function of producer supply.

For every good, there is a price that a consumer is willing to pay – this is represented by a demand curve. The demand curve is downward sloping because consumers prefer to have more goods for less cost. For every price, there is a quantity that a producer is willing to produce – this is represented by a supply curve. The supply curve is upward sloping because producers prefer to sell more goods at a higher price. The market-clearing price is that which equates the two forces of "supply" and "demand". This is the law of supply and demand (Figure 3.1). If supply exceeds demand, the price will be reduced to attract consumption. If demand exceeds supply, the price must be increased to induce producers to incur additional costs to produce it. The law of supply and demand can be applied to any item in the economy, including money. The "price" of money is the interest rate.

When economic agents are aggregated to represent all firms, all consumers, and all goods, the relationship becomes one between aggregate supply (AS) and aggregate demand (AD). As such, shifts in aggregate demand and aggregate supply produce movements in aggregate prices (inflation or CPI) and aggregate output (economic growth or real GDP).

Changes in monetary and fiscal policy will shift the aggregate demand curve, while changes in productivity and technology (e.g. factors that affect the cost of production) will shift the aggregate supply curve. Figure 3.2 illustrates the effects of different shifts in the curves. Oil

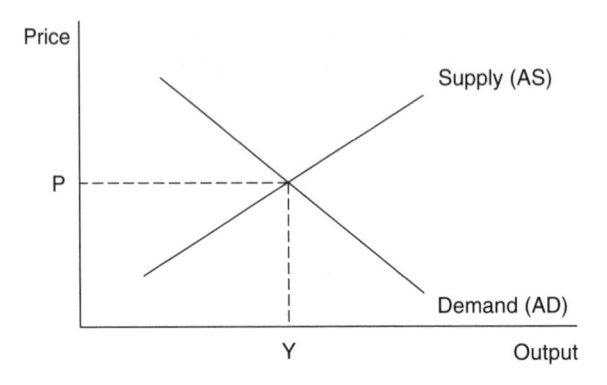

Figure 3.1 The law of supply and demand

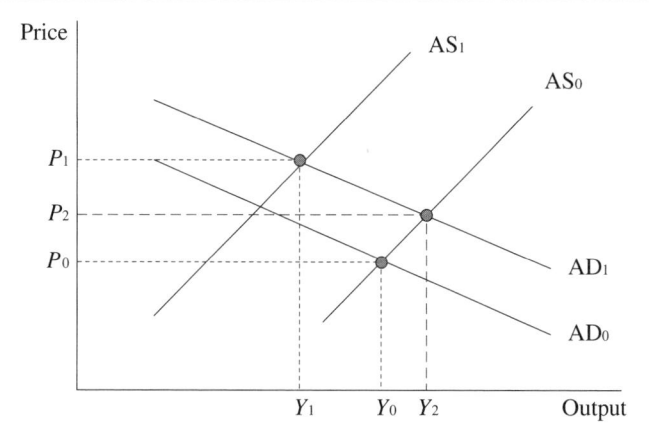

Figure 3.2 Shifts in supply and demand: manipulating inflation and growth

price shocks push back the supply curve, increasing prices and contracting output (P_1 and Y_1). Expansionary monetary or fiscal policy shifts out the demand curve, increasing prices and output (P_2 and Y_2). Changes in regulatory or legal parameters also influence the economy by creating incentives or disincentives that influence consumption, production, and investment – foreign or domestic.

```
↓ AS  ⇨  ↑ P  and  ↓ Y
↑ AD  ⇨  ↑ P  and  ↑ Y
```

Fiscal policy is implemented by adjusting the government budget surplus/deficit – that is, through changes in taxes and spending. Fiscal policy is a direct manipulation of GDP via the net of government revenues and expenditures (Equation 3.1) and an indirect manipulation of GDP via the effect of tax rates on consumption and investment. Monetary policy is implemented by adjusting the cost of money, either directly through base lending rates or indirectly through the money supply.[2] Monetary policy indirectly manipulates GDP via consumption, investment, and net trade (exports less imports).

Equation 3.1 Components of GDP

GDP = Consumption + Investment + Government + (Exports − Imports)

The magnitude of the effect on inflation and growth from a shift in the AS and AD curves depends on the slope of demand and supply. The curves are more inelastic (steeper) in the short run and more elastic (flatter) in the long run. In the short run, firms can only respond to increased orders by working existing labor and plant harder or longer. In the long run, new plants can be built, new machines can be purchased, and more workers can be hired. Consumers who own large gas-guzzling cars can only respond to higher fuel prices in the short run by curtailing their driving. Over the long run, however, consumers can switch to more fuel-efficient cars.

The degree of slack in the economy determines whether shifts in demand and supply have a larger impact on prices or output. If the economy is in recession, an increase in demand

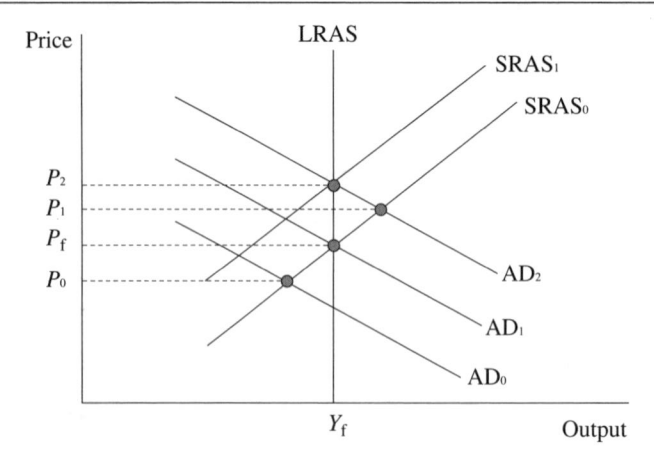

Figure 3.3 Keynesians versus Monetarists

puts less pressure on prices and there is more of an output response. On the other hand, if the economy is booming, an increase in demand puts more pressure on prices and there is less of a response in output. The reason is the feedback effect via wages and input prices. In bad times, workers are uncertain about their job security and suppliers are uncertain about their ability to remain in business. Hence, wage demands are put aside and suppliers let profit margins narrow. In good times, workers are more aggressive in their wage demands and firms can preserve their profit margins, thus increasing pressure in the overall price level.

Like any discipline, there are various schools of thought within economics. One school (Keynesian) advocates the importance of demand, while another school (Monetarist) advocates the importance of supply in the design of government policy to stimulate growth and curb inflation.[3] Essentially, the difference between the two schools is their different views about the slope of the supply curve (Figure 3.3). For Monetarists the aggregate supply curve is vertical (i.e. inelastic), while for Keynesians supply is positively sloped (i.e. elastic). As such, the Keynesian supply curve may be viewed as more of a short-term representation, while the Monetarist supply curve may be viewed as more of a long-term representation.

The Keynesian supply curve is associated with an inflation–output trade-off.[4] The inflation–output trade-off refers to the effect of increasing aggregate demand when the aggregate supply curve is positively sloped. As such, expansionary fiscal or monetary policy produces a higher level of real economic growth, albeit at the cost of higher prices. If the aggregate supply curve is vertical, however, attempts to increase aggregate demand produce only higher inflation, with no effect on real economic growth (Figure 3.3).

The different shapes of the aggregate supply curve reflect different degrees of wage–price flexibility as well as different inflation expectations. In the short run, there is considerable inertia in wages and prices as well as a slow adjustment in inflation expectations. As such, workers are initially fooled by the higher nominal wages generated by the policy stimulus and this money illusion prompts additional spending. Workers eventually observe that prices are higher as well, which in turn leads to the renegotiation of wage contracts and a retrenchment in spending. In the long run, inflation expectations as well as wages and prices fully adjust to the new level, such that there is no change in real economic activity.

Most economists agree that in the long run there is no trade-off between output and inflation. That is, attempts to move the economy beyond the equilibrium level of output will ultimately produce only higher inflation. In the short run, however, expansionary policy[5] can temporarily produce lower unemployment and higher economic growth.

The law of supply and demand is important for fixed income investors because the relative supply and demand for money directly affects the price of money – the interest rate. The monetary authorities control the supply of money, while the demand for money is related to economic activity. Hence, interest rate forecasts require a view on future monetary policy and economic growth.

The Business Cycle

An economic cycle may be viewed as the product of self-reinforcing effects. In good times, production and investment grow until the return on investment begins to decline, at which point production and investment are curtailed and a slump begins. Lower production eventually causes the return on investment to increase, and the cycle begins all over again (Figure 3.4).

The effect of a change in monetary (or fiscal) policy on the economy is analogous to tossing a stone into a still pond. The stone produces ever-widening ripples in the pond. In economic terms, these ever-widening ripples are feedback effects – produced by the interrelationships among economic variables. In the real world, our economic pond is bombarded by many stones being tossed into the water. A circular ripple generated from one stone eventually bumps into the ripple generated from another stone, producing a new pattern in the water. Such is the nature of a dynamic economy.

The interrelationships among economic variables mean that at times a given variable, such as the market interest rate, is the cause (e.g. the stone, or rather, the independent variable) and at other times it is the effect (e.g. the ripple, or rather, the dependent variable). The challenge is to determine where we are in the cycle. A business cycle consists of two types of circle: one virtuous and one vicious.

A virtuous circle might begin with a landmark trade agreement that shifts out the demand curve, increasing output and prices (Figure 3.5). The increase in demand boosts corporate profits. Businesses expand production to meet demand. In turn, business investment and employment rise. Rising income (via dividends and employment) boosts consumer confidence and consumption. Demand and business confidence are boosted further, and the cycle is repeated. Price increases reflect the abundance of demand relative to supply – a healthy economy.

A vicious circle might begin with an oil price shock that shifts back the supply curve, decreasing output and increasing prices. The sharp increase in oil prices reduces corporate profits. Marginal businesses close their doors; others are able to remain in business by cutting

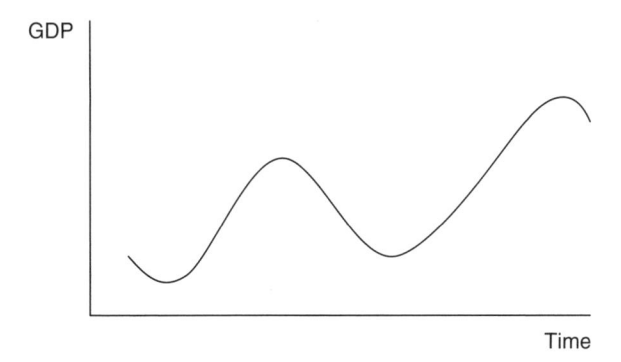

Figure 3.4 The business cycle

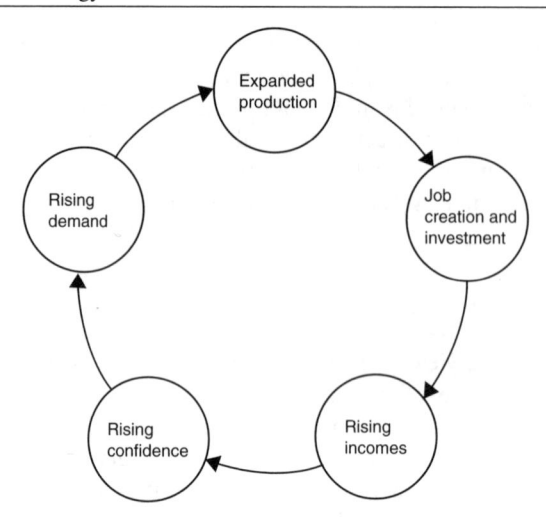

Figure 3.5 A virtuous circle

costs in other areas – such as jobs or investment in new projects. The decline in investment and employment in turn prompts a fall in income and consumption. Demand and confidence retract further, and the cycle is repeated. Price increases reflect the cost of doing business. High and variable rates of inflation make the evaluation of costs and benefits more uncertain.

The business cycle is important for fixed income investors because it aids in the evaluation of relative pressures on prices and interest rates – which is helpful for anticipating monetary policy. When the economy is growing quickly, the monetary authorities will be focused on inflation risk. When the economy is contracting, monetary authorities will be focused on the risk of a further deterioration in economic growth.

Economic Transmission Mechanism
Relative supply and demand → Business cycle phase → Spending or saving

3.2 INTEREST RATE THEORIES: FORECASTING MARKET DIRECTION

The yield of a bond has three components: (1) the risk-free real yield; (2) the expected rate of inflation; and (3) the premium for bearing risk. Interest rate forecasts require a view on each of these factors. The risk-free yield combined with the expected rate of inflation make up the nominal risk-free rate, which is examined in this section. The risk premium is examined in Section 3.4.

Equation 3.2   The components of a bond yield
Bond yield = Risk-free real interest rate + Expected inflation + Risk premium

The Risk-Free Real Yield

The risk-free real interest rate is a measure of the pure time value of money – that is, the strength of preference for consumption today as opposed to consumption in the future. A thriving economy is associated with vigorous investment and consumption – that is, a strong preference for money now. Hence, a thriving economy produces rising real interest rates. Conversely, a stagnating economy is associated with caution – that is, a strong preference to postpone spending for times that are more certain. Hence, an increased tendency to save will lead to falling real interest rates. In practice, real interest rates are inferred by stripping inflation expectations from the nominal yield observed in the market. In markets that have inflation-indexed government bonds (such as the US, the UK and the Euro area), risk-free real interest rates are directly observable.

Expected Inflation

We live in a dynamic world of changing prices and output. Based on past experience, we learn how inflation erodes our purchasing power – that is, how the same amount of money buys fewer goods. In order to maintain our purchasing power we allow for the effect of future price increases by adjusting the prices we set *today* for labor, capital, goods, and services. This behavior is particularly important in environments with high and variable inflation. Some economic agents will base their inflationary expectations on past performance (i.e. adaptive expectations); other agents will make their best possible prediction of the future using all available information (i.e. rational expectations). Whether one is backward- or forward-looking, monetary policy plays a key role in the formation of inflationary expectations.

Anticipating Changes in Monetary Policy (Part I)

Changes in monetary policy affect the performance of every asset in the economy. An increase in interest rates reduces the value of a fixed income portfolio (as price and yield are inversely related). Meanwhile, uncontrolled money growth that precipitates inflation – beyond what is expected – reduces the value in real terms of coupons and re-paid principal. As future monetary policy is a key risk factor for fixed income investors, substantial effort is made to anticipate actions by the central bank.

One way to anticipate monetary policy is to listen to what the policy makers have to say. Minutes of policy meetings and speeches (in many cases available on central bank websites) provide insight on the direction and timing of future policy moves – beyond the sound bites reported in the press. Press conferences are also valuable because insightful impromptu remarks can often be heard. It is important to note when the "doves" change their tune and start sounding hawkish (and vice versa).[6] Moreover, statements will tell you the underlying variables that have captured the current focus of the authorities. It is always worth going back to analyze what central bankers have said in light of what is actually done.

As monetary policy is ultimately based on an assessment of the economy, it is also important to monitor the fundamental data, particularly those indicators with the capacity to derail key assumptions of the base case scenario. When a central bank faces the dual objectives of price stability and full employment, it is particularly important to gauge the policy bias – such as whether the balance of risks to inflation is more to the upside or whether the balance of risks to economic growth is more to the downside.

In the early stages of the business cycle, there is plenty of slack in the economy. At this point, the central bank typically has a neutral- to accommodative-policy stance. In these circumstances (as well as in recessionary periods) the focus tends to be less on inflationary signals and more on leading indicators of economic recovery. In contrast, when the economy is in the advanced stages of the business cycle, the focus tends to be on the risk of inflation.

In assessing the upside risk to inflation, core price indices (excluding volatile food and energy components) are evaluated alongside key commodity prices, such as crude oil. The trend in wholesale prices and wage rates can be examined relative to consumer price trends to judge whether businesses feel sufficiently robust to pass input price increases on to the final consumer. Pass-through tends to be curtailed in sectors where there is greater competition or when the economy is sagging. Meanwhile, rising labor productivity (ahead of demands for higher wages) reduces the cost of doing business, which tends to subdue inflation.

In assessing the downside risk to economic growth, one might focus on the indicators of aggregate demand that are particularly sensitive to changes in interest rates – such as consumer spending on automobiles and homes as well as capital expenditure by business. Getting a handle on consumer spending is crucial as this is the dominant force in the economy (roughly two-thirds of GDP in the US and the UK). Consumer spending forecasts should be made in the context of changes in wealth (e.g. acceleration/deceleration in job losses, gains/losses in wages, weakness/strength in the stock market, and changes in the tax code). Imports also provide clues on domestic demand.

Business spending forecasts will rely on the outlook for corporate earnings and profits, both of which should be assessed within the context of whether declines or improvements have deepened or broadened across the economy. A large amount of excess production capacity (capacity utilization data) can thwart meaningful job growth and stall economic recovery. With inventory adjustments it is important to assess whether a build-up is voluntary or not; however, this can be difficult to judge. A buildup in inventories, if intentional is bullish on the economy (bearish for bonds). If unintentional, however, an increase indicates weakness ahead.

Relevant external factors include economic growth prospects in key export markets, currency strength, and exposure to event risk (such as Argentina's devaluation and default in 2002). Changes in the government's budget deficit/surplus must also be considered.[7]

Table 3.1 categorizes the economic indicators used by the market to anticipate monetary policy. Structural changes in the economy as well as a change in the focus of the monetary authorities will shift the relative importance of specific statistical reports.[8] Data that reflect a broader segment of the economy will have a greater impact in the market.

The lagged effect of monetary policy requires central bankers to be forward looking. As such, more forward-looking economic data – such as business and consumer sentiment surveys – may have larger significance than data released well after the fact (such as GDP). Sentiment surveys, however, register emotions and intentions for the future – not necessarily the same as what happens in reality.[9] Hence, reports on retail sales, manufacturing activity, and jobless claims are important for confirmation. Although unemployment data tend to be a lagging indicator of economic growth, reports of growing unemployment can increase consumer anxiety and curtail spending.

Many central banks have a price stability target in mind – whether inflation, money growth, or the exchange rate. Targets may be specific or vague. Even if a specific target is made public, there is likely to be some degree of tolerance for error that is not made public. In the event of extreme geopolitical or financial turmoil, however, the focus of the monetary authorities can be temporarily directed away from the domestic economy to the global economy.

Table 3.1 Economic data used to anticipate monetary policy

Direct measures of inflation	Indirect measures (via economic growth)
Consumer (retail) prices	Real GDP growth
Producer (wholesale) prices	Equity market weakness/strength
Core inflation (excluding food and energy)	Personal income and consumption
Crude oil and other commodity prices	Consumer confidence
Labor (employment) costs	Retail sales, home sales, auto sales
Average hourly earnings	Industrial production, factory orders
Currency strength/weakness	Capital spending by business
	Business outlook
	Corporate earnings (actual/expected)
	Business inventories (adjustments to)
	Durable goods orders
	Construction activity, housing starts
	Unemployment rate
	Initial and continuing jobless claims
	Non-farm payrolls
	Government budget deficit/surplus
	Trade balance (net foreign demand)
	Productivity growth

An important aspect of forecasting monetary policy is anticipating the method used to achieve price stability. Monetary policy is conducted by adjusting the volume of money and its price. Manipulation of the monetary base or the money multiplier effect will produce a shift in the money supply (Equation 3.3). The monetary base is equal to the currency held by the public plus commercial bank reserves and official foreign exchange reserves.[10] In a fractional reserve system – where banks are required to hold a fixed proportion of their deposits in the form of reserves – an increase in commercial bank reserves causes deposits to increase by a multiple of the initial amount of the reserve increase.

Equation 3.3 Money supply

Money supply = Monetary base × Money multiplier

The central bank controls the monetary base by direct injections or withdrawals of liquidity in its open market operations (OMO). Open market purchases of government securities by the monetary authorities increase the money supply (which reduces interest rates), while open market sales of government securities decrease the money supply (and increase interest rates). Central banks make daily injections/withdrawals of liquidity, ensuring the smooth operation of the financial system.

Alternatively, the central bank can manipulate the money supply by influencing the money multiplier – via the reserve ratio.[11] An increase in the reserve ratio reduces the volume of credit which produces the money multiplier effect, ultimately lowering the money supply and increasing interest rates. Conversely, a decrease in the required level of reserves increases the money supply, which reduces interest rates. In practice, reserve ratios are changed infrequently.

Changes in base lending rates directly affect the cost of borrowing reserves to meet obligatory reserve requirements. Reserves are non-interest bearing, so banks seek to keep them to a minimum. On the other hand, banks are penalized for having too few reserves. To avoid being penalized, banks that are short on reserves at the end of the day borrow from those banks – including the central bank – holding an excess. In the US the rate charged by the Federal Reserve is the discount rate, while the benchmark rate of interest charged by depository institutions trading reserves among themselves is the federal funds rate. In the US market, practitioners closely monitor changes made to the federal funds rate, while in the Euro area the focus is on changes made to the minimum bid rate on the ECB's main refinancing operation.

The Transmission of Monetary Policy

A change in the market for central bank reserves triggers a chain of complex economic interactions. For example, an increase in the base lending rate produces increases in other short-term interest rates.[12] A rise in short-term rates that is expected to continue also leads to increases (typically smaller) in long-term rates. The higher cost of credit makes current consumption more costly, which reduces demand for housing, business investment, automobiles, and other consumer durables – those items that are the most sensitive to changes in the cost of borrowing. The change in demand for these items has spillover effects into other sectors of the economy. The reduction in aggregate demand ultimately produces a slowdown in economic growth and subdues inflationary pressures.

$$\Delta \text{Central bank's base lending rate} \to \Delta \text{Aggregate demand}$$
$$\to \Delta \text{Economic growth, inflation}$$

Monetary policy also affects the yield curve and the performance of spread products. When the central bank raises interest rates, the yield curve tends to flatten and spread products tend to underperform government bonds. Rate changes by the central bank have a direct influence on the short end of the yield curve and an indirect effect on the long end of the curve (via changes in inflation expectations). Credit spreads tend to widen when the central bank raises rates because investors fear the rate increase will weaken the economy. That said, each spread product should be considered on its own merits.

The monetary authority's choice of policy instrument will affect the timing and magnitude of the impact on the money supply and, ultimately, the timing and magnitude of the impact of monetary policy on the economy. Still, even for the same policy instrument, such as a change in official interest rates, the ultimate effect on the economy will depend on the prevailing circumstances. Figure 3.6 illustrates the changing relationship between the US federal funds rate and real GDP. Indeed, the complex web of dynamic economic interactions makes the skillful conduct of monetary policy – such as the engineering of a soft landing from an overheating economy – as much an art as a science.

Predicting the timing and magnitude of monetary policy changes remains a challenge. The complex interrelationships within the economy mean that the full effect of a policy change takes time to work through the economy. Moreover, the dynamic nature of the economy means that a 50 bps cut in interest rates cannot be expected to produce the same result with the same lag as was achieved in the past.[13] Given the lagged and uncertain effect of a policy change, monetary authorities are less likely to respond to gradual adjustments in the economy. Hence, the pace of change in economic variables is quite important when anticipating a response from the central bank.

Economic Fundamentals 49

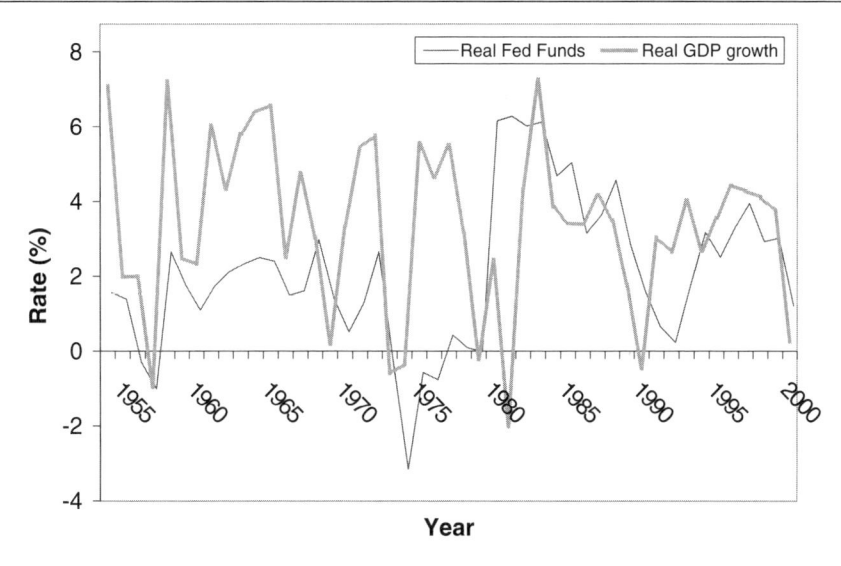

Figure 3.6 US federal funds rate and US GDP

Completing the Circle: The Determinants of Equilibrium Market Interest Rates

Classical Theory

The equilibrium interest rate equates the amount of funds that individuals desire to lend with the amount that others wish to borrow. Money demand (M_d) is a function of the price level (P), real aggregate output (Y), and the transaction velocity of money (V), such that $M_s = M_d = PY \div V$. As such, rising prices and real GDP increase the demand for money, while an increase in transaction velocity reduces the demand for money.

ΔEconomic growth, Inflation $\to$ ΔMoney demand $\to$ ΔInterest rates

Keynesian Theory

The equilibrium interest rate equates the supply and demand of money. Money is defined in terms of cash – that is, it pays no interest, in contrast to a bond, which does. The same equilibrium interest rate also equates the supply and demand for bonds. Money demand is a function of transactions demand (the cash required for planned transactions), precautionary demand (the extra cash held for unexpected transactions), and speculative demand (the cash used to speculate on future changes in interest rates). Transactions and precautionary demand are a positive function of income and a negative function of the interest rate; speculative demand is a negative function of the interest rate. Hence, money demand is a positive function of income and inversely related to interest rates.

ΔEconomic growth $\to$ ΔIncome, transactions $\to$ ΔMoney demand $\to$ ΔInterest rates

Summary

Table 3.2 displays a number of factors that influence market interest rates. This summary also includes aspects that were covered in Chapter 1.

Table 3.2 Factors that influence market interest rates

An increase in market rates may reflect:	A decrease in market rates may reflect:
Inflation (real, perceived, or expected)	Deflation (real, perceived, or expected)
A sharp decrease in the money supply	Strong growth in the money supply
Heavy issuance of bonds	Curtailed issuance of bonds
Reduced odds of monetary easing	Increased odds of monetary easing
Anticipated reversal in long bond positions	Asset allocation away from a weak equity market
Stronger-than-expected GDP data	Deterioration in confidence indicators
Required compensation for an expected depreciation in the local currency	Lower energy prices

3.3 YIELD CURVE MODELS: FORECASTING MOVEMENTS IN THE YIELD CURVE

As we saw in Chapter 1, the yield curve represents the relationship between the yield and maturity of a bond. By demonstrating the reward (in terms of yield) that is expected for commitments of different lengths, the yield curve isolates the pure price of time. Uses of the term structure of interest rates include:

1. Analyzing returns for investment commitments over different horizons
2. Assessing consensus expectations of future interest rates
3. Pricing bonds or options on bonds
4. Arbitraging between bonds of different maturities
5. Forming expectations about the economy.

As illustrated in Chapter 1, there are four classic yield curve shapes: rising (normal), falling (inverted), flat, and humped. Under normal conditions, yields rise continuously – possibly with some reduction in the rate of increase at longer maturities. An inverted or downward-sloping yield curve is typical when yields are currently high by historical standards. A flat curve indicates that interest rates are unaffected by maturity. With a hump-shaped curve, yields initially rise, but then peak and decline.

There are a number of theories that explain the shape of the yield curve. However, no single theory is conclusive in terms of both explanatory power and empirical evidence. The basic theories are broadly characterized below, including implications for practitioners.

The Expectations Hypothesis

According to the expectations hypothesis, the shape of the yield curve is determined by current market expectations of future short-term interest rates. A normal upward-sloping curve indicates expectations of rising interest rates throughout the relevant future – perhaps the result of central bank efforts to subdue inflationary pressures. On the other hand, an inverted curve indicates expectations of falling interest rates, with the timing of the downward movement in rates inferred from the maturity where the curve peaks. In an environment of well-contained inflation, a predominantly flat yield curve might reflect trust that the central bank will pre-empt inflationary pressures by raising short-term interest rates ahead of time.

Market expectations of rising rates in the long term generate a positively sloped curve because: (1) investors prefer to hold short-term investments as the value of longer term assets will fall as interest rates rise; (2) speculators anticipate the rise in rates and short sell the long end; and (3) borrowers wanting long-term funds borrow now when it is cheaper – all of which bids up the price of bonds at the short end of the curve relative to the long end. One implication[14] of the expectations hypothesis is that investors act only to profit from expectations about the future level of interest rates, without consideration for the risk that actual returns may deviate from their expectations. Based on the liquidity hypothesis, however, we know that accounting for such uncertainty creates a positive bias to the slope of the yield curve.

Although the expectations hypothesis accounts for all possible shapes in the yield curve, forward rates (e.g. the consensus expectation of future yields) are generally considered to be unreliable predictors of actual future interest rates.[15] De Bondt and Bange (1992) and Shefrin (2000) find a strong and predictable under-reaction bias in the inflation forecast which roundly rejects the expectations hypothesis.[16] De Bondt and Bange report three important features concerning the link between predictable interest rate movements and inflation forecast errors:

1. When the yield spread is above average, inflation forecasts tend to be too high.
2. When the 12-month-ahead inflation forecast exceeds the 6-month-ahead forecast, investors subsequently earned positive excess returns by holding long-term bonds.
3. Past inflation errors are positively correlated with future excess returns.

This means that excess returns are not only forecastable, but can be predicted by the extent to which the market has misjudged recent inflation. Hence, when spreads are high *and* investors have been under-reacting to declining inflation, a sell short/buy long strategy would capitalize on investor errors. The strategy is risky, however, because of uncertainty about what the central bank will do and because it relies on particular investor errors (Shefrin, 2000).

The Preferred Habitat Hypothesis

According to the preferred habitat hypothesis, the shape of the yield curve is determined by maturity preferences, which in turn affect the supply and demand for securities of different maturities. For example, pension funds and life insurance companies prefer long-term investments to match against their long-term liabilities. As such, they tend to dominate the long-term segment of the curve. Commercial banks, on the other hand, tend to restrict their lending and financing activities to short-term securities. Because bonds with longer maturities have greater convexity, there would seem to be a tendency to prefer the longer end of the curve (i.e. a convexity bias). Investors and issuers can be induced to depart from their preferred maturity range for a price – that is, at an appropriate premium reflecting the aversion to price or reinvestment risk when an alternative maturity segment appears to offer the best return for risk.

Since the preferred habitat premium responds to excess supply and demand conditions within a maturity range, all yield curve shapes are accommodated. For example, the preferred habitat premium would decrease with maturity as a result of a preponderance of investors and no offsetting actions by bond issuers at the long end. The preferred habitat hypothesis would seem to predict more variable demand in short term securities – in contrast to the larger variability observed at the long end – given the dominance of commercial banks at the short end.

The Liquidity (Risk Premium) Hypothesis[17]

According to the liquidity hypothesis, the yield curve is upward sloping (rising at a uniform rate) reflecting the premium that must be paid to bondholders for postponing consumption and assuming a higher level of risk with bonds of longer maturities. The return increment offered by longer maturities is a premium for bearing illiquidity and assuming the risk that there will be a difference between actual and expected interest rates. Moreover, risk increases as maturity is lengthened because bond price fluctuations increase with maturity – although at a decreasing rate.[18] As such, the liquidity risk premium should also increase with maturity, but at a decreasing rate. Hence, yield curve shifts reflect changes in the liquidity premium. During flight-to-quality events such as geopolitical or financial crises, for example, there is a surge in both the risk premium and the demand for short-term maturities.

Although there is strong empirical evidence of liquidity premia, the liquidity risk hypothesis fails to account for inverted, flat, or humped yield curves. Moreover, evidence suggests that the liquidity premium is unstable.[19] The implication for investors is that the liquidity hypothesis is only part of the story driving yield curve behavior. As such, the curve will be "normal" in the absence of other factors (discussed below). In the absence of other influences, investors would expect to earn higher returns, on average, from extending maturities.

The Stochastic-Process Hypothesis

According to the stochastic-process hypothesis, the shape of the yield curve is determined by predictable as well as unpredictable elements. The predictable component is specified by a mean-reverting process, whereby interest rates are more likely to fall/rise when they are above/below the long-term trend. In other words, there is the tendency for the yield curve to revert to its normal shape. The unpredictable component is the product of three items: (1) interest rate volatility (measured by the standard deviation); (2) the initial level of the interest rate; and (3) a stochastic process. Hence, by construction the term structure is more random during periods of high and volatile interest rates. The implication for investors is that defensive/neutral positions are prudent during periods of high and volatile interest rates.

Although this model is capable of producing any yield curve shape and preliminary tests of this model have been supportive (McEnally and Jordan, 1997), it has several drawbacks relevant for practitioners. First, mean reversion models are extremely sensitive to the period used to calculate the long-term trend. Second, there may be persistent factors that delay the reversion to trend for significant periods of time. Finally, the stochastic nature of the model reduces its value in forecasting the term structure.

Summary

There are a number of yield curve theories (Table 3.3) but the empirical evidence[20] permits only tentative conclusions as to their validity. Nevertheless, each theory seems to tell at least part of the story. Practitioners are thus advised to consider all of these influences when anticipating changes in the yield curve: (1) the natural upward bias of the curve due to a rising liquidity premium; (2) a convexity bias that weighs on yields at the long end of an investor's preferred habitat; and (3) the time trajectory of inflationary expectations. The "normal" upward-sloping curve occurs in spite of a convexity bias and in the absence of offsetting expectations of falling interest rates. Although analysts may disagree about the relative importance of risk premia,

Table 3.3 Summary of yield curve theories

Curve shape	Individual theory	Combined theories
Rising (normal)	• Risk premium increases with maturity. • Yields expected to rise. • Excess demand for short-term funds by commercial banks; excess supply of long-term funds.	The increase in the risk premium is large enough to offset the convexity bias, a decline in inflation expectations, and excess demand at the long end of the yield curve.
Falling (inverted)	• Risk premium alone cannot explain. • Yields expected to fall. • Excess demand for long-term funds; excess supply of short-term funds. • Convexity bias.	The increase in the risk premium is more than offset by the convexity bias, falling inflation expectations, and excess demand at the long end of the yield curve.
Flat	• Risk premium alone cannot explain. • Yields expected to remain unchanged. • Balanced demand and supply conditions across the curve.	The increase in the risk premium and excess demand for long-term funds is balanced by the convexity bias and an increase in inflation expectations.
Humped	• Risk premium alone cannot explain. • Yields are expected to first rise and then fall. • Extreme oversupply of intermediates.	Flight-to-quality demand at the short end combined with convexity bias and expectations of moderately declining interest rates from the middle of the curve.

convexity bias, and rate expectations, a general rule of thumb is that monetary policy actions are more important for shifts at the short end of the curve, while inflation expectations are more important at the long end. Ilmanen (1996) notes that no matter what you believe to be the correct yield curve theory, the forward curve[21] reflects break-even yields, and, assuming an unchanged yield curve, provides a visual indicator of relatively cheap maturity sectors.

Anticipating Changes in the Yield Curve

Curve allocation decisions require forecasting changes in the market's assessment of the different segments of the yield curve. As such, the investor must have a contrasting view – either with respect to a future action or with respect to the timing of a future action. One portion of the curve may be expected to flatten, while another portion of the curve may be expected to steepen.

The yield curve might be expected to flatten due to the unwinding of steepening strategies – perhaps due to market overshooting or because the cheap valuations which drove the steepening have become fairly valued. Profit taking and hedging could also cause the curve to flatten.

The yield curve flattens from the short end (up to 2-year maturities) when short-term rates rise relative to the long end. The short end of the market tends to be more sensitive to near-term central bank rate expectations, expected carry, sharp re-evaluations of risk premia, and temporal supply/demand imbalances. The short end will sell off when the central bank unexpectedly hikes base lending rates, when the market reduces its central bank easing expectations, when the market shifts to a tightening bias in anticipation of the end of an easing cycle, or if the central bank cut rates by less than what the market expects. Expectations of low carry can also produce curve-flattening from the short end. Finally, a sharp improvement in risk appetite (characterized by a reversal of flight-to-quality positions) tends to have a larger impact at the short end of the yield curve.

The yield curve flattens from the long end when long rates fall relative to the short end. The long end of the market tends to be more sensitive to inflation expectations and structural supply/demand imbalances. Structural factors that might produce flattening at the long end of the curve include: an aging population that buoys pension fund demand,[22] sustained budget discipline leading to a reduction in the supply of long-dated government bonds, and EMU convergence trades. Market expectations for lower inflation over the medium to long term and a falling risk premium due to improved economic conditions over the medium to long term would also produce curve flattening from the long end.

- *Anticipate steepening from the short end* – (1) if you expect more easing from the central bank than the market does; (2) with flight-to-quality events; (3) when there is high carry from a steep yield curve (i.e. demand creating demand); or (4) to correct excessive flattening.
- *Anticipate steepening from the long end* – as a result of (1) higher inflationary expectations (associated with an overheating economy or oil price shocks); or (2) an abundance of government debt as the result of a sharp increase in government budget deficits.

3.4 SPREAD THEORIES: ANTICIPATING CHANGES IN THE RISK PREMIUM

From Chapter 2, we know that spreads represent the risk premium over debt considered to be free of default risk – such as US Treasuries. The wider the spread, the higher the risk. The compensation required for bearing this additional risk is typically measured by the nominal yield spread – the difference between the yield on a given bond and the yield on a US Treasury of comparable maturity. As such, the yield spread is influenced by the level of interest rates.

The economic cycle and the risk appetite of investors determine the overall environment of yield spreads. Within this environment, the risk premium of a specific bond is also affected by the risk associated with the issuer, relative demand, liquidity, structure, and tax factors. Since the spread reflects compensation for additional risk, changes in *perceived* risk may cause spreads to change.[23] For foreign issued bonds, the spread is also affected by exchange rate risk, interest rate differentials, and political risk. These factors are discussed in more detail below.

Key determinants of the risk premium
Economic cycle, Risk appetite, Credit risk, Relative demand, Liquidity

Economic Cycle

The economic cycle is the main determinant of the environment for spread products. Spreads widen in anticipation of an economic slowdown, while spreads narrow in anticipation of economic expansion. During an economic slowdown, corporations experience a decline in revenue and reduced cash flow, making it more difficult to service debt obligations. To induce investors to hold non-Treasury securities, the yield spread against Treasuries must widen.

Conversely, during an economic expansion, revenue and cash flow pick up, increasing the capacity to service debt obligations.

Risk Appetite of Investors

A change in the willingness of investors to hold risky assets affects the overall environment for spread products; it may also affect market risk. Changes in risk appetite may be due to a change in preferences or due to institutional factors, such as the need to adjust portfolios following losses incurred on holdings of other assets. A flight-to-quality generally involves much wider credit spreads, reflecting a significant increase in the aversion to risk. Measures of risk appetite include JP Morgan Fleming's LCPI and Citigroup's Instability Index. The Instability Index, for example, tracks signals of deleveraging, debt market credit spreads (BBB industrials, emerging market Brady bonds, US swaps to Treasuries and Euro swaps to Bunds) and the implied volatilities across three asset classes (equity, debt, and foreign) for insight as to the demand for insurance protection from investors. An increase in the Instability Index is associated with a widening in the spread.

Issuer Creditworthiness

A change in the perceived creditworthiness of the issuer will affect the yield spread of an individual bond. Credit risks arise from the possibility that debtors will default on their obligations. An increase in credit risk will increase the spread, while a reduction in credit risk will reduce the spread. Intuitively, if IBM's credit improves then its bonds would be more valuable, so they would yield less – reducing the spread over Treasuries. On the other hand, if IBM's credit deteriorated, investors would demand more in return for bearing the additional risk associated with holding its debt – that is, a higher yield. Firms with better credit (i.e. a higher credit rating) pay less for issuing new bonds and benefit from a general widening in credit spreads at the expense of firms with lower credit ratings. In the case of sovereign debt, both the ability and willingness to pay is part of the risk of default. While it is generally true to say that a borrower's yield spread will narrow if its credit improves and vice versa, this is not the whole story. Relative demand for a particular borrower's credit is also important. Credit ratings are one measure of credit risk.

Relative Demand

The yield spread is also an indication of the relative demand for a particular borrower's credit or bond sector. Hence, the oversupply or the relative scarcity of one sector compared to another will cause spreads to move. Generally, an oversupply of a particular spread product will cause prices to fall and the spread to widen. Conversely, excess demand will cause prices to rise and the spread to narrow. That said, a burst of new supply may coincide with an overall market spread contraction, or a sharp decline in new supply may coincide with an overall expansion in market spreads. In the investment grade corporate market, heavy supply often helps spreads as the new primary valuations validate and enhance valuations in the secondary market (e.g. supply creates its own demand) (Malvey, 1997). The performance of alternative spread products and asset classes is another important factor, as changes in the prices of other assets affect the opportunity cost of holding a particular security. For example, abysmal performance in equities and uncertainty about the corporate sector might enhance the attractiveness of government bonds. This relative scarcity in government bonds would tend to keep spreads wide.

Liquidity

Larger issues pose less of a liquidity risk than smaller issues. Changes in the preference for holding longer-dated bonds relative to shorter-dated bonds also affect the liquidity premium. A common measure of the liquidity premium is the spread between bid and ask prices.

Structure

Many issues have embedded call or prepayment options. Hence, the spreads on these bonds will reflect changes in the value of the embedded option, which is determined by interest rate volatility and the direction of change in interest rates. In the case of a callable bond, an increase in interest rate volatility increases the value of the embedded call option and reduces the value of the bond, thereby increasing the spread against a comparable non-callable bond. An expected decline in the level of interest rates will also widen the spread, as declining interest rates increase the prospect that the issuer will call the bond.

Tax Factors

Tax exempt bonds, such as US municipal bonds, have an advantage over their non-tax exempt counterparts. The tax advantage means that municipal bonds will offer a lower yield. Expected changes in tax legislation affect the spread between municipal and government bonds.

Country Considerations

For bonds issued in a foreign country, spread changes are also associated with anticipated movements in exchange rates and interest rate differentials. Perceptions of political risk – which is analogous to the credit risk of corporate debt – are also a factor. For example, emerging market sovereign borrowers are perceived to be more likely to default on their debt than developed market sovereign borrowers. As a result, investors typically require additional compensation (i.e. higher yields) to hold emerging market bonds. This is, however, not always the case. For example, the debt of the Czech Republic was trading below the benchmark Euro area curve in 2002 and 2003.

The Spread Curve

There is a term structure of credit spreads, known as "the spread curve".[24] Analytically, the spread curve is comparable to the yield curve, except that there is an extra layer of risk. An analysis of the term structure of credit spreads helps one to distinguish between risk factors affecting the whole curve (e.g. parallel shifts in the average spread across the maturity spectrum) and those affecting certain maturity sectors.

Generally, the spread curve is upward sloping, such that spreads are wider at longer maturities. An upward-sloping spread curve is consistent with risk aversion as higher duration bonds have greater price volatility than lower duration bonds. The term structure tends to be steeper for issuers with lower credit ratings than for those with higher credit ratings. Still, the long end of the spread curve has a downward bias because longer maturity bonds have greater spread convexity.[25]

The spread term structure may reflect expectations about the timing of a default and the path of resolution and recovery thereafter. For example, an upward-sloping spread curve may reflect the belief that a default in the near term is unlikely, whereas going forward there is a greater likelihood of a significant deterioration in credit quality than of a significant improvement. On the other hand, bond spreads might decrease with maturity for borrowers facing near-term financing difficulties. In this case, the short maturity spreads reflect the high near-term risk of default, while lower spreads at the longer maturities reflect the potential for corrective measures to be put in place to secure the long-term sustainability of the debt (Cunningham et al., 2001).

Changes in market pricing can also skew the spread curve. Under normal conditions bonds are priced on a spread basis. When the probability of default is high, however, a bond will trade on a price basis. Price-based trades are preferred because of the change in focus to the cash at risk (from the yield sacrifice). Also, past debt restructurings have been executed on a price basis. When trading goes from spread based to price based, the spread curve becomes inverted.

Iwanowski and Chandra (1995) find that corporate spread curves tend to flatten as the Treasury curve steepens, and confirm other findings that corporate spreads tend to tighten when Treasury yields rise. On the other hand, Malvey (1997) shows that the US corporate spread curve is highly independent of changes in the shape and altitude of the benchmark Treasury curve. This independence is attributed to (1) rising the rapid growth of mutual fund and total return barbellers (relative to longer-term insurance and pension fund managers) which seldom modify investment policy to surf among ripples in the underlying benchmark curve; (2) the rise in popularity of spread duration in the measurement of risk; and (3) the existence of trading conventions which limit the movement of corporate spreads.[26]

Anticipating Changes in Spreads

Spread performance will depend on the market's changing focus on the various determinants of spreads.

- *Anticipate spread narrowing* when (1) there is a general improvement in the environment for spread product (economic recovery and reduced aversion to risk); (2) alternative asset classes are less attractive; and (3) a new issue is expected to be well received.
- *Anticipate spread widening* when there is (1) rising uncertainty in the banking sector; (2) seasonal funding; (3) reduced prospects of economic recovery; and (4) during an equity bear market.

3.5 VOLATILITY MODELS: ANTICIPATING CHANGES IN VOLATILITY

As shown in Chapters 1 and 2, interest rate volatility affects the value of convexity and the value of bonds with embedded options. Volatility is triggered by an abrupt change in perception – such as the reversal of a policy that has been maintained so long that two-way risk is no longer contemplated. Uncertainty about the timing of an anticipated shift in the bias of monetary policy – from growth to inflation or vice versa – can also produce volatility in market interest rates. The more ingrained a perception becomes, such as when it becomes clear that the market is in a trend, the larger the response will be when that perception is unfulfilled.

Market perception – in particular the strength of market perception – can be gauged by (1) determining what interest rate expectations are priced into the market (discussed in Chapter 8); or (2) comparing implied to historical option volatility. When implied volatility is below/above the historical trend over the last few years, option volatility is cheap/dear. Volatility becomes cheap when the market sees only one-way risk. As such, the best time to hedge will be when you do not want to.

Table 3.4 Anticipating changes in interest rate volatility

Indicators of increased volatility	Indicators of decreased volatility
• When the trend becomes unclear • When option volatility is dear (i.e. implied > historical)	• When the trend becomes clear • When option volatility is cheap (i.e. implied < historical)

Generally, volatility is a declining function of maturity[27]; that is, market yields on shorter securities tend to be more volatile than yields on longer securities. The selection of volatility along the yield curve affects the risk adjustment of the portfolio. In other words, investors buy volatility on a particular part of the yield curve and sell it at another part in order to secure desired risk exposure.

Within all sectors there are bonds that perform well for a particular volatility forecast. In practice, however, it is difficult to differentiate between the influences of liquidity and quality on spread changes coincident with volatility changes.

3.6 THE EFFICIENT MARKETS HYPOTHESIS

Eugene Fama's efficient markets hypothesis (EMH) is one of the most debated in finance. EMH – also known as the random walk hypothesis – claims that financial prices fully reflect all available information (Fama, 1970). Because news is random, market price movements are random, or very close to random. As such, price movements follow a random walk. By implication, a bull/bear market is generated by a series of good/bad surprises. In other words, a random process can generate patterns.

The efficient markets hypothesis has three forms: weak, semi-strong, and strong. The weak form states that all market information is already factored into the current market price.[28] The semi-strong form states that all public information is already factored into the current price. The strong form states that all public and private information has been incorporated. Essentially, the correct price for a stock or bond is the one shown on your Bloomberg screen.

EMH assumes that identical investors share rational expectations about asset prices and then efficiently discount information into the market.[29] By implication, there are no profitable strategies available that are not already priced into the market, making it all but impossible to outperform the market. Moreover, attempts to improve investment performance through market timing will most likely fail.

Supporters of EMH find no compelling evidence that bond prices are influenced by past price behavior (Faillace and Thomas, 1997). Moreover, numerous studies indicate that active managers have been unable to time the market successfully on a consistent basis. For example, Sharpe (1975) finds that those who attempt to time the market (i.e. anticipate market turning points) must be correct roughly 75% of the time to merely match the overall performance of the manager who does not time the market. One reason for the disparity is the higher transaction costs associated with a more active market-timing strategy. Another reason is that market-turning points can only be recognized in retrospect.

In bear markets, for example, three to four months out of ten are up months. A manager that anticipates a bear market too soon – parking funds in cash equivalents during good years – sacrifices higher returns. Meanwhile, a manager that gets into a bull market too late is susceptible to missing the lion's share of the gains, as a disproportionate share of the total gain from a bull market tends to occur at the beginning of a market recovery.

Although fund managers are able to match the performance of their selected benchmark index before charges, net of fees, they have been unable to outperform a buy and hold strategy. It has also been shown that managers who outperform in one time period do not have a better chance of outperforming in another.

How, then, does EMH account for the incredible investment results of Benjamin Graham, Warren Buffett, Peter Lynch, and many others, or explain the various strategies that have managed to beat the market in the recent past? Supporters of EMH characterize such examples as "anomalies"[30]. A counterview – which is taken up further in Chapter 5 – is that individuals systematically misprice securities. One of the catalysts for this alternative view was the US stock market crash in 1987. Survey evidence on this event determined that more than half of the market moves occurred in the absence of news on fundamentals (Shiller, 1987).

Implications for Fixed Income Investors

Given the wealth of evidence supporting both sides of the EMH debate, it seems reasonable to conclude that portions of the market are more efficient than others. Where information is less available, less reliable, or less thoroughly analyzed – such as emerging market debt – the potential for outperforming the market is the greatest.

The evidence on anomalies points to areas even in the US Treasury market where efficiency is imperfect. However, the intense level of competition in the market seems to ensure that EMH is at least a decent approximation of reality – meaning that particular anomalies, once discovered, will disappear.

- Earning excess returns depends on obtaining information that is not already discounted by the market or identifying anomalies not yet seen by the market.
- Inefficiencies still appear, but they last for only short periods. As such, it is a challenge to get a lot of money into a position to profit from the market's mispricing.
- If market efficiency is due to the intense level of competition, one can also assume that in a competitive market not everyone does equally well. As such, individuals have potential to outperform or underperform.

3.7 CHAOS THEORY

Chaos theorists believe that financial markets are complex adaptive systems. A complex adaptive system is one where the agents in the system interact with each other and continually adapt their behavior to changes in the environment. An essential element of a complex adaptive system is the feedback loop. Strong positive feedback loops mean that the dynamic system has a tendency for instability. The recurrence of financial bubbles and crashes is consistent with strong positive feedback loops.

To describe a complex adaptive system correctly, one needs non-linear mathematics – this is deterministic chaos. The nature of non-linear mathematics is that, in general, one can only forecast behavior over the very short-term, and then only when the dynamics are understood. Even with theoretically correct non-linear models, it is impossible to forecast long-term behavior.

In contrast, economic models are generally based on linear equations and static equilibrium relationships. When feedback loops are incorporated, they are generally negative loops – those leading to stability – rather than the destabilizing positive loops suggested by financial bubbles and crashes. Such misspecification, according to chaos theorists, produces inaccurate short-term forecasts.

Table 3.5 Random walk versus chaos versus practitioners

	EMH	Chaos	Practitioners
Is there structure in market movements?	No. Financial price movements are random.	Chaotic time series appears random if tested by traditional methods.	Yes.
Can trading rules work?	Any rule that works will eventually be priced out of the market.	Perhaps. The interaction is very complex due to many feedback effects.	Yes.
Is it possible to outperform the market in principle?	No one can predict something that is random.	Chaotic behavior is not easy to predict, but is not inherently impossible.	Yes. From time to time if you are skilled enough.
Is it possible to consistently outperform?	There will always be someone who is more lucky than average.	There will always be someone who is smarter than average.	No one can beat the market all the time; the best traders have an edge which improves their odds.

Source: Adapted from *The Psychology of Finance: Understanding the Behavioural Dynamics of Markets* (Revised), L. Tvede. Copyright 2002 © John Wiley & Sons Limited. Reproduced with permission.

Empirical research on economic chaos – that is, non-linear systems where the individual parts interact and exhibit feedback effects that alter behavior – suggests that economic and financial behavior beyond one year is unpredictable (Ploeg, 1985; Chen, 1986; Chirella, 1986; Rasmussen and Mosekilde, 1988). Hence, there is a conundrum: Improving the economic models (i.e. recognizing the full dynamics of the system) makes the systemic behavior more chaotic – that is, very messy and highly unpredictable.[31] In practice, chaotic outcomes are difficult to distinguish from random ones (Table 3.5).

Implications for Fixed Income Investors

Chaos theory has two implications for fixed income investors:

1. Long-term predictions (beyond one year) are meaningless.
2. Short-term predictions must weigh the broad implications of simple economic models and the highly specific implications of complex models.

3.8 ECONOMIC FUNDAMENTALS: USES AND MISUSES

Practitioners trading on economics alone (e.g. fundamentals), believe that the economic cycle is the most important determinant of the bond price. Moreover, they believe that the cycle is predictable.

The Power of Economics

- *Structural framework* – Economics provides an understanding of the transmission mechanism of various exogenous changes in the economy – while holding all other things constant.

Of course, all other things do not in reality remain constant. Hence, forecasts involve some judgment as to the relative importance of shocks. An independent assessment of the economic outlook is useful for identifying market interpretations of the economic data that are too extreme and for correctly anticipating economic shifts not already reflected in the market consensus.

- *Long-term predictive power* – The long-run economic cycle is closely correlated with changes in bond yields, and trends in both tend to persist for a year or longer (Steward and Lynch, 1997).

The Limitations of Economics

- *Short-term predictive power* – Market interest rates have been shown to deviate substantially over the short-term from the level consistent with economic fundamentals. We shall revisit this issue in Chapter 6.
- *Preferences* – Economics has nothing to say about how preferences are formed, yet preferences are vital for outcomes. We shall revisit this issue in Chapter 5.
- *Motives* – Economics focuses on the optimal policy choice, not whether the optimal policy will be chosen (i.e. political risk). We shall revisit this issue in Chapter 4.

Economics provides an understanding of the transmission mechanism (e.g. how the cycle operates). Where we are situated in the business cycle will often be subject to debate, as this involves an assessment of the sensitivities and of the timing of feedback effects. While chaos theory provides a strong case for the importance of using non-linear equations to represent financial markets, it is lacking in practical implications for investors. To get a better handle on market dynamics, we need to examine the motives behind the choices individuals make as well as the formation of preferences. In other words, we need to understand politics and psychology. These topics are discussed in Part II.

NOTES

1. That is, choosing Option A precludes the possibility of choosing Option B.
2. Monetary policy is discussed in more detail in section 3.2.
3. According to Monetarists, changes in the money supply have no long-run effect on real output, unemployment or real interest rates. Instead, real output in the long run is determined by supply side factors (technology, population growth, the flexibility of markets, and the efficiency of the institutional framework of the economy). As such, monetary policy can only contribute to long-run growth via the achievement of price stability. Alternatively, Keynesians believe in the effectiveness of aggregate demand management.
4. The trade-off in the theoretical model is actually between inflation and unemployment, represented by the Phillips curve. For purposes of simplification, the trade-off is represented here as one between inflation and output.
5. In the case of monetary policy, only unanticipated changes produce these temporary effects. That is, an anticipated monetary expansion translates directly into higher prices (via inflation expectations), with no effect on output. Fluctuations in fiscal policy have real effects, whether anticipated or not.
6. A dovish policy maker is inclined to lower interest rates while a hawkish policy maker is inclined to raise rates.
7. A large fiscal stimulus might offset the need for the monetary authority to act, or might tip the balance of risk from growth to inflation – prompting a contraction in monetary policy.
8. For example, there was a period when US money supply data generated the greatest price action. These days passed as the Federal Reserve stopped targeting bank reserves in 1982. Moreover, the relationship between money and economic growth broke down.

9. For example, US consumer confidence surveys in 2002 were grim, while spending continued relatively unabated.
10. Balance of payments surpluses increase foreign exchange reserves and increase the money supply unless the central bank makes an offsetting adjustment in commercial bank reserves (i.e. sterilization).
11. The reserve ratio is the amount of funds that commercial banks and other depository institutions must hold in reserve against deposits.
12. Changes in official interest rates also influence expectations about the course of future monetary policy, which in turn affects inflationary expectations, the setting of wages and prices, asset prices, and the exchange rate.
13. As a general rule of thumb, it takes 12–18 months for the full impact of a rate hike/cut to feed through the economy.
14. For other implications of the expectations hypothesis, see McEnally and Jordan (1997).
15. The failure of the expectations hypothesis is attributed to market inefficiency. Research by Froot (1989), De Bondt and Bange (1992), Campbell (1995), and Shefrin (2000) confirms the failure of (or fails to support) the expectations hypothesis. McEnally and Jordan (1997) cite a number of reasons why the term structure may do a poor job of forecasting actual interest rates.
16. The De Bondt and Bange study is based on the period 1953–87. Shefrin (2000) updated this study through 1998.
17. The liquidity hypothesis can be viewed as a special case of the preferred habitat hypothesis.
18. Theoretically, long bonds should fluctuate in price more than short bonds because of the mathematics of bond price calculations (see Chapter 1). However, McEnally and Jordan (1997) observe that bond price volatility increases with maturity, at first at a very rapid rate, but then at a much lower rate as bond maturity lengthens.
19. Fama (1984) shows that liquidity premia vary over time, which effectively reduces the forecasting efficacy of the term structure.
20. For a review of the empirical evidence in more detail, see James C. Van Horne's *Financial Market Rates and Flows*, 4th edition (Englewood Cliffs, NJ: Prentice-Hall, 1994), Chapters 4 and 5. Also recommended is Campbell and Shiller's, "Yield Spreads and Interest Rate Movements: A Bird's Eye View." *Review of Economic Studies*, May 1991, pp. 495–514.
21. The forward curve plots forward (as opposed to spot) interest rates against maturity.
22. Demographic effects are discussed in Chapter 5.
23. Trainer (1997) finds that the market's perception of risk is quite variable.
24. The "spread curve" is similar to a yield curve but plots spread against maturity (instead of yield against maturity). One could also plot the spread plus benchmark yield against maturity.
25. Analogous to interest rate convexity, high spread convexity adds value to a bond.
26. Some dealers trade corporate debt by industry grouping (all industrials, all utilities), while others prefer curve segmentations (all longs, all intermediates, all shorts) or a blend of the two. The net effect is that the main areas of the corporate curve (short, intermediate, long) tend to trade in their own universes over short intervals.
27. This is indicated by the market pricing of options on Treasuries over the maturity spectrum. See Dialynas and Rachlin (1997).
28. This directly contradicts the assumptions of technical analysis (discussed in Chapter 6).
29. Although EMH theory is based on rational investors and perfect information, Fama argues that neither is a necessary condition for an efficient market.
30. Fama (1998a, 1998b) is not persuaded by the evidence on EMH anomalies.
31. Game theoretic models, other than the most simplistic, have similar limitations.

Part II
Enhanced Tools for Establishing a View on Interest Rates

When playing a game, one needs to understand the nature of the game and the nature of the players before devising a winning strategy. Part I presented the nature of the *game* – that is, the key structural relationships and fundamental transmission mechanisms of economics and finance that are relevant for fixed income practitioners. In Part II, we turn our attention to the nature of the *players*. The two key players in the fixed income game are the government and investors[1] (Figure II). Chapter 4 examines government policy from a political perspective, and Chapter 5 analyzes the investor from a human perspective.

Practitioners in any field come across the practical limitations of theory, and in this respect economics is no different. In the remainder of Part II an attempt is made to tackle these practical issues. Chapter 6 introduces technical analysis, while Chapter 7 discusses a number of other analytical tools used to anticipate market dynamics. Finally, Chapter 8 presents an interdisciplinary framework to assist in the construction of a fixed income strategy.

Investors → Debt market dynamics ← Government

Objectives → Government policy ← Constraints

Objectives → Investor activity ← Constraints

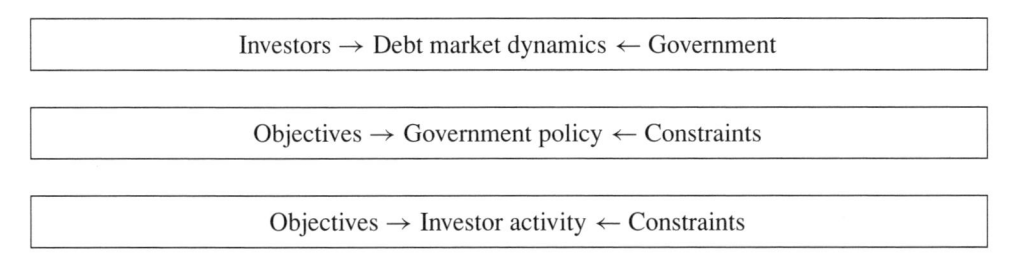

Figure II The fixed income "game"

---

[1] For simplification, "investor" is used to represent all private sector participants in the fixed income market. In Chapter 8 the distinction is made between different types of investors in the context of tailoring specific fixed income strategies to relevant investment objectives and constraints.

4
Government Policy: The Interface between Economics and Politics

The monetary, fiscal, and regulatory policies implemented by a government are a reflection of both economic and political factors (Table 4.1). On the one hand, the government has economic objectives (such as economic growth) and economic constraints (such as available policy instruments). On the other hand, the government has political objectives (e.g. redistribution) and political constraints (e.g. elections). Moreover, political goals are often achieved using economic tools, in which case the economic policy chosen is not necessarily optimal. Economic policy, even if it is the optimal one, must be implemented through a political process. As such, political factors are crucial for understanding debt market dynamics.

Table 4.1 Government policy objectives and constraints

Objectives	Constraints
Economics – "grow the pie"	Policy instruments
Politics – "divide the pie"	Elections

4.1 THE POLITICAL ECONOMY PERSPECTIVE

The term *political economy* was originally used to describe the discipline we now know simply as "economics". Today the distinction is made between economics (the effect of policy) and politics (the selection of policy). Political economy focuses on the range of political considerations that influence or constrain actual economic policy outcomes. The basic premise of political economy is that economic policy is the result of a decision-making process that balances conflicting interests – either about the policy itself or about the distribution of the policy's benefits. Hence, only when there is a conflict of interest do political considerations become relevant.

4.1.1 Political Business Cycles

The concept of a trade-off between inflation and output was introduced in Chapter 3. Most economists agree that in the long run there is no such trade-off. That is, attempts to move the economy below the natural rate of unemployment will ultimately only produce higher inflation. In the short run, however, expansionary policy can temporarily reduce unemployment and boost economic growth – an outcome particularly desirable for an incumbent politician facing an upcoming election.

A further incentive to manipulate the business cycle is that the benefits of expansionary economic policies – rising employment, wages, and profits – tend to come ahead of the costly inflation that materializes later. Meanwhile, the costs of contractionary policies – particularly higher unemployment – precede later reductions in inflation. Hence, an inflationary bias is generated as politicians find it easier to spend than to tax.

In countries with representative democracies, policy makers are held accountable to voters through elections. Given that election cycles are typically short, so too must be the time horizon of politicians seeking to remain in office.[1] Although elections keep politicians accountable for their actions, the re-election constraint means that the chosen policy may differ from the one that is socially optimal.

Overwhelming evidence suggests that voters are influenced by the state of the economy and that the focus is typically on short-term outcomes. In a study of the period 1916–1976, Fair (1978) finds that macroeconomic performance strongly affects voting in US presidential and legislative elections, and that voters do not look back more than a year or two when judging economic performance. Lewis-Beck (1988) finds that a similar relationship holds in the UK, France, Italy, Spain, and Germany; and Madsen (1980) confirms this result for Denmark, Norway, and Sweden.

Being well aware of the fact that economic conditions before an election significantly affect voter choices, there is a strong incentive for policy makers to destabilize the economy for political gain. A well-timed economic stimulus gives politicians the advantage of a booming economy just before an election, with most of the associated inflationary costs following once the election is over. This is the essence of political business cycle (PBC) theory.

Drazen (2000) cites the classic example of US President Richard Nixon prior to the 1972 election. The US government budget, which was balanced in 1970, was taken to a $10 billion deficit in 1971 as Social Security benefits and personal tax exemptions were increased and the investment tax credit was restored. In 1972 the budget deficit rose to $12 billion with the help of a 20% increase in Social Security benefits – announced two weeks prior to the election in a letter from President Nixon to 24,760,000 recipients. Thirty years later, the parallels with US President George W. Bush's fiscal record are striking.

Empirical evidence as a whole supports the existence of some pre-electoral manipulation of economic policy. Tufte (1975, 1978) finds strong evidence that economic activity in industrialized countries exhibits a clear political cycle. Haynes and Stone (1989), in a particularly rigorous study, find a 4-year cycle in US economic growth, unemployment, and inflation. Economic growth peaks in the quarter of the US presidential election, unemployment troughs in the quarter after the election, and inflation peaks five years after the quarter of the election.

Looking beyond the US, Alesina et al. (1992) examine 18 OECD democracies over the period 1960–93. While statistically significant political cycle effects in economic growth are found for only a handful of countries (Germany, Japan, New Zealand, and the UK), Alesina et al. find the PBC effect on inflation to be widespread across countries.[2] A political cycle in inflation is particularly noteworthy in Denmark, France, Germany, Italy, and New Zealand. In a similar vein, Willett (1988) argues that PBCs were an important influence – at least as significant as supply shocks – in the escalation of inflation in the US during the 1970s. Of particular interest to fixed income investors, Williams (1990) finds that the 3-month US Treasury bill rate is in part explained by a political cycle.

Even casual observation suggests that governments do not attempt to generate PBCs at every election. Indeed, some studies investigating the prevalence of PBCs often find negative results. Frey and Schneider (1978) explain that we often see "ideological" behavior when an election looks safe and PBC behavior when the election is expected to be close or the government fears losing its position. Moreover, Willett (1988) notes that a systematic replay of the PBC game would become highly transparent to voters and effectively neutralize the political gains from such a strategy. Finally, not every public servant can be expected to subordinate social welfare for personal gain.[3] Although one should not expect to see a PBC at every election, it is important to recognize the powerful incentives that produce them.

In many countries elections do not have preset dates – that is, the executive or legislative authority has some ability to call an early election on relatively short notice. When election timing is uncertain, political economy arguments suggest reverse causation – that is, the government opportunistically manipulates the *timing* of an election to take advantage of autonomously favorable economic conditions. Drazen (2000) observes that the empirical evidence as a whole does not suggest causation from economic conditions to early elections. This behavior, however, is found to be particularly strong in Japan (Ito, 1990; Alesina et al., 1993).

Apparently no government is completely independent of the support of the populace. Frey and Schneider (1978) find that political–economic cycles operate in authoritarian regimes. Even in the absence of elections, the dictatorial regime must balance the risk of being overthrown against improvements in economic and political conditions.

4.1.2 Budget Deficits and Monetary Policy

Thus far we have treated the government as a single entity. In fact, fiscal and monetary policies are often formed by separate authorities. Government revenues and expenditures (including taxes and debt issuance) are typically determined by the fiscal authority, while the regulation of interest rates and money supply falls under the domain of the central bank. Though separate, one authority is not necessarily independent from the influence of the other. Indeed, there are numerous examples of a 'tug of war' between the fiscal and monetary authorities.[4]

Sargent and Wallace (1981) use an intertemporal budget constraint to illustrate how the generation of large budget deficits pressures the monetary authority to print money. Government spending (G_t) in a given time period is limited to the resources that can be generated through taxes (T_t), new borrowing or debt (D_t), and the creation of money (M_t). When the government has borrowed in earlier periods, it also faces the cost of servicing previously issued debt (D_{t-1}). Rearranging terms, Equation 4.1 depicts this constraint in another way – such that the government budget deficit ($G_t - T_t$) plus the cost of debt service on government bonds issued in the previous period (D_{t-1}) are financed partly through the Ministry of Finance (or Treasury) with the new issuance of government debt, and partly through the central bank by monetization.

Equation 4.1 The Intertemporal budget constraint[5]

$$(G_t - T_t) + D_{t-1} = D_t + M_t$$

One can see from Equation 4.1 that budget deficits require the cooperation of investors and/or the monetary authority. The amount of government debt that can be issued is ultimately a function of how much debt domestic and foreign individuals wish to hold. In the absence of monetary accommodation, heavy government borrowing causes real interest rates to rise.[6] Rising interest rates not only neutralize the expansionary effects of budget deficits (as individuals and businesses become less willing to borrow at the higher cost), but also reduce the attractiveness of holding debt (given that bond prices and yields are inversely related). As the size of government debt grows larger and larger, it becomes more difficult and eventually impossible to satisfy the budget constraint through debt issuance alone.

Sargent and Wallace (1981) show how the monetary accommodation of budget deficits becomes inevitable when the real rate of interest payable on bonds exceeds the growth rate of the economy. A monetary authority that readily accommodates fiscal borrowing by monetizing outstanding government debt, however, will most likely channel deficit spending pressures into rampant inflation. Burdekin and Langdana (1992) illustrate this point using a number of historical examples, including the classic case of the German hyperinflation in 1919–1923. Accordingly, lower deficits imply less pressure for monetary accommodation, with implications for a more subdued inflation rate.

The arithmetic of the government's budget constraint illustrates how budget deficits might be restrained – and unsustainable fiscal policy reversed – through the control of the money supply.[7] The ultimate effect of budget deficits on monetary policy in practice is a function of the institutional environment. As such, inflationary pressures (and outcomes) will vary considerably, depending on whether monetary policy is controlled directly by elected officials or those assured of political independence.

4.1.3 Central Bank Independence

Optimal monetary policy requires a long time horizon; however, politicians (and the public) have neither a long time horizon nor an understanding of the long lags of monetary policy. An effective way to mitigate against short-run political pressures that generate excess inflation is to put monetary policy in the hands of unelected technocrats with long terms of office.[8] As such, an independent monetary authority is expected to exhibit greater willingness to deliver price stability.

> **The policy maker's time horizon determines whether policy is evaluated in terms of long-run benefits or short-term costs.**

Indeed, the more independent central banks tend to deliver lower inflation rates.[9] This result is confirmed in a number of empirical studies, including Grilli et al. (1991) and Cukierman (1992). Moreover, studies by Alesina and Summers (1993) and Alesina and Gatti (1995) find that central bank independence (CBI) achieves low inflation without the cost of higher variability in economic growth or unemployment.

Evidence also suggests that governments run smaller budget deficits in countries where the central bank is independent, as opposed to countries where the monetary authority is controlled by the government. Parkin (1986) finds that the choice of central bank institutions affects not only low and predictable inflation, but also fiscal discipline. In a cross-country study over the period 1960–1983, Burdekin and Laney (1992) show that the fiscal authority is deterred from running a deficit when the expectation is that deficits will not be accommodated in the future.

Finally, a number of studies indicate that the causality between monetary and fiscal policy can run in both directions. Ahking and Miller (1985) find a two-way causality between budget deficits and base money growth in the US during the 1950s and 1970s, but only a one-way causality (from deficits to money growth) in the 1960s. Bradley and Potter (1986) show causality from fiscal to monetary policy, while Turnovsky and Wohar (1987) suggest that it flows the other way.

4.1.4 Policy Objectives

When attempting to anticipate policy, it is important to determine the credibility of the objectives relative to the available instruments. In the case of monetary policy, the authorities effectively have one instrument – control of the price of money. In some cases, however, the monetary authority is charged with the dual objectives of price stability and full employment (or economic growth). This presents a dilemma as the pursuit of price stability can exacerbate unemployment – and vice versa. Rogoff (1985) shows how the appointment of a conservative central banker does not fully eliminate the inflation bias as long as the monetary authority places any weight on unemployment (below the natural rate). Hence, even independent central banks may retain a degree of inflationary bias.

4.1.5 The Monetary Policy Mechanism

In Chapter 3, we saw how the money supply is directly linked to inflation and ultimately to market interest rates – both of vital interest to fixed income investors. In purely economic terms, the supply of money is treated as an exogenous (or independent) variable. Allowing for considerations of political economy, however, it is clear that monetary policy reflects a number of influences, including fiscal deficits, political independence, and policy objectives (Equation 4.2). While budget deficits and full employment objectives tend to increase monetary accommodation, central bank independence and price stability objectives tend to contain expansionary tendencies.

Equation 4.2 The monetary policy mechanism

Monetary policy $= F$ (Budget deficit, Independence, Policy objectives)

It is important to note that monetary authorities will not always respond to a particular stimulus in the same way. Intuitively, monetary officials change, decision procedures change, and learning occurs. Empirical evidence also suggests that monetary reaction functions are not stable. In a cross-country study on single factor determinants of monetary policy, for example, Willett et al. (1988) find that no single factor dominates across countries or time periods, although almost all the factors examined have some explanatory power for particular times and places.[10] While past observations can provide useful insight to future policy, it is important to be alert to possible regime shifts.

4.2 ANTICIPATING CHANGES IN MONETARY POLICY

As we have seen, institutional considerations have significant implications for monetary policy. In this section, we examine the policy-making structures of the US Federal Reserve and the European Central Bank. Although both central banks can be characterized as highly "independent" in a relative sense, we shall see that they are not completely immune from political influences.

4.2.1 Fed Watching

Few factors move the US bond market more than the Federal Reserve does. With the US Treasury market serving as the benchmark for global debt markets, "Fed watching" captures a global audience.

The monetary authority of the US, the Federal Reserve, is charged with promoting "maximum employment, stable prices, and moderate long-term interest rates". The "Fed" derives its authority and duties from the US Congress, and sets monetary policy through the Federal Open Market Committee (FOMC). The FOMC consists of the seven members of the

Board of Governors, the president of the Federal Reserve Bank of New York, and presidents of four other regional Federal Reserve Banks, who serve on a rotating basis. Although the Fed Chair wields just one of 12 FOMC votes, there is little doubt of the Chair's immense power.

The Board of Governors (BoG) consists of seven members including a Chairman and Vice Chairman – all appointed by the President of the US and confirmed by the US Senate. The full term of a Board member is 14 years, and terms are staggered so that one expires in January of an even-numbered year. Terms for the Chairman and Vice Chairman of the BoG are four years, but can be extended to the full term length of 14 years.

Presidents of each regional Federal Reserve Bank are appointed to five-year terms by the board of directors of their respective Federal Reserve banks (12 in all), with approval by the BoG. The terms of all 12 regional presidents run concurrently, ending in years numbered 1 and 6 (e.g. 2001 and 2006). The regional presidents serve one-year terms on the FOMC on a rotating basis beginning, January 1 of each year.

The Fed has taken steps to improve its transparency. By law the FOMC must meet at least four times a year, but since 1980 has held regularly scheduled meetings eight times a year. Although meetings are closed to the public, the minutes of FOMC meetings are released to the public about six weeks after the fact. Until the expiration of the Humphrey Hawkins Act in 2000, the Fed Chair was required to report twice a year (in February and July) to both houses of Congress on monetary policy and the economy. Nevertheless, the semi-annual monetary testimony has continued. The market reaction to Chairman Alan Greenspan's Congressional testimony has been known to extend for weeks.

Under the helm of Greenspan, Fed moves have been highly correlated with each other. That is, during each phase of an interest rate cycle, the Federal Reserve has implemented a long series of small interest rate changes – in lieu of fewer, but larger, changes. For example, Greenspan cut interest rates 25 times (21 of which were 25 basis points) during George H. Bush's presidency. In 2001 the Fed made 11 cuts, most the size of 50 basis points. There is a slight bias against changing interest rates during an election year,[11] and the Fed has been known to act on behalf of the global economy. For example, the Fed responded to threats to global financial stability produced by the Asia crisis in 1997, the Russian devaluation and default in 1998, and the Brazil crisis in 1999.[12]

The Fed has taken great care to communicate its intentions to the financial markets, but in some cases has caught markets by surprise. Indeed, over the years the market has learned to decipher the cryptic language of Greenspan, Fed Chairman since 1987. In 2006, term limits require that Greenspan's tenure comes to an end. Without a doubt, there will be an adjustment period (potentially more surprises) as markets get accustomed to the communication/policy style of the new Fed Chairman.

Political Economy Considerations

Despite empirical studies that rank the US Federal Reserve near the top in terms of central bank independence, a substantial body of literature finds that the Federal Reserve can be heavily influenced by pressures from Congress, the executive branch, and private interests – though not a simple captive of any one group. Although the long terms of office mean that the Fed is not completely dominated by the President, the appointment process ensures that the Fed's powers with respect to the executive branch are limited. Nevertheless, the authority of the Fed versus the President only becomes an issue when the two disagree.

Woolley (1986) and Beck (1987) argue that the Fed may be especially willing to accommodate executive branch pressures during election years in order to prevent sharp movements in interest rates. Similarly, Lombra (1988) finds a persistent tendency for the Fed to stabilize the short-run environment – in response to both political and economic factors, but not according to any simple rule. Given that policy makers operate in an atmosphere of great uncertainty with respect to important structural relationships and the path of a dynamic economy, they usually (and understandably) confine their efforts to stabilizing short-run nominal interest rates.

Kane (1988) notes that while the executive and Congress try to influence Fed policy goals, they want to be able to avoid blame for unpopular policies – allowing the President and Congress to "Fed-bash" when politically expedient. Indeed, it has not been unusual to see battles between the White House and the Fed (perhaps most famously during the early years of Paul Volcker's Chairmanship). More recently, in a semi-annual testimony to Congress, Greenspan expressed vociferous disapproval of George W. Bush's proposed tax cuts. Although the Fed must in the long run obey the dictates of the political system, in the short to medium run it does have some flexibility.

4.2.2 ECB Watching

The European Central Bank (ECB) is the monetary authority of the Euro area, which was implemented in January 1999. The ECB derives its authority from the Treaty establishing the European Community (as amended) and its mandated primary objective is the maintenance of price stability.

The Governing Council of the ECB formulates the monetary policy of the Euro area, including decisions on intermediate monetary objectives, key interest rates, and the supply of reserves. The Governing Council consists of the six members of the Executive Board (including the President and Vice President of the ECB) and the governors of the Euro area national central banks – of which there are 12 (as of 2003). Terms of office are eight years and are not renewable for both the Governing Council and Executive Board. The term for national central bank governor must not be less than five years.

Monetary policy decisions are based on a simple majority-voting rule, where each member of the Governing Council has one vote. In the event of a tie, the President of the ECB has the deciding vote. The voting record is not published, which serves to deflect political pressure from the national representatives. At the time this book was going to press, the ECB was in the process of revising its voting procedures – subject to the unanimous approval of EU governments – in order to accommodate a large influx of new members.[13] Under a plan endorsed by the EU, voting rights are to be rotated, with the five biggest economies sharing four votes and the remaining economies sharing 11 votes. The six Executive Board members would keep a permanent voting right.

As an independent central bank, the ECB is instructed not to seek or take instructions from any other body – in particular EC institutions or a member state government. By Treaty, independence is preserved in that the ECB has sole responsibility for deciding/executing operations in the foreign exchange market, and cannot provide credit to the public sector. Similar to the Fed, the ECB has its own budget, and members of the Governing Council have long terms of office.

Precise reporting obligations – including an annual policy report presented to the European Parliament – exist to ensure accountability to EC institutions as well as the public. The President of the ECB also appears before the European Parliament's Committee on Economic and

Monetary Affairs each quarter to report on ECB policy and answer questions (transcripts of these hearings are available on the ECB website).

While the Governing Council has yet to make the proceedings of its policy deliberations public, it has gone beyond reporting requirements by publishing a *Monthly Bulletin*, which provides a thorough assessment of the economic situation. The President and Vice President of the ECB also hold a press conference immediately after the conclusion of each month's policy meeting. A statement on the economic situation and an assessment of the risks to price stability, as well as other issues discussed, is followed by an extended question and answer period.[14]

With the purpose of providing an anchor for inflation expectations and a benchmark for ECB performance, the Governing Council has defined more clearly the objective of price stability. Since 1998 price stability has been defined as a year-on-year increase below 2% in the Euro area's harmonized index of consumer prices (HICP). In 2003, the Governing Council further clarified the aim of maintaining inflation close to 2%, thus providing a floor for inflation expectations.

Price stability is to be maintained over the medium term, reflecting that monetary policy cannot fine-tune changes in prices over short horizons – that is, changes in monetary policy only affect prices with a considerable (as well as variable) lag and the magnitude of the eventual impact is difficult to estimate. A medium-term focus means that policy must be forward looking and that excessive activism (the introduction of unnecessary volatility) is to be avoided. The major implication for the financial markets, however, is that a medium-term focus means that inflation target overshooting/undershooting need not imply an imminent rate hike/cut.

The ECB's assessment of risks to price stability rests on two pillars: (1) money growth, reflecting the monetary origins of inflation over the medium to long term[15]; and (2) a wide range of economic and financial indicators that affect prices over the short to medium term, as near-term developments may become entrenched.

The appropriate conduct of monetary policy in an uncertain world is a challenge for any central bank. Uncertainties about economic relationships and possible changes in the structure of the economy are particularly relevant in the case of a new currency area. Institutional changes also affect the transmission of policy. Most relevant in this respect is that 10 countries are scheduled to join the EU in 2004 – Poland, the Czech Republic, Hungary, Estonia, Latvia, Malta, Lithuania, the Slovak Republic, Cyprus, and Slovenia – with the first new members adopting the euro possibly as early as 2006.

Political Economy Considerations

European Monetary Union (EMU) is a classic example of political goals implemented using economic tools, as many of the participating countries have been persuaded to join more by political factors than by an economic cost–benefit analysis. Even the credibility benefit used by high-inflation economies to justify membership is a political argument, as credible monetary policy is inherently a political goal.[16] Moreover, the decision to create a common currency is inherently a political phenomenon – an outcome of treaty negotiation, parliamentary ratification, and popular referenda.

Eichengreen and Frieden (1993) note that the political nature of EMU stems from specific political goals (economic cooperation makes political cooperation easier) and the conflict over objectives (the degree of anti-inflation commitment). Given that ECB policy is set by majority, the highly anti-inflationary stance associated with the German Bundesbank can be superseded. Garrett (1993) argues that Germany made such concessions because it had other goals that gave it a strong interest in making sure that EMU came into being. Specifically, Germany was interested in smoothing European acceptance of its rapid reunification.

Drazen (2000) points to a number of theoretical studies having implications for the ECB. Notably, decision by committee leads to compromise positions on difficult issues and imparts a degree of inertia. Although this means that policy will not be idiosyncratic, it imparts a degree of instability to decisions, particularly if they are adopted by majority rule. Moreover, the difficulty of reaching agreement will affect the nature of proposals as well as the time it takes to reach agreement.

The ECB is a relatively new institution that is not fully understood. Minutes from policy meetings are not released, and the numerous policy makers have added to the confusion by making diverse and often contradicting comments. Information is scattered and European-wide data come late. Indeed, financial markets have found it difficult to correctly anticipate ECB monetary policy – particularly when compared to other central banks. Ross (2002) attributes this in part to the large number of monetary policy meetings (bi-monthly until February 2002), the unique circumstances of the ECB (its relatively young age and the need to establish its credibility as a politically independent institution), and the absence of a consistent policy on communicating bias on the future direction of interest rates.

The ECB is widely viewed as too slow and cumbersome. The preferred policy has been to keep interest rates on hold and to keep them high, illustrating the difficulty of persuading enough policy makers to adjust the course of monetary policy. Certainly, the ECB seems to require stronger signals to persuade it to act. The impending enlargement of the Euro area poses both a challenge and an opportunity. On the one hand, the larger size will complicate an already complex monetary transmission mechanism. On the other hand, a revision to the voting rules can be seen as an opportunity to increase the efficiency of decision making.

4.3 IMPLICATIONS FOR FIXED INCOME INVESTORS

Beware of Upcoming Elections

Although one should not expect to see a political business cycle maneuver at every election, it is important to recognize that there are powerful incentives to produce them. If you suspect that one is being engineered, empirical evidence suggests positioning for economic growth that peaks in the quarter of a US presidential election and inflation that peaks five years after the election.

Budget Blowouts are Bond Bearish

As we have seen, an explosion in fiscal deficits requires the cooperation of investors and/or the monetary authority. With monetary accommodation, the result is rampant inflation which diminishes the value of nominal debt held by investors. Without monetary accommodation and capital inflows, there is the potential for sharply higher real interest rates. Moreover, heavy debt issuance will depress bond prices. Investors required to stay in fixed income should consider inflation-indexed bonds.

Independent Central Banks are not Devoid of Politics

The empirical evidence is clear – central banks with greater independence deliver better inflation performance. However, the need for accountability as well as the policy-making process itself involves some degree of political maneuvering.

Distinguish between Ability and Willingness to Pay

Unlike ordinary debt, sovereign debt repayment is not about the ability to pay, but is rather about the *willingness* to pay. Since the sovereign borrower, with few exceptions, has the technical ability to meet debt obligations, repayment decisions are inherently political. The probability of default depends on the government's budget position – the government being more likely to default on its debt the higher the level of expenditures.

Political Crisis Spells Economic Crisis

An economic crisis will undoubtedly be exacerbated (if not instigated) by a lack of political will to implement corrective policy measures, and it may be impossible to achieve that political will without an economic crisis in the first place. Nevertheless, fixed income investors should be aware that political risk combined with fragile fiscal fundamentals is akin to pure nitroglycerine. The most vivid recent examples include: Japan (1990–2003), Indonesia (1997–2003), and Argentina (2001–2003). In all of these cases (which had yet to be completely resolved as of 2003), a protracted political impasse served to prolong and deepen the economic pain.

* * *

The government plays a key role in debt market dynamics, and politics brings an important perspective to understanding government policy making. The government, however, represents only part of the equation. In the next chapter we look to the field of psychology in an attempt to glean some additional insight into the motivations of investors.

NOTES

1. Because politicians must win elections in order to implement their preferred policies, even the most partisan policy maker can display office-motivated behavior.
2. One reason the evidence on economic growth is less solid may be that it is difficult to time the economic response to pre-electoral stimulation.
3. Perhaps the best contemporary example is former US President Jimmy Carter, who arguably showed high integrity and altruistic motives, but failed to win re-election in 1980. During his administration, Carter was unable to tackle the problem of stagflation (high unemployment combined with high inflation).
4. A recent example is the policy battle between Japan's Ministry of Finance and the Bank of Japan (which was made independent in 1999).
5. The budget constraint can be extended to include the foreign sector. Using the national savings identity, the budget deficit is financed by net domestic saving and a current account deficit. Despite spiraling budget deficits during the Reagan administration, US interest rates fell as foreign capital inflows helped finance the deficit.
6. From the law of supply and demand, an increase in the demand for money increases the price of money. In contrast, budget surpluses (as was the case during the Clinton administration) allow interest rates to fall.
7. There is strong empirical evidence which supports the premise that government behavior is consistent with the intertemporal budget constraint. See Barro (1979), McCallum (1984), Hamilton and Flavin (1986), Trehan and Walsh (1988), Kremers (1988, 1989), Hakkio and Rush (1991), and Joines (1991).
8. While legislating a price stability objective may improve inflation performance, the effectiveness of such a mandate remains in doubt without a suitable enforcement mechanism (Burdekin and Willett, 1992).
9. The degree of central bank independence is a function of statutory policy independence, the proportion of government appointees on the policy board, and legislated objectives.

10. The factors include international reserve increases, import price shocks, wage pressures and budget deficits. Although Willett et al. (1988) find considerable evidence of monetary accommodation of wage increases and budget deficits, the authors caution against making the assumption that wage/price shocks will always be validated.
11. US President George H. Bush blamed central bank rate hikes as the reason for his electoral defeat in 1992.
12. Some might argue that the lack of inflationary pressures in the US at the time afforded the Fed such latitude.
13. By the end of the decade, membership in the Euro area could conceivably double. It is difficult to get 24 people to agree on anything, let alone the management of monetary policy.
14. Transcripts of the press conference are released on the ECB website on the same day.
15. The ECB's reference value for M3 money growth (4.5%) is not a monetary target. However, deviations from the reference value are analyzed closely in the context of other economic data (such as changes in velocity and distortions from changes in tax rules) to determine risks to price stability.
16. The reputation of monetary authorities in pursuing announced policies (such as a price stability target) has a large impact on how the policy affects the economy. For example, a central bank that is prone to delivering higher-than-expected inflation will over time lead to the adjustment of inflation expectations and higher equilibrium inflation.

RECOMMENDED READING

Burdekin, R. and Langdana, F. (1992). *Budget Deficits and Economic Performance*. New York: Routledge.
Drazen, A. (2000). *Political Economy in Macroeconomics*. Princeton: Princeton University Press.
Willett, T.D. (ed.) (1988). *Political Business Cycles: The Political Economy of Money, Inflation, and Unemployment*. Durham: Duke University Press.

5
Human Factors

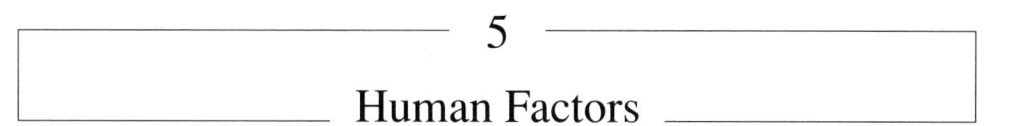

The basic premise of economic models is that an individual's "preferences" are held constant. In other words, the determination of preferences lies outside the realm of economic study. Nevertheless, an understanding of how preferences change is crucial for anticipating market behavior, particularly over the short term. Recognizing that the market consists of a heterogeneous group of individuals, human behavior is analyzed from the perspective of two disciplines: sociology and psychology.

5.1 GROUP BEHAVIOR: A DEMOGRAPHIC APPROACH

Demography is the study of population statistics. The combination of this sociological approach with economics makes a powerful forecasting tool. Demographic considerations provide a context for demand pressures and the historical trends that can result. As such, demography provides a meaningful yardstick to evaluate historical norms – which is useful for investors assessing relative value. Demography can also help to ascertain whether (and when and how sharp) US savings rates, for example, might swing to more "normal" (higher) levels – a current issue that has particular relevance for fixed income investors.

Although we are unique as individuals, as a group we have a number of common tendencies. Sociologists characterize behavioral patterns by age group and track the impact as successive generations age over time. This technique explicitly assumes that behavioral patterns are stable – that is, a 40-year-old today will act like a 50-year-old 10 years later. In other words, the 30-year-olds of the future are expected to behave like the 30-year-olds of today – raising young children, buying houses in the suburbs, and filling those homes with furniture and appliances. Similarly, today's 30-year-olds are expected to behave, in 20 years' time, like today's 50-year-olds – who have more senior jobs and discretionary income to invest for retirement. If particular generations occupy a dominant segment of the population, the aging process can have significant implications for consumption and investment – and ultimately, interest rate trends.

The characterization of behavior by age group captures a number of important socioeconomic variables that affect human behavior, including income level and family status. For example, a 20-year-old is more likely to be single than a 30-year-old, and a 30-year-old is more likely to be a borrower than a 50-year-old. Young seniors – concerned about outliving their capital – tend to seek investments with growth potential and inflation protection, while older seniors tend to focus on assuring a fixed income stream. The behavioral life cycle is summarized in Table 5.1. Most spending tends to occur during the 20s and 30s. Financial planning increases in importance as we move into our 40s and 50s. During the 60s and 70s, our spending shifts to health and travel.

Human behavior is relatively stable with respect to age when it comes to many activities. According to Foot and Stoffman (1998), we attend school, leave home, rent apartments, start families, buy homes, and make intensive use of hospitals at a similar age. Although people

Table 5.1 The behavioral life cycle

Age	Characteristic behavior	Investment phase
20s	Urban lifestyle: single, enter job market and rent; possibly emigrate.	*Spending and borrowing phase* • Assets low relative to liabilities. • Long investment horizon.
30s	Suburban lifestyle: raise families, buy homes and furnishings; focus on childcare and education.	
40s	Gradual increase in discretionary income.	*Saving and investment phase*
50s	High pressure and time-consuming jobs; care for ill parents and teenagers.	• Build investment portfolio as income begins to exceed expenses. • Relatively long investment horizon, but preservation of capital becomes more important.
60s	'Young' seniors: major job responsibilities; retire and relocate; travel; care for elderly parents.	
70s	'Mid' seniors: travel and health care.	*Spending phase*
80s	'Senior' seniors: home care and health care.	• Financially independent. • Living expenses covered by investment income.

Source: Adapted from Foot and Stoffman (1998).

in the industrialized world are living longer and healthier lives, and are delaying marriage and childbirth longer than previous generations, a 28-year-old woman is still about five times more likely to have a baby than a 38-year-old. This stability makes demographic forecasting an effective tool over the long term. Nevertheless, large shocks – such as sharp downturns in the economy and the disruption of war – have had a distinct impact on the fertility rate,[1] which in turn affects the age distribution of the population.

As can be seen from the population pyramid displayed in Figure 5.1, the US has a population bulge in the group aged 30 to 49. This is the "Baby Boom" generation, born in the 20-year span from the conclusion of World War II through the mid-1960s. The baby boom ended in the mid-1960s with the introduction of the birth control pill and as increasing numbers of women entered the workforce, postponed childbirth, and decided to have fewer children. The US also has a smaller population bulge in the group aged 5 to 19 – the children of the Baby Boomers born between 1980 and 1995 (called the "Echo" generation).

The parents of the Baby Boomers belong to a much smaller generation as they were born during the hardship years of the Great Depression and World War II. This generation – which was able to afford a house full of children on one salary – benefited from good timing and its small numbers. This cohort entered the workforce during the post-war reconstruction of the 1950s, and its small size meant less competition for jobs and promotions. Many retired early with the help of their Baby Boomer children – who, in turn, drove up the value of their assets (Figure 5.2).

Baby Boomers represent nearly one-third of the population of the United States. The early Boomers, now heading into their early 50s, have little in common with the late Boomers (called "Generation X") in their mid-30s. Foot and Stoffman (1998) explain how the masses of early Boomers took the traditional jobs, and drove up rents, house prices, interest rates (in the 1980s),

Human Factors 79

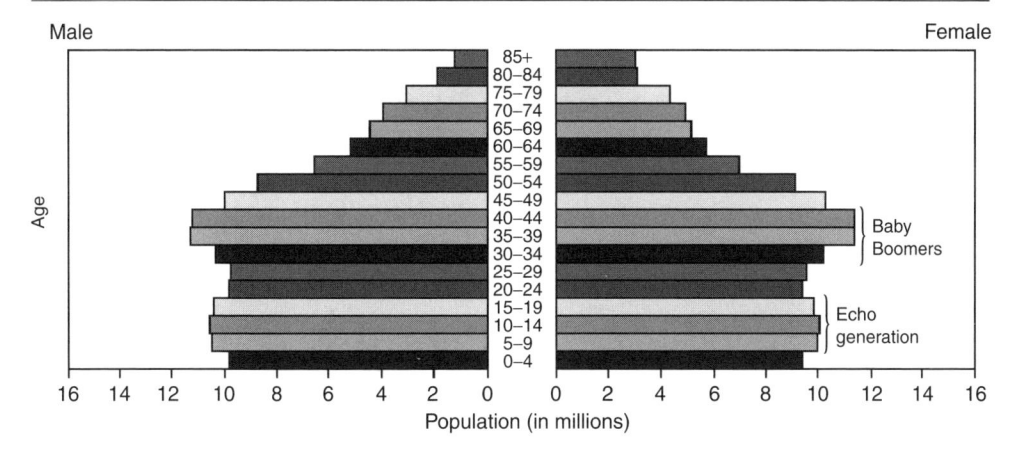

Source: US Census Bureau, International Database.

Figure 5.1 US population pyramid, 2000[2]

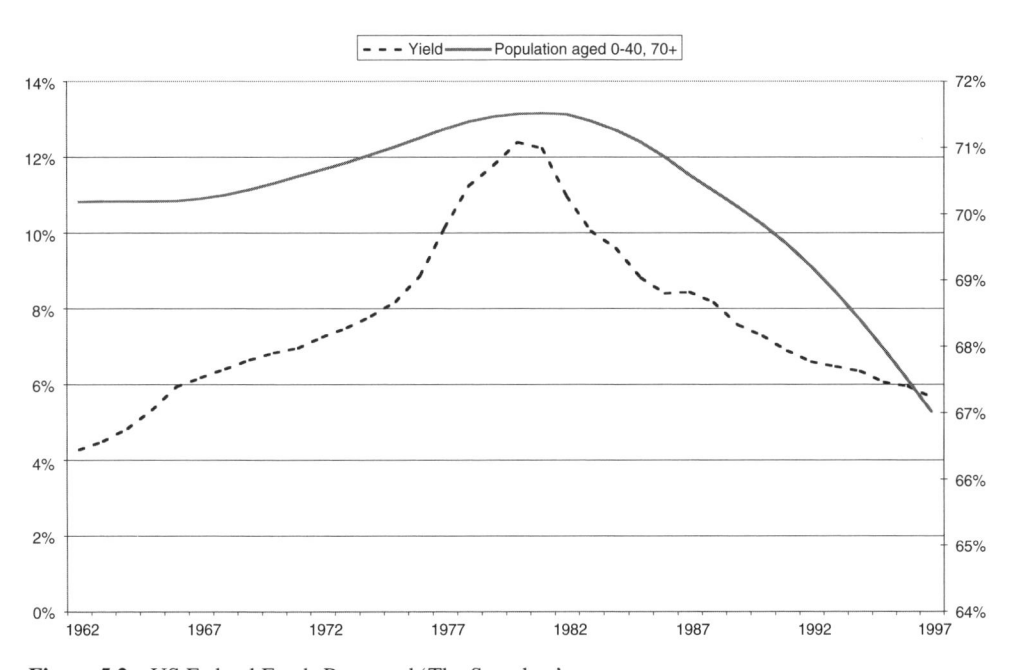

Figure 5.2 US Federal Funds Rates and 'The Spenders'

Figure 5.3 Japan's population pyramid, 2000

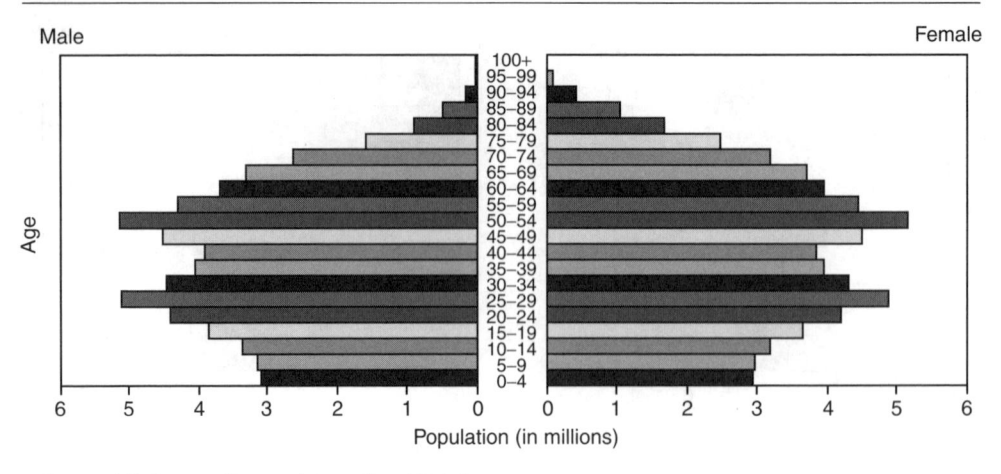

Source: US Census Bureau, International Database.

and equity prices (during the 1990s). Competition has been keen for those born in the early 1960s, many of whom were still waiting to buy their first house in the mid-1990s. In the intense competition for jobs among its large peer group, Generation X boosted the service economy – by selling its valuable time to hurried and harried early Boomers.

Because younger populations tend to spend more than older populations, countries with younger populations tend to have higher interest rates (as excess demand for money boosts the price of money). A comparison of Figures 5.1 and 5.3 shows that the population in Japan is much older than that in the US. In fact, Japan has the most rapidly aging population in the world. The reason is that Japan's fertility rate started to decline in the 1940s, in sharp contrast to the US where fertility did not begin to fall until the 1960s.[3]

During the 1990s when Japanese real interest rates fell into negative territory, 38% of Japan's population was aged 40 to 60 – the saving and investing years (Figure 5.4). Not only were interest rates pushed to historical lows, but also equities were cashed in by retirees. At the same time in the US, the spending and borrowing generations dominated the population. Demography suggests that Japan's experience of plunging interest rates and equity prices during the 1990s appears to be particularly prescient for the US – where 37% of its population are expected move into the saving and investing years by 2010.

As can be seen from Figure 5.5, the US is also relatively young compared to the European Union (EU). The post-war baby boom was less pronounced in Europe largely due to the destruction of World War II and post-war emigration. Italy had no post-war baby boom at all. The decline in fertility in the 1960s was also not as sharp. For demographers, the slower economic growth that has been observed in the EU relative to the US is the consequence of an older population. With the benefit of its Echo generation, the US is expected to maintain its age advantage for the foreseeable future (Foot and Stoffman, 1998). Although demography implies that US interest rates should be higher than those in the EU, currently this is not the case – in part because of smaller, less liquid, and more segmented European capital markets. Once European capital markets become completely integrated, this anomaly is expected to disappear.

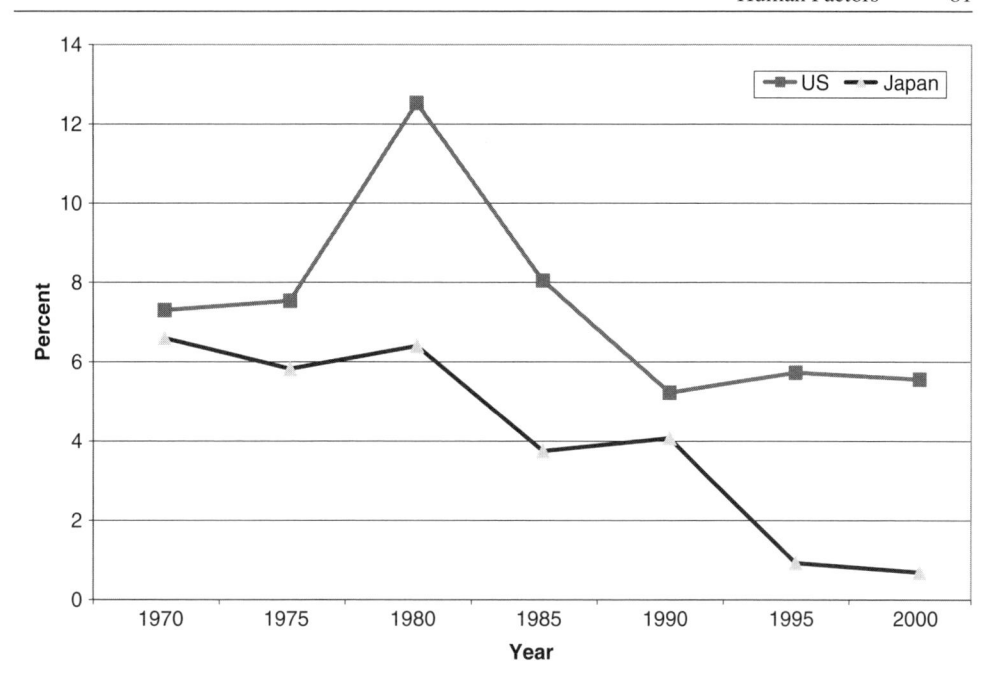

Sources: Bank of Japan and US Federal Reserve.

Figure 5.4 US and Japanese official interest rates, 1970–2001 (5-year rolling average)

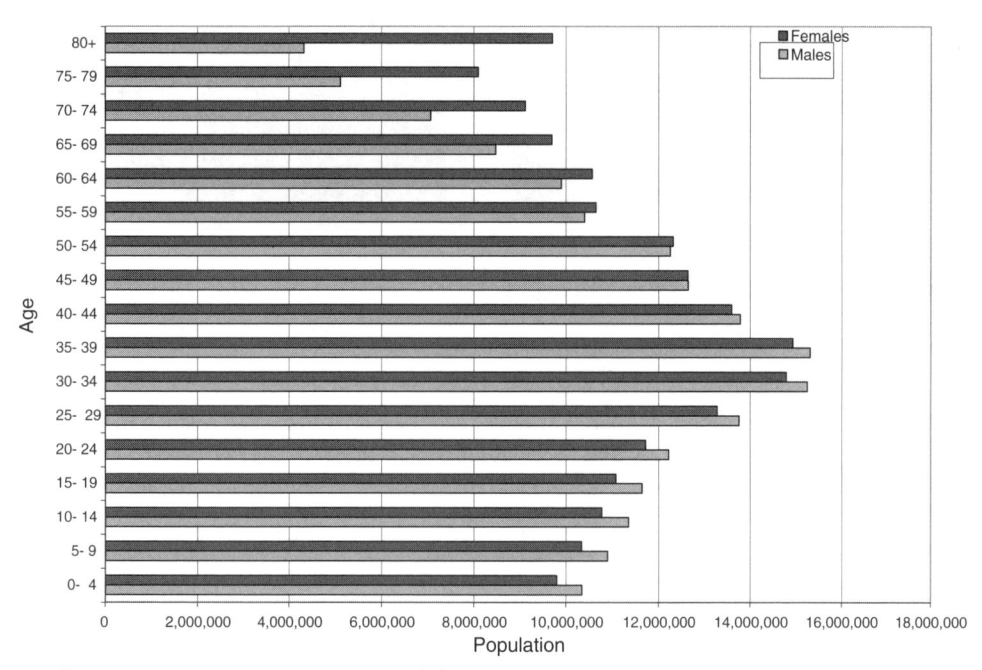

Source: Calculated using data from the US Census, International Database.

Figure 5.5 EU population, 2000

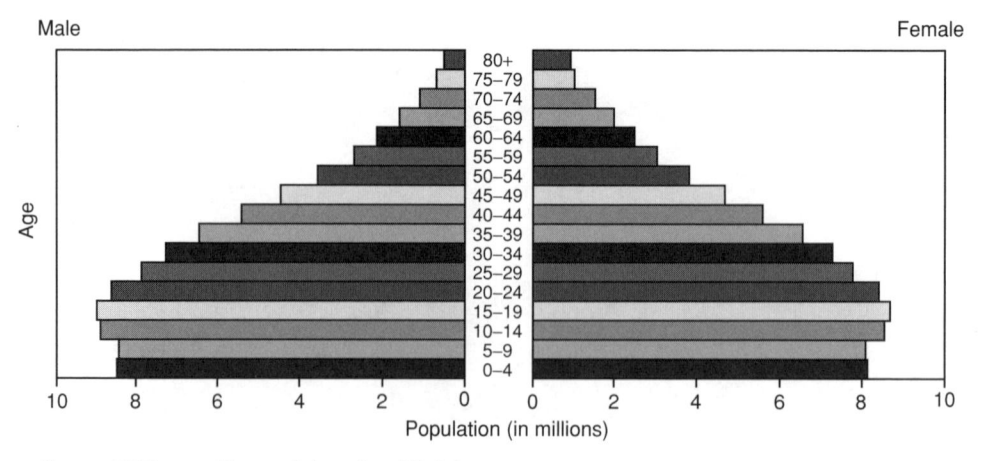

Figure 5.6 Brazil population pyramid, 2000

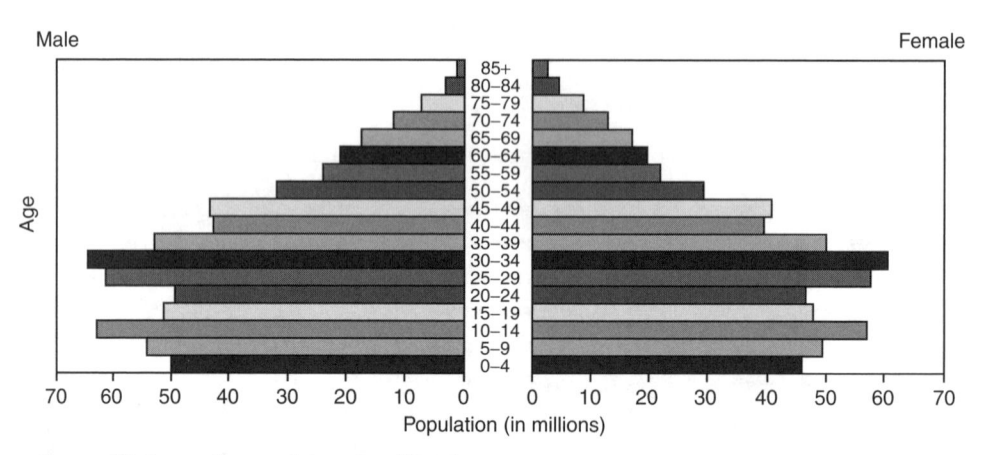

Figure 5.7 People's Republic of China population pyramid, 2000

Although the US is young compared to Japan and the EU, it is mature relative to emerging market economies where roughly half of the population is under the age of 25. The population structure of Brazil is a case in point (Figure 5.6). Note that the People's Republic of China – the most populous country in the world – is developing a generational bulge as a consequence of its strict population-control policies (Figure 5.7).

Young economies with high growth rates and ample job opportunities provide an excellent source of demand for manufactured goods in more developed countries. However, a young economy with a high unemployment rate is particularly prone to instability. Population projections by the United Nations forecast a 58% increase in the population of developing countries over the period 2000–2050 – a sharp contrast to the 2% growth expected in developed countries.[4] As such, looming generational bulges in some of the world's most unstable countries point to growing geopolitical risks on the horizon.

Implications for Fixed Income Investors

By 2005, 25% of the US population will be between the ages of 45 and 65 (compared with 20% a decade earlier), while the share of the population aged 20 to 40 will fall. As such, demographic considerations imply that US interest rates will continue to fall over the coming years as the Baby Boomers move out of the spending and borrowing years into the saving and investment phase of the lifecycle. This tendency would be reinforced if the US curtails its immigration levels, as has been indicated by the current Bush administration. In contrast, demography implies that interest rates in Japan will begin to rise as the dominant segment of its population starts to spend and borrow. In other words, the US and Japan may be set to reverse their relative roles as importers and exporters of capital.

Demography implies that the long end of the US yield curve will have a flattening bias over the coming years as aging Baby Boomers underpin demand from pension funds.[5] Moreover, a combination of rising life expectancy and historically low interest rates will fuel demand for more risky fixed income products (including those with longer maturities) to offset the risk of retirees outliving their capital. Sharp losses sustained in the equity market during 1999–2002 may further enhance Baby Boomer demand for longer dated corporate bonds. Finally, the growing geopolitical risk implied by population trends is bullish for short-term government debt – the preferred safe-haven trade.

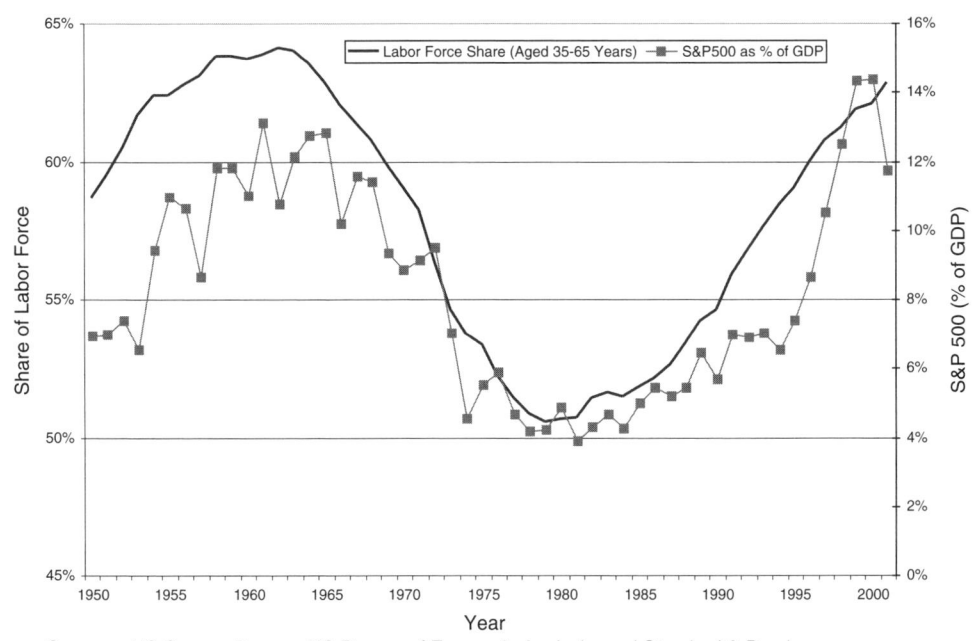

Sources: US Census Bureau, US Bureau of Economic Analysis, and Standard & Poor's

Figure 5.8 Aging and asset prices

The Limitations of Demographics

Demography is a useful analytical tool for anticipating changes in trends over the very long term.[6] Moreover, the effects of war, immigration, and technology can be seen to have even larger significance when seen through their secondary impact on demographic trends. Although demography arguably affects market dynamics, shifts are gradual, which means that demographic effects can get swamped by the cyclical ebb and flow of economic activity (Figure 5.8). As such, for some practitioners the implications of demography will be beyond their investment time horizon.

Like economics, demography assumes that preferences – in this case with respect to age group – are stable. Anyone familiar with the financial markets, however, knows that preferences exhibit a high degree of volatility around the trend. As such, we now turn our focus to psychology – another discipline focused on human behavior – with the goal of improving our ability to first understand, and ultimately anticipate, more short-term market dynamics.

5.2 THE INHERENTLY HUMAN NATURE OF MARKETS: A PSYCHOLOGICAL APPROACH

Market fluctuations register the human reaction to events, not the events themselves.

Any given market price and any given market movement is the cumulative result of millions of individual actions – each of which is the outcome of a potentially fallible and emotion-laden decision-making process. As such, investors ignore the psychological underpinnings of the market at their own peril. Psychology is the discipline that examines the human mind and behavior – including how humans experience emotions, process information and make decisions that guide behavior. Psychology is well equipped to provide valuable insight into the decisions investors make in an environment of uncertainty.

Behavioral finance – a relatively new discipline at the intersection of economics and psychology – applies psychological concepts specifically to financial decision making. In contrast with the efficient market view that mispricing is a random and brief departure from fundamentals, behavioral finance asserts that certain psychological phenomena produce behavioral biases. This makes market practitioners prone to specific errors which, in turn, cause prices to deviate systematically from fundamentals. Mispricing can persist for long periods because market participants learn slowly from their mistakes.[7]

The decision-making process can be reduced to two components: (1) the 'objective' processing of information in and of itself; and (2) the 'subjective' attitude and mood of the decision maker which puts the information into context. Although these components are irrevocably linked in practice, for explanatory purposes they are segregated here. Within each of these two components are a plethora of psychological phenomena which predispose market participants to commit specific cognitive errors (Table 5.2). These phenomena are discussed subsequently.

5.2.1 Information Processing

Physiologically, thinking involves the millions of neurons in the brain and the connections among them. These neural connections recognize complex patterns, classify new information into patterns, and draw associations between new data. In short, we are predisposed to think in terms of patterns. In fact, the underlying premise of analysis is based on replicating a pattern.

Table 5.2 Decision making and market bias

Component	Behavioral phenomena	Market bias
I. 'Objective' Information Processing	Representativeness (heuristic) Conservatism (heuristic) Gambler's fallacy	Overreaction (by amateurs); underreaction (by experts)
	Confirmation bias Selective exposure Selective perception False consensus effect Ego-defensive attitudes Hindsight bias	Overconfidence; over trading
II. 'Subjective' Attitude and Mood	Prospect theory Regret theory Cognitive dissonance Ego-defensive attitudes	Sell winners too early and hold on to losers
	Mental accounting Concorde (sunk cost) fallacy Hindsight bias	Distortions in risk assessment; take on more risk than perceived
	Anxiety Groupthink Adaptive attitudes Social comparison	Volatile decisions; overshooting

When a computer evaluates a new piece of information, a scenario is completely reconstructed from scratch by rerunning a computer program using *all* available data – the old as well as the new. On the other hand, when humans evaluate a new piece of information, the original scenario is merely given a face-lift. In other words, the new piece of information is fit into an already recognizable pattern.

Psychologist William James (1907) documents how individuals settle into new opinions. We meet a new experience that puts some of our old opinions under strain, producing "inward trouble". We seek to escape from this inward trouble by modifying the old opinions. However, we try to save as many of the old opinions as possible, such that our new opinion preserves the older stock of truths with a minimum of modification. Even the most violent revolutions in our beliefs leave most of the old order standing. In short, the mind resists change.

Pattern formation first involves the assembly of all the bits of information – including old opinions if they exist. The next steps involve discarding the pieces that are irrelevant and filling in the missing connections. In order to better understand market dynamics, we must understand how humans, both individually and collectively, filter out discordant "noise" and extrapolate from input.

Pattern Formation
Information bits → Filter out noise → Fill in connections → Pattern

A lesson from cognitive psychology is that humans can only handle so much information at once. Miller (1956) finds that we are only able to handle six or seven things at one time. A limited capacity to handle information, combined with the information overload of the present Information Age, points toward the importance of neural filters.

Meanwhile, Gestalt psychologists have shown that when faced with an incomplete picture, we mentally try to fill in the missing portions. In other words, humans extrapolate from experience and input in order to create more complete mental images. This is done by assimilation, whereby incidents are placed into a familiar and understandable (pre-existing) theme.

As a means of filtering out noise and assimilating masses of information fragments, we resort to rules of thumb (called *heuristics* in the field of psychology). A rule of thumb is a "rough and ready" procedure when an exhaustive examination of all available options is not feasible. In other words, we use old patterns to process new information. McGuire (1969) explains that an attitude (or expectation) is formed based on: (1) survival or safety (i.e. adaptive attitudes); (2) self-esteem (i.e. self-realizing attitudes); (3) defense mechanisms (i.e. ego-defensive attitudes); and (4) facts and experiences (i.e. knowledge attitudes). It is the reliance on these "rules of thumb" and the nature of these attitudes that leads to biased decisions and makes investors vulnerable to committing systematic errors. These patterns persist because people are slow to learn from their mistakes – a lesson from cognitive psychology.

Psychology tells us that our ability to understand abstract or complex ideas depends on carrying in our mind a working model of the phenomena. We construct *mental models* of reality to help anticipate events. Ongoing research shows that our use of mental models is frequently flawed – either the result of incomplete or unstable representations, or the improper application of accurate representations. Moreover, we have a tendency to create mental models based on superstitions and unwarranted beliefs (akin to *magical thinking*). In such cases, we believe that a certain behavior leads to a desired effect, even when we know of no explanation and when, in fact, there is none. For example, critics of technical analysis might argue that the use of trendlines is such a ritual.

We are susceptible to magical thinking because as pattern-seeking creatures we distrust chaos and disorder. Similarly, we have an aversion to ambiguity. As a result, it is psychologically more palatable to believe that a precise answer is more certain and therefore deserves a higher level of confidence than an approximate answer. Hence, we seek explanations – even for the unexplainable – because the alternative is too uncomfortable. This accounts for a willingness to listen to the predictions of market forecasters even when it is clear that no one has the ability to predict the future (Shermer, 2000).

Overreaction Bias

Research from behavioral finance finds that investors tend to overreact to news. Specifically, investors are overpessimistic about recent losers and overoptimistic about recent winners. De Bondt and Thaler (1985) find that investors – both experts and amateurs – tend to overweight the most recent information and underweight the information that came previously.[8] Howe (1986) also finds investors to be overpessimistic about recent losers.

The tendency to overreact to news in general is based on the erroneous extrapolation of new pieces of information into the future (called the *representativeness* heuristic).[9] The representativeness effect is essentially naïve trend projection and a failure to recognize the laws of probability – specifically regression toward the mean. One manifestation of this phenomenon is that people think they see patterns in truly random sequences. De Bondt (1991) finds that for all but the shortest predictions, economists find it difficult to do more than extrapolate the historical rate of growth. The representativeness heuristic leads to excessively volatile predictions and the tendency to revise too much. An overreaction to *bad* news in particular is linked to representativeness as well as an emotional aversion to loss (discussed in Section 5.2.2). Together the phenomena of representativeness and loss aversion explain why investors are especially bearish when bond prices are on the decline.

Underreaction Bias

Research from behavioral finance also finds evidence of an underreaction to new information. Bernard (1992) and De Bondt (1993) find that positive surprises are followed by more positive surprises, and vice versa. Cutler et al. (1991) examine aggregate time series of security returns (including bonds) and find generally, though not uniformly, underreaction over horizons of one-month to one-year. Chopra et al. (1993) find systematic underreaction in stock prices over a 3- to 12-month horizon in contrast to overreaction at very short (within a 1-month) and long (3-year) horizons.[10]

The tendency to underreact (e.g. revise too little) is based on the anchoring of future predictions to *significant* past events (called the *conservatism* heuristic). Anchoring means that people are slow to change their beliefs in the face of new evidence.[11] As such, predictions do not sufficiently reflect new information – or rather, more permanent changes in circumstances get mistaken for temporary ones. Salience is key. When the past is more relevant, recent information tends to be overweighted. For example, the price paid for a bond and the highest price reached since purchase become irresistible anchors, or rather, clues to future movements for the individual investor (which are irrelevant to the market as a whole).

Hence, different perceptions produce different biases and failures of judgment. Some individuals are subject to an overreaction bias produced by the representativeness heuristic, while others are subject to an underreaction bias produced by the anchoring and adjustment heuristic. Interestingly, research indicates a systematic difference in perceptions between individual investors and Wall Street strategists. De Bondt (1998) finds that individual investors are prone to betting that trends continue, while experts show a tendency to inappropriately predict trend reversal in the wake of above-average performance. This is *gambler's fallacy* – the false belief that the probability of a random event is dependent on preceding events. For example, a gambler may have the false belief that 'red' is increasingly likely following a succession of 'black' outcomes at the roulette table. Similarly, when recent performance has been above average, a strategist tends to have the false belief that future performance will be *below* the mean – instead of *closer* to the mean – in satisfying the law of averages.

Overconfidence Bias

Overconfidence causes errors. Research shows that we tend to overestimate our ability to make correct forecasts and complete difficult tasks successfully. In one study, for example, individuals rated themselves above the mean in almost every positive personal trait (De Bondt, 1993). Experts, particularly the "super analysts", are the worst offenders. The experience of Long-Term Capital Management (LTCM) – helmed by Nobel laureates Myron Scholes and Robert Merton, and the pioneer of fixed income arbitrage, John Meriwether – is a notorious example. Arguably, extreme overconfidence was at least partially responsible for the astonishing degree of leverage (between 20:1 and 30:1) employed by LTCM which put the lion's share of its capital at risk on a regular basis (Lowenstein, 2000). Overconfidence can also lead to increased trading activity. As we all know, high turnover strategies tend to underperform buy and hold strategies in rising markets because of transaction costs. Finally, experts that focus on economic fundamentals tend to downplay the importance of errors. Meanwhile, those that rely on technical analysis tend to produce excessively volatile predictions.[12]

Overconfidence stems from a tendency to test our beliefs by seeking evidence that verifies them and ignoring evidence that refutes them (called *confirmation bias*).[13] For example, analysts may seek evidence that confirms their previous analysis, or investors might ignore evidence that refutes a previous investment decision. We also have a tendency to pay attention to media reports that reinforce our pre-existing attitudes (called *selective exposure*). Katz and Lazarsfeld (1955) show that people selectively read newspapers and magazines or watch TV – looking for those pieces that reinforce attitudes already held, and shunning those that might change their mind. Similarly, there is a tendency to misinterpret information in a way that confirms our behavior and attitudes (called *selective perception*). Finally, there is a tendency to overestimate the extent to which other people share our attitudes (called the *false consensus effect*). The false consensus effect can lead investors to take on exposure in mature trends when they should not.

Confirmation bias, selective exposure, selective perception, and the false consensus effect are all mechanisms that cause investors to put too much weight in their beliefs – even when new information contradicts them. Ego-defensive attitudes and hindsight bias (discussed in Section 5.2.2) are other psychological phenomena which complement confirmation bias and reinforce overconfidence.

5.2.2 Attitude and Mood: The Effect on Risk Tolerance and Judgment

The pleasure of pulling down profits is great, so the investor puts a lot on the line from a psychological standpoint.

GALLEA and PATALON (1998)

Although the calculation of risk is an objective mathematical calculation, the tolerance for risk is a subjectively emotional experience. Our psychological reaction to potential loss affects the decisions and errors we make. This section highlights a number of psychological phenomena which affect risk tolerance and judgment.

Loss Aversion

Fear is a stronger emotion than greed. We learn from a young age to avoid sources of pain. Hence, it may come as no surprise that humans have a skewed intolerance for loss (called *Prospect Theory*). Not only do we prefer the option that offers the best chance of not losing, but we are also willing to take more risks to avoid losses than to realize gains. Kahneman and Tversky (1979) demonstrate that the pain of loss is far more significant than the satisfaction of gain by a factor of 2.5 to 1. Moreover, we seem to assign more value to a gain of a given size than to an equal loss. Thaler et al. (1997) show that pain avoidance dominates pleasure seeking as a motivator.

Similarly, we avoid actions that confirm we have made mistakes (called *Regret Theory*). Regret minimization is the reason why we stubbornly hold on to bonds that are doing badly – because the loss doesn't feel like a loss until we sell. We avoid selling at a loss in the hope that the price will recover so that we can break even before closing a position. That is, we hope to avoid the feeling of pain and regret when the loss is booked, so we gamble that the price will eventually rise.

The evidence is clear that many run contrary to the conventional wisdom of "cutting losses and letting winners run".[14] Shefrin and Statman (1985) find that investors are predisposed to holding losers too long and selling winners too early. Odean (1998) finds that investors who are loss averse realize their paper gains 1.68 times more frequently than they do their paper losses. In a study of 19,000 off-floor trades in the Treasury bond futures market of the Chicago Board of Trade, off-floor traders held initial paper losses longer than trades showing initial paper gains (Heisler, 1994).

There are a number of psychological phenomena that assist us in the aversion of pain – including cognitive dissonance and ego-defensive attitudes. When faced with a contrary view or a conflict between expectations and an actual outcome (an unpleasant inconsistency), we tend to resolve the dissonance by choosing a comfortable route (called *cognitive dissonance*). The tendency is to try to avoid the discordant information (or distort it) and to avoid action that highlights the dissonance (Festinger, 1957). This explains why investors are slow to sell in a downtrend and slow to buy in an uptrend. It takes time to reconcile the new bullish/bearish environment with their existing bearish/ bullish attitude.

We also adapt our attitudes so that they seem to confirm the decisions we have made (called *ego-defensive attitudes*). The ego-defensive attitude protects us against being confronted with our own mistakes. In other words, denial protects the ego. This trait bears most of the responsibility for the fact that individual investors quickly close off good positions and let the bad ones run. It also explains why turnover is normally lower in bear markets than in bull markets (Tvede, 2002).

Distortions in Risk Assessment

We tend to think of money (especially the risk associated with it) in separate categories, optimizing each "account" rather than the whole (called *mental accounting*). In other words, we make distinctions between paper and realized losses, and between losses and gains – with each category savored separately (as opposed to the net gain or loss). Mental accounting is the reason we are far more willing to gamble with a year-end bonus (especially if it is higher than anticipated) than with our monthly salary (Shefrin, 2000). Statman (1994) shows that we are more inclined to gamble with losses than with gains. When deep "in the red", for example, people turn into risk seekers – accepting worse than normal odds in the hope of recouping their losses.

Similarly, individuals will make different choices depending on how a problem is presented (called *frame dependence*). For example, investors allocate more of their portfolio to stocks than bonds when exposed to an impressive history of long-term stock returns; and vice versa when exposed to volatile short-term stock returns (Benartzi and Thaler, 1995). We tend to base decisions on past efforts rather than on future prospects. For example, many investors attempt to recoup losses by investing even more money on the same item – instead of assessing the current rationality of the investment irrespective of the loss (called the "*Concorde*" or *sunk cost fallacy*).[15] Mental accounting is one technique which allows us to propel this fallacy and distort our perception of actual risk.

Finally, we have a tendency to be "Monday morning quarterbacks" – as appropriate actions are always clear in retrospect, even if we had no clue to begin with (called *hindsight bias*). This overestimation in the ability to predict outcomes, leads us to be insufficiently surprised by events. As a result, hindsight bias can seriously distort judgments. For example, an investor that believes an up-move in the bond price was actually fairly predictable might have intense regret for closing a long position too early, and attempt to get back in at the level where the bond was mistakenly sold.

The Impact of Emotion on Judgment

Emotions affect the way investors evaluate alternatives and are a crucial determinant of our risk-taking behavior (Lopes, 1987). As emotions oscillate between hope and fear, our tolerance for risk changes. Fear reduces risk tolerance and induces a focus on unfavorable events, while hope increases risk tolerance and induces a focus on favorable events. Greed is the operative emotion during bull markets, while fear is the operative emotion during bear markets. Our most recent experience also affects our tolerance: a loss/win makes us less/more inclined to gamble, while a loss on top of another loss is especially painful.

Lopes (1987) documented the range of emotions experienced by investors over the investment horizon (Table 5.3). Fear leads to the desire for security, while hope leads to the desire for potential upside. One of these poles dominates. Together they determine risk tolerance.

Table 5.3 Emotional time line

Investment horizon time line	Emotion
1. Ponder alternatives, and decide amount of risk to bear.	Hope (or fear).
2. Ride financial roller coaster (e.g. watch decisions play out), and decide to keep or alter initial strategy.	Anticipation (or anxiety).
3. Learn investment outcome.	Pride (or regret).

Source: Adapted from Lopes (1987).

We are, through a long process of evolution, acutely uncomfortable and anxious in the face of uncertainty. Anxiety not only affects our tolerance for risk, it also affects our judgment and interferes with problem solving. A number of studies show that we prefer a certain gain of a small size to a highly probable gain of much larger size, even if the latter's statistical value is higher (called the *certainty effect*). We prefer certainty, because uncertainty generates anxiety. Ambiguity and uncertainty elevate anxiety, and anxiety increases the volatility of our predictions and the likelihood of mistakes.

Our disposition to change our attitudes is dramatically increased when we get very stressed. Attitudes are fairly solid because they are tied to what we think, do, and feel. However, they can be dissolved quickly by adrenalin (Tvede, 2002). Changes in attitudes that might normally take weeks or months can take place in a matter of hours, minutes, or seconds when we are stressed – such as when there is a sudden plunge in market prices.

Carl von Clausewitz commented on the difficulty of holding onto one's original strategy or seeing how it should be altered when one's nerves are wracked by uncertainty amid a never-ending stream of new information from the battlefield. He also noted how fears are a fertile breeding ground for lies and untruths. Today, practitioners face a media deluge of news and opinions from the "financial battlefield". According to Lifson and Geist (1999), instant information leads investors to make too many emotional decisions – one of which is likely to be wrong.

Research shows that when people are presented with messages designed to produce more or less anxiety, they tend to ignore the messages creating the greatest amount of fear (Janis and Feshbach, 1953). This helps to explain why people who are bullish tend to ignore those calling for a market decline. Investing increases anxiety and in that arena people have a bias to seek and hold onto majority opinion for comfort.

5.2.3 Social Psychology: The Herding Phenomenon

Men go mad in crowds, and they only recover their senses slowly and one by one.
CHARLES MACKAY (1841)

Herding is a deeply ingrained psychological tendency. Like many other species, living with the herd was once in the best interest of survival for humans (both individually and collectively). While survival is no longer an issue, people still turn to crowds for safety. From an early age we are rewarded for conforming to society's norms and we learn to self-censor our creative (i.e. "dangerous") thinking to avoid the pain of rejection. The greater the uncertainty or stress we face, the stronger our desire to follow the crowd.[16]

These factors make us susceptible to "groupthink", a well-known phenomenon in social psychology where individuals conform to the thinking of the group, even if it is faulty. Asch (1955) demonstrates the power of the group with a study showing how one in three would even deny the totally obvious. Janis (1972) demonstrates how highly cohesive groups are in danger of reaching terrible collective decisions.

Groupthink is supported by a number of psychological phenomena observed from individual behavior, including a tendency for individuals to develop the same attitudes as people with whom they associate (called *adaptive attitudes*). For example, we are influenced by what we read, what people we know say and do, and what the price movements are telling us that other people are doing (Sherif, 1937). Adaptive attitudes along with the phenomenon of anchoring and adjustment – together underpin a dynamic in which long-established trends are not easily reversed. There is also the tendency for individuals to use the behavior of others (such as experts or the consensus) as a source of information about a subject that is difficult to understand (called *social comparison*).

As part of the crowd we feel, think, and act in a manner quite different from when we are on our own. As a group, people become primitive and action oriented, tending to react to emotion rather than intellect (e.g. peer pressure). Group members tend to believe others, particularly group leaders, more than they believe themselves. This is reinforced by the *persuasion effect* from Gestalt theory: we are swayed more by a credible source than a credible argument.

Research indicates that groupthink mainly occurs in situations of high stress and complexity. In the context of financial markets, the uncertainty in asset price movements propels many investors to look for a leader who will tell them what to do. For technical analysts, that leader is the price action itself. For others, the leader will be an expert opinion.

Unfortunately, even the experts are motivated to follow the crowd. In a highly competitive atmosphere where bad recommendations could mean getting fired, survival instincts come to the surface. In this case, survival means conforming to the consensus opinion. Logically, if you are wrong – it is not so bad if all your competitors are also wrong. What is not acceptable, however, is to be wrong when everyone else is right.[17]

It is indeed sobering to understand the fragile base on which majority opinion is built. But we are not finished yet. As a final point, it is important to make the distinction between attitudes and actions. Psychology tells us that the action and timing of the action depends on the intensity of the attitude and whether the attitude is associated with pleasure or pain. In terms of the markets, this is particularly relevant as most analysts responsible for generating trade ideas are not accountable for the outcome that results.

The Psychology of Trends and Reversals[18]

A trend often runs far longer than anyone expects, and the underlying psychological dynamics provide some insight into this phenomenon (Table 5.4). After taking big losses from the previous downturn, most investors have a difficult time dealing with the new bullish trend. In other words, the rising price is inconsistent with their attitude that the bond is a "loser" (i.e. cognitive dissonance). Instead of admitting the error and buying the bond back to profit from the new trend, they remain on the sidelines. As the bond continues to rally, investors with long positions vacillate between greed and fear. Greed says to stay in and fear says to get out. Hindsight bias and regret minimization are in operation as investors that sold just before the rise hope the price will drop a little so that they can get back in with some honor intact; they buy on the dips produced by others taking profits.

Rising prices soon catch the interest of analysts who then issue bullish recommendations. The trend starts to feed on itself as the representative effect[19] takes hold, and investors use mental accounting to play with "house money". Bullishness begets further bullishness. The media rationalizes the trend. Those still out of the market are plagued by hindsight bias and regret. Ego-defensive attitudes and overconfidence mount.

Table 5.4 The psychological dynamics of a rising trend

Market phenomena	Key psychological phenomena
1. An increased number of investors are attracted to market gains	Cognitive dissonance Conservatism Hindsight bias Regret theory
2. News is interpreted in a way that supports the trend	Confirmation bias Selective exposure Selective perception Adaptive attitudes Social comparison
3. The trend starts feeding on itself. The market becomes the subject of social small talk	Representativeness Magical thinking Mental accounting Confirmation bias False consensus effect Hindsight bias (for those out of market) Regret theory (for those out of market)
4. Bad news is ignored. The market is flush with liquidity	Cognitive dissonance Representativeness Confirmation bias Selective exposure Selective perception False consensus effect

Source: Adapted from *The Psychology of Finance: Understanding the Behavioural Dynamics of Markets* (Revised), L. Tvede. Copyright 2002 © John Wiley & Sons Limited. Reproduced with permission.

Bonds rally enough to resolve the dissonance for the majority of investors.[20] Those who got out too early are plagued by hindsight bias and regret. Many are willing to buy at the slightest sign of weakness; those not in the market feel ridiculous. Any price drop is very limited before the next rise starts. The new rise is not just provoked by new investors but also early sellers who want to get in again. Financial liquidity increases and there is a false consensus effect. Stop-loss buy orders are triggered for short sellers. Greed takes hold and fear is forgotten. The mere fact that there is a trend makes people believe that it will continue, and bad news is ignored. The trend feeds on itself.

At the late stages of a bull market, the professionals will sense something is wrong and start selling their major positions, using short-term rallies to unload. The new amateurs on the scene see this as an opportunity to buy. The market jerks up and down, spreading uncertainty. Doubt prompts more and more amateurs to sell. The dynamics for a falling trend are the mirror image of those for a rising trend: when prices begin to drop at the start of a new bearish trend (i.e. at the reversal of an uptrend), most investors are not worried as their courage has been bolstered by the previous persistence of rising prices.

The Dynamics of Market Manias and Panics

Manias and panics are cases of extreme crowd behavior. The frequent recurrence of manias and panics shows how easy it is to succumb to the psychology of the crowd. Classic examples include Holland's Tulip mania in 1636, the South Sea Bubble in 1711, the California Gold Rush in 1840, and the Wall Street crash in 1929. More recent examples include the bursting of Japan's double bubble (equity and real estate) in 1990, and the episode of "Irrational Exuberance" in the US information technology sector almost a decade later. In 2003, the question in many investor's minds was whether they were witnessing a bond market bubble – particularly in Japanese government bonds. What is it that makes normally prudent investors cavalierly disregard warnings, throw caution to the wind, and become speculators?

Behavioral finance attributes price bubbles to trend-chasing based on extrapolative expectations – effectively the representativeness heuristic *en masse*. Shiller (1987, 1988) determines that most sellers in the 1987 stock market crash did so in anticipation of further price declines. Moreover, smart money investors aggravate the effect by buying in anticipation of further buying by uninformed investors. Technical analysts describe this process in terms of accumulation, distribution, and liquidation.[21]

Alternatively, Gladwell (2002) uses biology to explain a number of (non-financial) examples of contagious behavior, deemed "socioeconomic epidemics". A viral epidemic is the result of: (1) contagious behavior; (2) geometric progression (e.g. small changes having big effects); and (3) critical mass. In the socioeconomic context, Gladwell translates these channels into: (1) transmitters; (2) a message with impact; and (3) the environment or context.

If we extend this concept to financial markets, it would seem that manias and panics are the consequence of: (1) the fast and wide dissemination of information via the media and internet; (2) the numerous positive feedback loops within financial markets; and (3) the appearance of a new trend. Geometric progression is assisted by a positive feedback loop, where price gains attract more investors, which in turn produce further price gains. At some point, the new trend is considered the normal steady state (Table 5.5).

Another theory is that large-scale events in biology, geology, and economics are not necessarily the result of a single large event, but rather the unfolding of a chain reaction of smaller

Table 5.5 Factors generating a critical mass

Biological	Socioeconomic	Financial
1. Contagious behavior	1. Transmitters	1. Media and internet dissemination
2. Geometric progression	2. Message with impact	2. Positive feedback loops
3. Critical mass	3. Environment	3. Appearance of a trend

events in a type of avalanche effect. Bak et al. (1996) apply the avalanche concept to financial markets. They explain how stock prices climb when the ratio of trend followers to "fundamentalists" begins to grow. As prices increase, a larger number of fundamentalists sell and leave the market, replaced by a growing number of trend followers who are attracted to rising prices. When the relative number of fundamentalists is small, financial bubbles occur because prices have moved far above the fair price a fundamentalist would pay: a steepening pile of sand which increases the possibility of an avalanche. Conversely, when the number of fundamentalists is large, market prices typically lock into a trading range defined by the give and take of fundamentalists and trend followers.

5.2.4 Implications for Fixed Income Investors

Although our human tendencies are beneficial in social as well as survival circumstances, when it comes to investing they can be costly. As such, an investor employing the lessons of psychology will need to actively decouple emotion and decision-making. A number of practical suggestions as to how this can be accomplished are presented below.

[1] Beware of an Inherent Bias to Follow the Crowd

Members of the financial community watch the same quotes on their terminals and read the same articles. Day in, day out, the crowd influences our thinking. The longer a rally continues, the more the analyst gets caught up in the bullish sentiment, ignores the warning signs, and misses the reversal. The analyst has joined the crowd.

To avoid the crowd mentality, it is important to think independently and be strong enough to execute independent, non-emotional decisions. Emotional independence is supported by following an objective trading plan that has been worked out in advance – including specific indicators to watch and how to interpret them. Knowing the exact conditions in which one enters and exits a trade avoids the impulsive trading that usually leads to error. A plan also assists in cutting losses when they are small and reasonable. It is important not to change the plan while positions are open, as this is when we are most vulnerable to being pulled into the crowd.

Since the practitioner is arguably the weakest link in any investment strategy, Elder (1993) argues that it is as important to study the changes in our mental state as we trade as it is to study the trades themselves. One suggestion is to identify the aspects of our personality that contribute to successful investing as well as those aspects that must be constantly guarded against. To this end, it is necessary to keep a detailed record of the reasons for going into a trade, and for getting out – including one's state of mind as well as the supporting analysis. These details will help to add valuable structure to the decision-making process and will help to avoid mistakes being repeated.

Finally, independent analysis requires just that – forming your own view independent of the opinion around you. The consensus opinion and the recent trend should be of no relevance to your fundamental view. Otherwise, this information "frames" your mind and biases the analytical process. Listening to experts for guidance is your conscious decision not to think for yourself.

[2] Beware of an Inherent Bias toward Unwitting Speculation

Psychology suggests that even expert investors can be unwitting speculators, making investment errors grounded in a distorted perception of risk. We think we are investing, but we act speculatively. Then, without realizing it, we end up with a speculator's return. Gallea and Patalon (1998) note that most investors have fooled themselves into believing that they are making rational, as opposed to emotional, decisions.

As such, practitioners need to be vigilant about maintaining the integrity of their information processing and ensuring that investment decisions are not influenced by gains and losses already made. In other words, it is important not to compartmentalize risks and returns.

It is easy to say that we should ignore the noise in the market but quite another matter to master the psychological effects of that noise. Consequently, investors need a *process* that allows them to resist their innate biases. Charlie Munger suggests a two-track analytical check: first, for known facts and rational factors that govern the situation; then for signs of subconscious psychological misjudgment (either your own or those of others).[22]

[3] Beware of an Inherent Bias against Selling

Investors are psychologically biased toward a "buy and hold" strategy. If prices are rising, there is the fear that one is making a mistake by selling too soon. If prices have fallen below the purchase level, there is the hope that the pain of loss can be avoided. Daily conditioning from the media tends to reinforce current trends, and analysts are eight times more likely to produce buy recommendations than sell recommendations (Cassidy, 1999). Selling requires accepting new negative information, a 180-degree reversal in prior thinking, and going against the crowd (selling when news is positive and everyone loves the bond). Alternatively, a deluge of information and associated analysis can produce "analysis-paralysis". The course of least resistance is inaction (e.g. holding on).

In order to offset the bias against selling, investors should have a clear selling target in mind before a bond is purchased. Remember that the entry price has only personal significance; it has no significance to the market. In addition, over the investment horizon practitioners should frequently revisit the question: Given what you know today, would you buy the bond at today's price? If the answer is no, the bond should be sold. Finally, once we own a bond, there is a tendency to hear only the positive aspects about it and to dismiss the negative. The same tendency exists for analysts that recommend the investment. Hence, the techniques discussed in Item [2] should remain active throughout the investment horizon.

[4] Beware of an Inherent Bias toward Overconfidence

We tend to overestimate our abilities – particularly if we have managed to put a succession of profitable trades together. There is a tendency to attribute our success to skill as opposed to random luck. Moreover, our existing attitudes act as a subconscious anchor in the evaluation of new information. As a result, we tend to think much like a racehorse that runs with blinders. As such, learning is slowed and the ego grows. A large ego seriously elevates misjudgment risk.

A *proactive* approach to learning – making it a conscious part of the investment process – will help to keep the ego on the sidelines. When losses are made, it is important to identify the mistake and realign the ego – that is, don't blame the market, but accept responsibility for the losses. The tendency will be to engage in hindsight bias and to adopt an ego-defensive attitude. The key is to be methodical. Remember: no one can predict the future.

5.2.5 Limitations of the Psychological Approach

Psychology provides valuable insight into the subconscious biases of individual analysts and investors as well as the market as a whole. Although psychology explains why we as individuals react as we do, it does not allow for an objective calibration of these reactions; this makes it difficult to put into practice as a forecasting technique. Even at the theoretical level, there is no clear answer to the question: "What compels individuals to react at the same time?"

In the next two chapters, we consider a number of techniques used by practitioners to quantify qualitative behavioral influences and anticipate short-term market dynamics. Chartists study the price patterns that develop as a reflection of mass market psychology. Others study the flows of different types of investors. Effectively, these techniques attempt to put "socio-epidemic" and "avalanche" theories into practice. In other words, technical analysts may be seen as applied social psychologists.

NOTES

1. A high fertility rate is associated with a young population, a booming economy and/or a large influx of immigrants (who tend to move during the prime child-bearing years).
2. The US Census Bureau has a fantastic international database of population pyramids, historical as well as projected. See www.census.gov/ipc/www/idbpyr.html.
3. The earlier decline in Japanese fertility is linked to the devastation and knock-on effects of two atomic explosions during World War II.
4. Based on the 2002 Population Report. See www.un.org/esa/population/unpop.htm.
5. Over a much longer horizon, however, demography implies a steepening bias at the long end of the curve in the absence of policy changes that address skyrocketing government pension liabilities. Based on estimates by BCA Research (2003), for example, in the absence of policy changes the aging of Japan's population is expected to push the net government to GDP ratio to more than 300% by 2025.
6. For small, open economies foreign demographic shifts may be more relevant than domestic shifts.
7. Behavioral finance rests on two major pillars: limited arbitrage and investor sentiment. For more information on the aspects associated with limited arbitrage, see Shleifer (2000).
8. In an examination of US stock returns dating back to 1993, De Bondt and Thaler (1985) show how a portfolio of "loser" stocks held for three years outperformed the general stock market by nearly 20% and outperformed a portfolio of "winner" stocks by nearly 25% (the winners underperformed the market by 5%). Meanwhile, De Bondt (1998) finds overpessimism on the part of experts after 3-year bull markets and overoptimism after 3-year bear markets. The overreaction result has been corroborated by De Bondt and Thaler (1987), Chopra et al. (1992), and Lakonishok et al. (1994). All the studies relate to the stock market. Haugen and Baker (1996) and Fama and French (1998) examine non-US evidence.
9. The representativeness heuristic was documented by psychologists, Kahneman and Tversky (1973, 1974).
10. Further evidence of underreaction in stock prices: Jegadeesh and Titman (1993) and Chan et al. (1996) find underreaction over a 6- to 12-month horizon; Rouwenhorst (1997) documents underreaction in international equities.

11. Edwards (1968) identified the phenomenon of conservatism. Edwards found in his experiments that individuals would update their views in the right direction, but by too little. According to Edwards, a first approximation is that it takes from two to five observations to do one observation's worth of work in inducing a change in opinion.
12. Shefrin (2000) notes that an optimal forecast is much less variable than the process being predicted – minimizing the likelihood of mismatch between the forecast and actual outcome. Technical analysts are prone to making excessively volatile predictions because they rely on representativeness as a rule of thumb.
13. Einhorn and Hogarth (1978) find that we are prone to search for confirming evidence.
14. A classic example is rogue trader Nicholas Leeson's failure to cut losses, which led to the collapse of Barings PLC.
15. Named after the supersonic aircraft, the Concorde, whose cost rose so steeply during its development that it soon became uneconomical. Nevertheless, the British and French governments continued to support it to justify the past investment.
16. In theory, one's confidence and self-esteem are bolstered under stressful conditions by mutual support. In practice, Kazdin (2000) finds no evidence of a causal relationship between stress and groupthink.
17. Scharfstein and Stein (1990) document the herding of portfolio manager stock selections to avoid looking bad.
18. This section follows an excellent discussion in Tvede (2002: 219–222).
19. Just because the market has gone up a long way, investors believe it will keep going up.
20. This is why a roaring bull market near its end draws in the most inexperienced of investors.
21. Accumulation is the purchase by informed investors in anticipation of future price increases; distribution involves the selling by the smart money investors who bought early to the uniformed investors who buy late; liquidation involves the return of prices to fundamental values.
22. Quoted in Hagstrom (2000).

RECOMMENDED READING

Foot, D.K. and Stoffman, D. (1998). *Boom, Bust & Echo 2000: Profiting from the Demographic Shift in the New Millennium*. Toronto: Macfarlane Walter & Ross.

Mackay, C. (1841). *Extraordinary Popular Delusions and the Madness of Crowds*. New York: Three Rivers Press (reprinted 1980).

Tvede, L. (2002). *The Psychology of Finance: Understanding the Behavioral Dynamics of Markets* (revised). New York: John Wiley & Sons.

APPENDIX: SUMMARY OF PSYCHOLOGICAL PHENOMENA

Behavioral tendency	Description
Adaptive attitudes (*Social psychology*)	We develop the attitudes of those with whom we associate.
Anchoring (*Cognitive psychology*)	Decisions are influenced by a framework through which information is interpreted.
Certainty effect (*Behaviorist school*)	Certain gains of a small size are preferred to a highly likely gain of much larger size.
Cognitive dissonance (*Cognitive psychology*)	When reality diverges with our attitudes, we try to avoid it or distort it.
Confirmation bias (*Cognitive psychology*)	Conclusions are biased by what we want to believe, even if new information contradicts it.
Ego-defensive attitudes (*Psychoanalytic theory*)	Attitudes are adapted to confirm the decisions we make.
False consensus effect (*Gestalt theory*)	We overestimate the number of people that share our opinions.
Hindsight bias (*Cognitive psychology*)	We overestimate our ability to predict the outcome of past events.
Magical thinking (*Behaviorist school*)	We think that certain behavior leads to a desired effect, even when we know of no explanation.
Mental accounting (*Cognitive psychology*)	We compartmentalize phenomena and try to optimize each individually rather than the whole.
Overconfident behavior (*Cognitive psychology*)	We overestimate our ability.
Persuasion effect (*Gestalt theory*)	We are persuaded more by a credible source than by a credible argument.
Prospect theory (*Behaviorist school*)	We are irrationally less willing to gamble with profits than with losses.
Regret theory (*Cognitive psychology*)	We avoid actions that confirm we have made mistakes.
Representativeness effect (*Gestalt theory*)	We think that the trends we observe are likely to continue.
Selective exposure (*Cognitive psychology*)	We expose ourselves only to information that confirms our behavior and attitudes.
Selective perception (*Cognitive psychology*)	We misinterpret information in a way that confirms our behavior and attitudes.
Social comparison (*Social psychology*)	We use others (the smartest or the majority) for guidance on subjects we find difficult to understand.

6
Technical Analysis: Applied Social Psychology

History does not repeat itself, but it does rhyme.

MARK TWAIN

Technical analysis is a widely used tool to determine the strength of market trends and identify potential turning points. The basic premise of technical analysis is that, *en masse*, investors and speculators tend to do similar things when faced by similar circumstances. As a result, characteristic patterns in price action emerge which are repeated again and again. These past reactions are used to assess the likelihood of future price movements.

The basic principles of technical analysis are: (1) prices are determined solely by supply and demand; (2) supply and demand are affected by various factors – including fundamentals, the prevailing mood in the market, and investor perception of value; (3) prices discount all information – including economics, politics, psychology, etc.; (4) prices tend to move in trends that persist over time; and (5) history repeats itself.

The basic tool of technical analysis is the chart, which is used to identify trends and patterns in historical prices.[1] Chart patterns represent the behavior of the masses, which is considered to be more predictable than individual behavior. Since the market is human, it is prone to swings in optimism and pessimism. The chart is used to assess these swings.

The prices at which bulls (e.g. the buyers) and bears (e.g. the sellers) are willing to trade change with perceptions of value (the meaning of news) and the prevailing mood in the market. Consequently, prices move up or down because of changes in the relative aggressiveness of bulls and bears. Kahn (1999) explains that markets rise because of fear among bears and greed among bulls, whereas markets fall because of fear among bulls and greed among bears. A rally continues as long as bulls are greedy enough to meet sellers' demands. When the buyers feel much stronger than the sellers, the market rises quickly. The job of the technical analyst is effectively to determine when the buyers are strong and when they start running out of steam.

6.1 FUNDAMENTALISTS VERSUS TECHNICIANS

Fundamental and technical analysts agree that price is determined by supply and demand, and that the price fully discounts all known information in the market, but this is where agreement ends. The "fundamentalists" claim that price adjustments reflect new information immediately, while "technicians" claim that this information is reflected gradually. If information is reflected immediately, price movements are random, and price patterns are meaningless. Technicians believe that the patterns in their price charts hold useful information, particularly in the absence of changing fundamentals. Fundamentalists point out that any random process can generate patterns. In other words, fundamentalists and technicians find themselves firmly entrenched on opposite sides of the fierce and ongoing debate about the efficiency of markets.[2]

The primary focus of fundamental analysts is the reason for the underlying price action, whereas the focus of technical analysts is the price action itself. Although technicians acknowledge that fundamentals underlie market dynamics and drive prices in the long run, the underlying fundamentals are irrelevant for technical forecasts. Instead, technicians focus on those price levels seen to be important by a large number of market participants.

Fundamental analysis examines economic variables (such as GDP and inflation) in order to anticipate where the market is likely to head in the future, while technical analysis examines market information (such as prices and volume). Economic data are available with a lag and are revised regularly, whereas market information is real-time and never revised. Fundamentalists and technicians are most at odds at the start of a reversal of a major trend, when the fundamental reason for the change is yet unclear.

Fundamentalists and technicians both agree that sometimes markets reflect changes in sentiment, quite apart from any change in fundamentals. However, technicians attribute a more important role to sentiment and believe that it can influence market prices for prolonged periods of time. Kahn (1999) aptly notes that the biggest mistake a fundamentalist makes is thinking that the market price is the same as the fundamentally determined value; whereas the biggest mistake a technician makes is thinking that they are different.

6.2 THE BASIC TOOLS OF TECHNICAL ANALYSIS

Price, volume, and sentiment are the three main areas that technicians consider. The primary tool, however, is the price chart. There are a number of ways to draw a chart – using line, bar, candlestick or point-and-figure methods – and sometimes the different methods will indicate different levels of resistance and support. Charts can be based on daily, weekly, or monthly price action. Daily charts are best suited for 3- to 9-month analyses, while weekly or monthly charts are best for longer horizons. Long-term charts provide invaluable perspective on the trend and key support/resistance levels that is impossible to achieve with the use of daily charts alone.

Technical analysis can be as simple as drawing a trend line on a chart or as complicated as using impulse waves, as in Elliott wave analysis. For the purpose of this book, however, we focus on the basic essentials. Whether using simple or advanced techniques, the recommended approach is to weigh the implications of a number of indicators.

Dow Theory

The cornerstone of technical analysis is Dow Theory. Charles Dow (1850–1902), editor of the *Wall Street Journal* in the late nineteenth century, devised the following principals:

- Market indices discount everything – that is, all important information held by the market is discounted in the stock price.
- The market has three trends: (1) primary trends extending over several years; (2) secondary trends lasting from 3 weeks to several months, often comprising a correction of up to 66% of the preceding primary phase; and (3) minor trends lasting for up to 3 weeks, which are sensitive to stochastic exogenous disturbances and have little or no relevance to the prediction of other movements.
- A primary trend has three phases. In the first phase of a bull market, far-sighted investors accumulate stock while the majority sells in the belief that there is worse to come. Meanwhile,

the media and expert analysts reflect the negative mood. In the second phase, there is price acceleration as a result of professionals buying the market following the emergence of a small trend. The third phase reflects exaggerated optimism. Market participants become increasingly confident of easy profits. Professionals sell to the amateurish general public following euphoric media coverage that the party will go on forever.
- Volume supports the trend – that is to say, volume expands in the primary direction of the market trend and decreases during a corrective phase. The significance of a price movement is strengthened if it appears at high volume or turnover. If volume is high when the market rises and poor when it drops, this will indicate that the market will go up.
- Market indices must confirm each other in order to signal a bull/bear trend.
- The trend is assumed to be intact until a clear signal is given to show that it has reversed.

Support and Resistance

As the masses slowly join a trend or a new pattern, momentum builds until the price reaches levels that exhaust excess supply or excess demand. These levels – denoted "support" and "resistance" – provide important price signals for technical analysts. Support and resistance reflect the clustering of customer orders just above or just below previous highs or lows.[3] Clustering can reverse, pause, or accelerate the short-term trend.[4] In a rising trend, the last top is the most important; in a falling trend, the last bottom is the most important.

> **Rule:** If price action fails to exceed a certain level, then that level becomes important.

- *Support* is the level at which demand exceeds supply – that is, the aggressive selling of bears has waned sufficiently to be offset by the increased aggressiveness of bull buying. When a falling movement stops, it has found support. Support represents a concentration of demand sufficient to pause the prevailing trend. In a rising trend old tops act as support; in a falling trend, old lows act as resistance.
- *Resistance* is the level at which supply exceeds demand – that is, the aggressive buying of bulls has waned sufficiently to be offset by the increased aggressiveness of bear selling. When a rising movement stops it has met resistance. Resistance represents a concentration of supply sufficient to pause the prevailing trend.

Evaluation of the importance of a support/resistance area involves the consideration of: (1) how long the price has been consolidating in the area (the longer the better as traders remember this price); and (2) turnover (high turnover makes the area stronger as many investors have gone in at this price). The more important the support/resistance area, the more significant is a market move out of the area (i.e. the breakout). The further the market moves away from an area of support/resistance, the more the market will be convinced that the breakout is valid. The longer markets are plagued by uncertainty (i.e. the longer they fail to move), the more aggressive will be the breakout when it finally comes.

A note of caution: Some traders are inclined to enter and stop out positions at price levels (or implied yields) with round numbers. The professionals are aware of this tendency and sometimes try to flush out these positions. Hence, stops should not be placed on levels with round numbers.

Trend Analysis: "The Trend is your Friend"

Not all market participants have access to the same information at the same time. Moreover, they do not reach the same conclusions or act on them with the same speed or enthusiasm. As such, trends represent the slow dissemination and assimilation of news. According to Dow, a trend must be confirmed by peaks and troughs. A rising trend is intact as long as all new peaks and troughs are rising; a falling trend is intact as long as all peaks and troughs are falling.

> *Trend-following Tactic:* **Get in early and stay with it until it changes.**

In an uptrend (bull market), the price action moves like a staircase, with the reaction highs and lows moving higher. As prices climb upwards they encounter different support and resistance areas. The small daily fluctuations between these areas are fairly noise-sensitive and unpredictable. Similarly, in a downtrend (bear market), the price action moves in a series of declining steps – with reaction highs and lows moving ever lower.

Table 6.1 Trend trading rules

- Go out of a trend when its trend line is broken.
- Trade with the trend for your time frame.
- Use dips or retracements (such as 33% or 66%) against the trend as entry points.

Moving Averages: Simple Trend Identification

A simple average is defined over a fixed period of time, whereas a moving average (MA) drops the oldest price and adds the newest price as one goes forward in time. There are a number

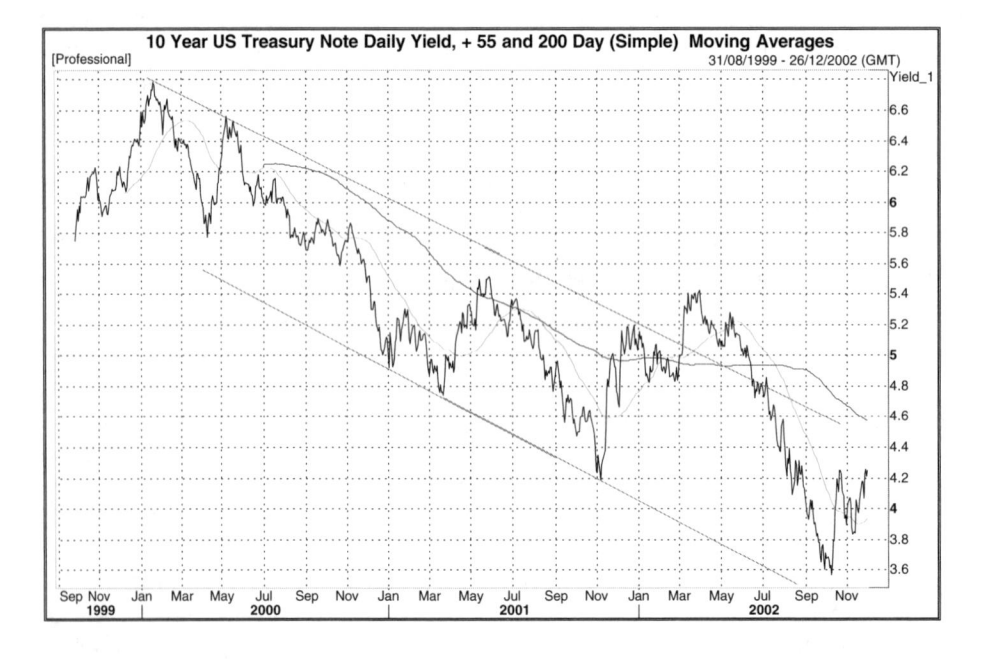

Source: Reuters. Reproduced with permission

Figure 6.1 Trend identification

of ways to calculate a MA – including simple, weighted, and exponentially smoothed. MAs may also be based on the high, open or low price. An exponential MA gives greater weight to the most recent mood of the crowd; hence, it responds to changes faster than a simple MA. In practice, the exponential MA is the preferred measure.

The MA is a lagging indicator of the underlying trend which smoothes away short-term volatility. The greater the number of days involved in the calculation, the slower the response. Widely used periods are 20-, 55-, and 200-day MAs and 55- and 200-week MAs. The MA tool is used by many professional investors, which means that there is a degree of self-reinforcing impact.

A buy signal is a *golden cross* – when a short rising average breaks up through a long rising average. For example, if the 55-day MA breaks up through the 200-day MA this is potentially a very bullish signal of short-term trend reversal (Figure 6.1). A sell signal is a *death cross* – when a short falling average breaks down through a long falling average. For example, if the 55-day MA, breaks down through the 200-day MA, this is potentially a very bearish signal.

Because an MA is a lagging indicator, one should not expect to capture the entire move. The advantage of the MA indicator is that it keeps you in the trend longer than other signals that knock you out too soon when whipsaws occur. In a ranging market, however, whipsaws will generate MA buy signals at the highs and sell signals at the lows. Hence, MAs should be avoided in trendless markets.

Table 6.2 MA trading rules

- **Buy signal** – when MA rises and prices close above it; cover short positions when prices close above the MA.
- **Sell signal** – when the MA declines and prices close below it.

Conviction of the Trend

Once a trend has been identified, the next task is to determine its strength, or rather, momentum. Together speed and power determine market momentum. Speed is the slope of the trend. Power is the conviction of the participants (measured by volume or open interest). Intuitively, the more people become involved and the more prices move, the more robust the trend.

> ***Rule:*** **If the speed of rising prices is declining, be forewarned that a market top may be near.**

Trend continuation patterns include "pennants", "flags", and "wedges". Trend-following techniques include simple (or exponential) MAs and some momentum indicators such as the MACD (discussed below). Trends are where the big money is earned. When a trend has been established it often runs far longer than anyone expects. A market will tend to continue in the same direction until some force acts upon it. For technicians, that force manifests itself in a clear reversal pattern.

Trend Reversal

At the end of an uptrend, the prevailing sentiment is very bullish and usually everyone is fully invested – both reflecting the general euphoria in the market. As a result, the trend is inevitably

Table 6.3 Characteristics of primary trend reversals

- A sudden acceleration of the trend (indicating an influx of new buyers) and unusually high volume (indicating distribution).[5]
- A serious interruption in the trend's pattern of rising (or falling) peaks and troughs; the interruption is of certain scale and over a long enough period for the psychology to suffer serious damage.
- Significant movement against the trend, making many investors insecure.
- A lack of breadth (e.g. smaller issues have stopped following the trend as investors are concerned about their ability to get out quickly).
- A long stalling phase where the trend comes to a standstill for so long that gradually long-term investors lose all patience and abandon positions – reflected in falling momentum. Falling momentum means that the bulls are losing their conviction.

at its steepest angle. The initial falls in a bull run (or rallies in a bear market) often occur after a sudden increase in the angle of the trend (over a number of months), and will always run counter to the prevailing market sentiment. This is why the technician invariably disagrees with the fundamentalist at the start of trend reversals. Although the fundamentals may still be very bullish, if "everyone" is fully invested the market cannot rise further.

In order to have a reversal, there must be a prior trend. There also needs to be a break in the major trend-line. All primary trend reversals are different. However, almost all of them have some or all of the characteristics listed in Table 6.3.

Falling momentum can be detected from: (1) divergence (when prices are rising but the rate and/or power of the rally declines); and (2) reversal patterns. Some reversal patterns occur more frequently than others, but reversal patterns do not work all of the time. Most importantly, reversal patterns are not a pattern until they have been *completed*. Since the market cannot be forced into a pattern, it is not advisable to trade a pattern before it has completed. Just about every part of a trend at some stage has the potential to look like a reversal pattern, which is why it is important to wait and have a clear understanding of the difference between reversal and continuation.

There are many chart patterns that signal a reversal – including, for example, "double tops/bottoms" and "triple tops/bottoms". The best-known and most reliable reversal pattern is the head and shoulders reversal pattern (Figures 6.2 and 6.3).[6] Many other patterns are simply variations of this formation, which consists of a left shoulder, head, right shoulder,

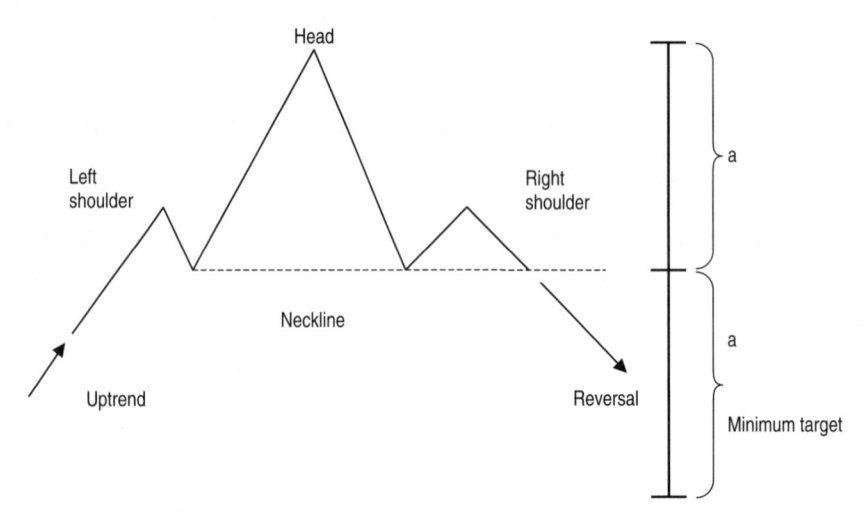

Figure 6.2 The head and shoulders reversal pattern

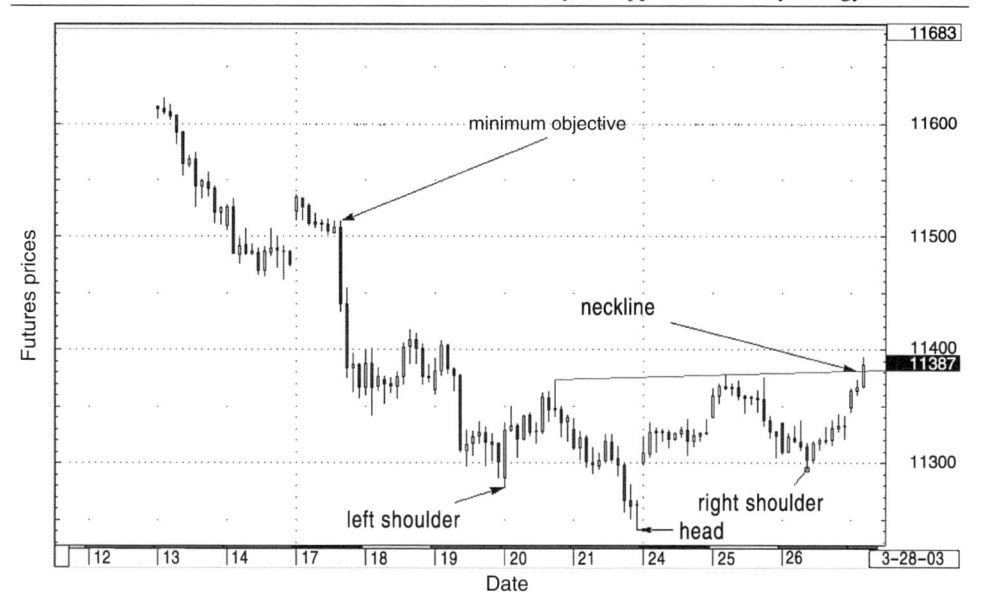

Figure 6.3 Head and shoulders reversal of a downtrend in German 10-year Bund futures

and neckline. At the left shoulder stage, there is no suggestion of a counter-trend. The news – which is discounted in the price – is usually the most bullish (or bearish during a downtrend) in the formation of the head. The neckline is the trigger point.[7] The head and shoulders pattern works best when a market rally/sell-off has over over-extended.

In a rising market, prices make higher highs and higher lows as the trend continues upward. The left shoulder is simply part of this pattern. Prices rise to the top of the shoulder and fall in a normal correction. Next, prices rise to another new high. At this point it cannot be predicted that this is going to be the head of the pattern and the final push in the rally. Momentum readings will indicate that the bulls are losing power even though the market continues higher. As prices fall back, they now fail to set a higher low and fall back to the previous low – this is the "neckline". The right shoulder begins to form: as the market attempts to make a higher high, momentum decreases further and prices fail to reach the previous high (the head) and fall again to the neckline. The weaker the market, the smaller the right shoulder.

> *Rule:* **Set minimum price targets based on the distance between the head and the neckline.**

Price Momentum Indicators

Price momentum indicators are used to determine trend integrity and establish when trends might reverse. They are also useful to help time trades closer to local reversion points. The basic idea is to look for a market that is losing momentum, and go the other way. Momentum indicators are considered to be more predictive than MAs because momentum measures the speed of price movements, not the prices themselves (i.e. MA indicators lag and momentum indicators lead). There are many ways to measure momentum – including the MACD, the RSI, and stochastic oscillators. The MACD is best used in trending markets, while the RSI and stochastic oscillator are best used in trendless markets. Momemtum indicators get you closer to the turning point of a trend, but at the greater cost of getting whipsawed.

The **moving average convergence-divergence** (MACD) is a lagging indicator showing the convergence/divergence of two exponential moving averages. The basic premise of the MACD indicator is that as a market moves higher, the shorter of two MAs is above the longer MA. Because the shorter average reacts faster to price movements, the longer average will always lag behind. When the shorter average crosses below the longer average, it is a signal that the trend may be reversing. Hence, crossovers of the faster MACD line and the slower signal line identify shifts in the balance of power between bulls and bears.[8]

Table 6.4 MACD trading rules

- **Buy signal** – when the fast MACD line rises above the slow signal line.
- **Sell signal** – when the fast MACD line falls below the slow signal line.

Divergences are another use of the MACD. When there is a divergence between the trend in the MACD and the price action of the security being analyzed, there is a possibility of a price trend reversal. In rising markets, divergence occurs when the market makes higher highs and the MACD makes lower highs. In falling markets, divergence occurs when prices reach lower lows and the MACD reaches higher lows (Figure 6.4, Panels 1 and 2).

Because the MACD is a lagging indicator of price momentum, it is best used as a confirmational tool in combination with other indicators. Caution is warranted in sideways markets when multiple crossovers of the MACD and signal line can occur over a short period of time.

Market top signal: **When volatility and momentum go crazy.**[9]

The **relative strength index** (RSI) is a coincident indicator of oversold (or overbought) levels. The basic premise of this indicator is that prices are "elastic" in the sense that they can move only so far from a mean price. As such, rapid price advances result in overbought situations and rapid price declines result in oversold situations – both of which are expected to be reversed *eventually*. The RSI filters out normal volatility while maintaining the significance of single large price moves. The more often prices move higher in the period (the number of up closes) and the greater those changes become (the magnitude of those closes), the higher the RSI value.

The RSI is constructed on a scale from 0 to 100. A relatively high RSI (55–75) normally accompanies an uptrend and a relatively low RSI (25–45) normally accompanies a downtrend. Generally, an RSI above 70–75 indicates excessive bullishness (an overbought situation), and a value below 25–30 indicates excessive bearishness (an oversold situation).[10]

A chart of RSI and the price indicates how an instrument's momentum is changing over time and is helpful in identifying overbought and oversold situations (Figure 6.4, Panels 1 and 3). Divergence occurs when the RSI and the price move in different directions – an advance warning of a potential reversal in the price trend. Because a divergence can remain in existence for a long period of time, it is prudent to wait for the price to reverse before trading on the potential reversal. It is important to note that a divergence between momentum indicators and price does not always result in the anticipated move.

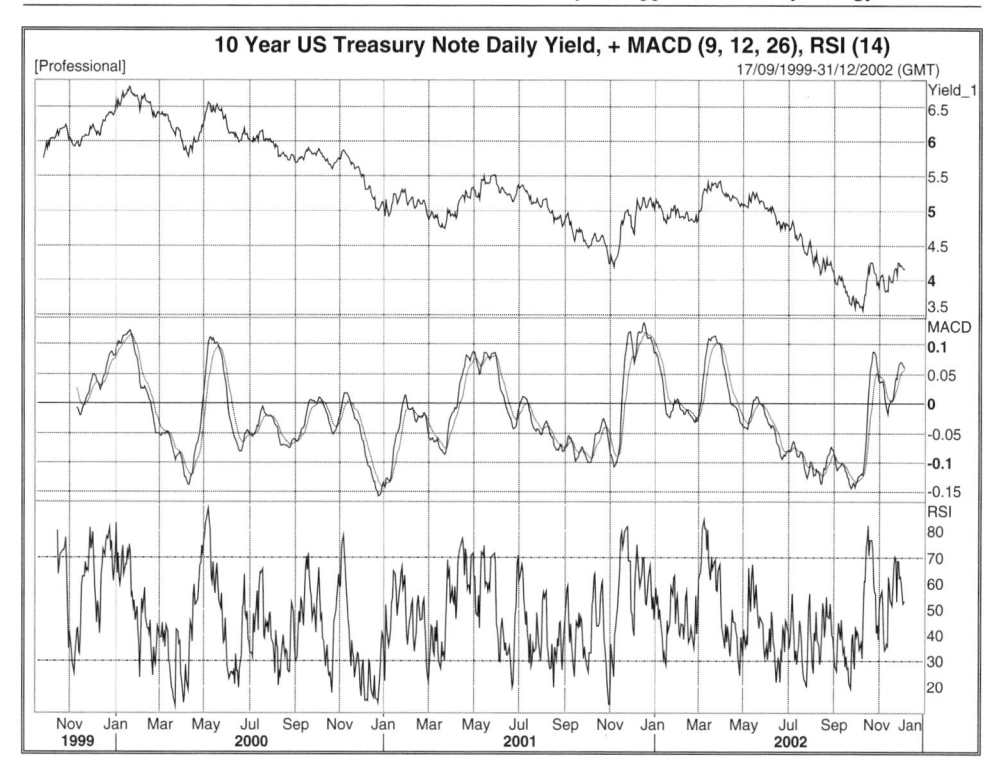

10 Year US Treasury Note Daily Yield, + MACD (9, 12, 26), RSI (14)

Source: Reuters. Reproduced with permission

Figure 6.4 MACD and RSI signals

Table 6.5 RSI trading rules

- **Close short positions when oversold** – when the RSI declines below its lower reference line and then rallies above it; wait for other indicators to confirm a buy signal.
- **Sell when overbought** – when the RSI rises above its upper reference line and then crosses below it.

The **stochastic oscillator** tracks the relationship of each closing price (current momentum) to the recent high–low trading range (recent momentum).[11] The basic premise of this indicator is that markets tend to close at the top of the day's range in an uptrend, and close at the bottom of the day's range in a downtrend.[12] When prices trend higher and closing prices begin to sag within the range, this signals weakness – that is, the bulls are becoming weaker relative to the bears. The stochastic oscillator filters out market noise and weeds out bad signals. However, momentum can change when there is no change in the price trend. Hence, the stochastic oscillator is best used in combination with other indicators.

Like the RSI, the stochastic is scaled from 0 to 100. At a reading of 0, the oscillator implies that the security's close is at the lowest price that it has traded during the period; whereas a reading of 100 indicates that the security's close is at the highest price that it has traded during the period. Values above 80 are considered to be in overbought territory, giving an indication

Table 6.6 Stochastic oscillator trading rules

- **Buy signal** – the indicator falls below 20, then rises above 20, indicating a return of interest in the security. Requires confirming evidence to avoid whipsaws or failed signals.
- **Sell signal** – the indicator rises above 80, then falls below 80.

that a reversal in price is possible, while values below 20 are considered as oversold. In a strong trending environment, the stochastic oscillator can stay in overbought or oversold territory for some time while price continues in a single direction, providing little interest. Hence, this indicator is best applied to flat or choppy markets.

Open Interest: Gauging the Degree of Participation in a Market Move

The degree of participation in a market move is extremely insightful for anticipating market trends. For example, it makes a big difference whether a million investors put on a €1 trade or whether a single investor puts on a €1 million trade. The value is the same, but the implication about behavior is entirely different. Consequently, a price move that occurs on strong volume helps to validate that move and suggests that it will probably continue. A price move that occurs on light volume suggests that there is very little sponsorship for the price move and it probably will not be sustained. It is difficult to find volume data for bonds; instead market participation can be tracked though the futures and options markets.

In the bond (or equity) market, the amount of paper bought equals the amount of paper issued. In the futures, options, and forwards markets, however, there is no limit to the number of buy and sell contracts that can exist (other than there must be an equal quantity of both). Consequently, the number of contracts outstanding[13] (open interest) depends exclusively on appeal in the market.

Table 6.7 Open interest trading rules

When open interest rises
- During a price rally, this is a bullish signal. It suggests that new longs have entered the market and that it is safe to add to long positions.
- While futures prices fall, this is a bearish signal. It suggests that new short positions have been established and that it is safe to sell short.
- While futures prices are in a trading range, this is a bearish signal. Commercial hedgers are more likely to sell short than speculators.

When open interest falls
- During a rally, this is a bearish signal. It suggests that the rally is due to short covering rather than new long positions. Hence, sell and get ready to sell short because participants are getting out of the market.
- During a decline, this is a bullish signal. It suggests that the sell off was due to long liquidations that eventually will be exhausted. Hence, cover shorts and get ready to buy.
- In a trading range, this is a bullish signal. It identifies short covering by major commercial interests, particularly if open interest is falling sharply.

When open interest is flat
- During a rally, it is a signal to tighten stops on long positions and avoid new buying.
- During a decline, it is best to tighten stops on short positions.
- In a trading range, this does not contribute any new information.

Technicians gauge the quality of a market move by comparing daily changes in open interest in the futures market with the direction of the futures price. Rising open interest in an uptrend is bullish; whereas rising open interest in a downtrend is bearish. Similarly, declining open interest in an uptrend is bearish; whereas declining open interest in a downtrend is bullish.

Daily statistics are kept on open interest in the futures and options exchanges (Table 6.8). A 10% change in open interest deserves serious attention, while a 25% change often gives major trading messages. Open interest is considered to be more important at the end of a trend. For example, historically high open interest at the end of a long trend, combined with a strong reversal, warns of an impending change in trend.

Table 6.8 Sources of open interest data

Market	Futures and options	Exchange
Euro area	Schatz, BOBL, and Bunds	EUREX
Japan	Euroyen	TIFFE
UK	Gilts	LIFFE
US	Treasury Notes and Bonds	CBOT

6.3 THE CONTRARIAN APPROACH

It's always the darkest before the dawn.

The contrarian approach is based on the idea that the vast majority of investors misjudge the timing of market tops and bottoms. The basic principal of contrarian investing is that if there are no bears left and everyone has invested, then there is no one left to buy the market and push it higher. Hence, the path of least resistance is down.

Contrarians use crowd opinion as an entry and exit technique – which allows them to buy low amid the dire news at market bottoms and sell high amid the exuberant news at market tops. Although the essence of a contrarian strategy is buying and selling when the crowd is not, it is only in the timing that contrarians seek to be different. After taking their positions, contrarians wait for the new trend to materialize. They then stick with the crowd for most of the ride.

> **Contrarian investing is all about timing.**

Betting against the crowd – including the highly visible experts that form mass opinion – is difficult to do. As we learned in Chapter 5, herding is a deeply ingrained psychological tendency. Hence, contrarian investors need a detached, independent view and the courage to execute it. Contrarians can often pull the trigger too early. This means that, for a time, they are not only alone but also wrong.[14] Contrarians must be willing to wait three or more years for a payoff; but this may be too long for professionals whose performance is gauged in terms of weeks or quarters.

Contrarian investing requires more than a bullish or bearish majority. It requires investing against opinion when it reaches an extreme – when opinion has been translated into action by the vast majority. However, gauging extreme sentiment can be quite subjective.

Contrarian Indicators

Data considered to be mean reverting (as opposed to trend following) are useful for constructing contrarian indicators. The best practice is to look for confirmation from several sentiment indicators and to consider fundamental factors as well, before trading on these signals. If you believe that the indicators are not consistent with the fundamentals, you might re-evaluate whether the market has an extreme bullish or bearish position based on your own subjective analysis.

The Call-to-Put Ratio (CPR)

The CPR[15] is the ratio of open daily call option trading volume to open daily put option trading volume. Call options indicate bullish sentiment, whereas put options indicate bearish sentiment. Users of CPR believe that when investors become more optimistic, option traders increase their holding of call options relative to put options. An abnormally high reading of this ratio signals considerable optimism. A sell signal is generated when the CPR's 10-day average exceeds its 1-year average by a factor of 1.4 (that is, 1.4 calls traded for every put); a buy signal is when this ratio reaches 0.8 (that is, 0.8 calls traded for every put) (Crescenzi, 2002). The CPR has been a good guide for calling tops and bottoms in the bond market.[16] The most reliable and widely tracked options followed by bond market participants are the options on futures that trade at the Chicago Board of Trade (CBOT), which provides daily call and put volume on its website.

Extreme Positions taken by Speculators

Extreme positions taken by speculators have frequently foreshadowed market tops and bottoms. Speculators tend to put too much weight on their recent experience and extrapolate recent trends that are at odds with long-run averages. As such, they tend to accumulate large positions toward the end of a cycle, letting greed dictate their actions. The US Commodity Futures Trading Commission (CFTC) publishes a weekly *Commitments of Traders* (COT) report which provides information on the positions (open interest) of speculators in US futures and options markets.[17] The COT report also discloses the positions of non-speculative accounts. A high level of bullish futures traders (70%) is considered a sell signal, while a low level of bullish futures traders (30%) is considered a buy signal.

Extreme Positions taken by Investors

Futures market data are a tremendous resource for gauging speculative excess in the bond market because speculative trading is high in the futures market. For a more complete picture of where non-speculative investors stand, it is important to look outside the futures market. A useful proxy for sentiment in the underlying bond market is the activity of fixed income portfolio managers, who are the major players in this market. The best way to judge how fixed income portfolio managers are positioned is to follow surveys on aggregate duration.[18] When portfolio managers are bullish on bond prices, they increase duration above the benchmark. Aggregate duration is generally maintained between 95 and 105% of the performance benchmark (such as the Lehman government bond index) except under extraordinary circumstances. At 95%, the market is extremely oversold and ripe for reversal; while at 105%, the market is extremely overbought and set to fall. For intermediate trends, 97% and 103% are seen as extreme positions (Crescenzi, 2002).

Investment Advisory Opinions

When 60% of investment advisers are bearish, contrarians view this as a buy signal. If 20% are bearish, this is a sell signal.

Risk Reversal

The risk reversal is the price of puts relative to calls. In theory the price of a put should equal the price of a call. If the price is not the same then there is a bullish or bearish bias.

Banner Headlines

Most buying or selling climaxes occur when the tone and volume of information accelerates to a crescendo of banner headlines, exacerbating the excessive euphoria/pessimism of investors. Look for indications in the media that things have begun to appear completely obvious (e.g. "the death of fixed income") and that everybody seems to agree. When banks have all fired their equity/fixed income analysts, this is a signal for contrarians to get into equities/fixed income. The market is considered ripe for reversal when media reports start to predict that rises/drops will continue for years.

"Things are Different this Time"

A firm belief that the market trend will continue forever is a contrarian sell signal. Perhaps the ultimate signal to sell is when the chairman of the central bank becomes a believer in the "new economy".

6.4 THE "SMART MONEY" APPROACH

The smart money approach keeps an eye on the professionals and imitates what they do.

Distribution of Open Interest

The COT report mentioned in the previous section indicates how open interest is distributed among large hedgers, large speculators, and small market participants. Hedgers have performed the best, followed by speculators (Tvede, 2002).

Confidence Index

Barron's produces an index based on the yield of the 10 top-quality US corporate bonds divided by the yield on the Dow Jones average of 40 bonds. The index is less than 100, reflecting the fact that high-grade bonds have lower yields than average bonds. The closer this index approaches 100, the smaller the difference in yield between top-quality and normal corporate bonds. A narrow yield difference (a high ratio) indicates that investors are confident and happy to invest in normal bonds. Confidence is a buy signal. Alternatively, a wide yield difference (a low ratio) indicates that investors are not willing to invest in riskier issues except at high yields – a sell signal. The problem with this approach is that it focuses only on demand and ignores the fact that supply can also affect yields.

Treasury Bill–Eurodollar Yield Spread

The TED spread is a more global version of the Confidence Index. The higher the Eurodollar yield compared to T-bills, the less confident investors feel – indicating a flight to quality.

6.5 IMPLICATIONS FOR FIXED INCOME INVESTORS

Trading Practicalities

Technical analysis is better suited than fundamental analysis for predicting short-term market movements. In particular, technical analysis more quickly identifies the end of a trend. For investors with a longer investment horizon, such as corporations and asset managers, technical analysis is useful for timing transactions and for cross-checking fundamental views. With the help of technical analysis, losses can be kept to a minimum if markets should take an unexpected turn. According to Kahn (1999), the worst case is that you put on a bad trade based on a false breakout; the best case is that you never miss a large move.

Trading Discipline

Without a plan, traders can get shaken out of bear/bull strategies by a short-term wave of optimistic/pessimistic news. A technically based strategy does not involve reading newspapers, following economic data releases, tracking comments by government officials, or listening to tips and rumors. Instead, it involves following objective rules – essentially trading from a plan. In this case, the trading plan requires the investor to know where the major short- and long-term support/resistance levels are and where the market is positioned in relationship to major trendlines and MAs.

The objective rules of technical analysis provide the investor (contrarian or otherwise) with some emotional distance from the crowd. As we saw in Chapter 5, humans follow the herd for their psychological safety. Going against the crowd allows investors to capitalize on repetitive group behavior, but it requires that the investor weigh the psychological discomfort of standing alone against the financial discomfort of following the crowd past the end of a trend.

Self-fulfilling Dynamics

Whether you believe in technical analysis or not, if the big institutional players are looking at technical indicators, you at least need to understand them. Technical levels become self-fulfilling when thousands of investors draw the same lines on the same charts – particularly during periods of below-average liquidity. As such, technical analysis is not just a technique for reading the mind of the market, but is itself part of the underlying market psychology. If enough traders and dealers use the same chart systems, technicals will generate valid signals and profitable strategies, regardless of whether the charts mean anything. Technicians, however, argue that the market is too extensive to be manipulated by any one technique. Moreover, many in the market prefer to trade on hunches, rumors, fundamentals or other techniques.

6.6 THE LIMITATIONS OF TECHNICAL ANALYSIS

A Focus on the Past

The major drawback of technical analysis is that it relies on past behavior to predict the future. Critics argue that this is particularly problematic given the evolutionary nature of financial markets. However, this is a criticism that can be leveled at all models. Moreover, psychology teaches us that humans are creatures of habit and that groups are particularly predictable. Technicians recognize that the patterns of the past may not be representative of the future. As a result, they stress the importance of using several techniques before making investment decisions.

Price Patterns are Subjective

Although technical analysis has many objective rules and techniques, experience and judgment still play a large role in the analysis as technical patterns are rarely crystal clear. As a result, technicians recommend that signals are confirmed by other indicators – the more the better. It is also important not to force the pattern onto a chart, but to let the market tell you what it is doing. When markets are trading in ranges for long periods of time, attention to fundamentals is prudent as well.

Predictive Power

Individual patterns and indicators have failed at various times. In other words, technical analysis works sometimes, but so does flipping a coin. Hence, the successful distinction between a trend and a range requires knowing when to use a particular method. Technical analysis is most effective in trending markets. When institutional investors dominate the market, however, the price action tends to be choppier – that is, short-term trends are less clearly defined. The reason is that there is less "dumb" money to which to sell late in the game at the top of the trend. In addition, professionals do not sell at one price level; instead they scale out as the market goes up and scale in as the market goes down.

Because no single technique works all the time, technical analysis (like any method) should be used to build a body of evidence in forming a trading decision. A strong complement to technical analysis is an understanding of the fundamentals that ultimately direct market valuation levels. There are also other analytical tools, such as flow and quantitative analysis, that can be used. These are discussed in the next chapter.

NOTES

1. Technical analysis also analyzes volume and open interest to a lesser extent.
2. The efficient markets debate is introduced in Chapter 3, and taken up again in Chapter 8.
3. Banks have order books which list customer order levels. The assumption is that similar types of customers target similar levels, and this in practice tends to be true.
4. Osler (2001) shows that within these price clusters, a further distinction can be made between take-profit and stop-loss orders. Take-profit orders tend to cause the trend to reverse (if there are a sufficient number of them) or to pause. Stop-loss orders tend to accelerate and intensify a prevailing trend or to extend the trend.
5. When distribution is over there are no more buyers and the market collapses. A broker can recognize the last phase of a distribution from the limited amount of sale orders above the current price – indicating that the large professional investors have finished selling.

6. The head and shoulders pattern can sometimes appear as a continuation pattern.
7. In addition to the chart pattern, other indicators are used to confirm the reversal – including momentum, volume, and trend-break.
8. The MACD line is the difference between the 12- and 26-day exponential moving averages. The signal line is the 9-day exponential MA of the MACD indicator. The fast MACD line reflects mass consensus over a shorter period, while the slow signal line reflects mass consensus over a longer period. Traders sometimes vary the calculation period of the signal line and may use different moving average lengths in calculating the MACD dependent on the security and trading strategy.
9. Michael Marcus, as quoted in Schwager (1989).
10. This does not mean that the market will immediately reverse once either of these levels is reached. More likely, the market will pause to consolidate. An oversold market usually stops going down although it does not always start to go up. Use an oversold condition to close out short positions but wait for other indicators to confirm a buy signal.
11. The stochastic is calculated as the ratio of the difference between the current closing price and the lowest low, divided by the difference between the security's highest high and lowest low.
12. This concept can also be applied to weekly and monthly data.
13. For example, one open interest constitutes a buyer and a seller of a futures contract.
14. Success as a contrarian investor requires a long-term view and a willingness to hold securities for two to three years. Gallea and Patalon (1998) note that out of favor securities often pose less downside risk, since the bad news has already been built into the price.
15. Bond investors prefer CPR because call volume generally exceeds put volume. Call volume is greater because the bond market is more concerned about sudden increases in prices than decreases. Conversely, the stock market follows the put-to-call ratio (PCR). Equity investors prefer the PCR because put volume generally exceeds call volume.
16. Meyers (1989) and Shefrin (2000) find empirical support for the CPR as a contrarian indicator. However, both studies use very short sample periods. Note that it may take days or weeks for the turn in the market to occur.
17. The COT report is discussed in more detail in Chapter 7. Activity in the contract on the 30-year Treasury bond (as opposed to the 10-year Treasury note) is where most of the speculative flow has resided because it has been the more volatile instrument; hence, it has been a better sentiment indicator.
18. Stone and McCarthy Research Associates and Ried–Thunberg take weekly surveys on aggregate duration.

RECOMMENDED READING

Gallea, A.M. and Patalon, W. (1998). *Contrarian Investing: Buy and Sell When Others Won't and Make Money Doing It*. New York: New York Institute of Finance.

Murphy, J. (1999). *Technical Analysis of the Financial Markets*. New York: New York Institute of Finance.

7
Other Techniques for Short-Term Analysis

In this chapter we examine other methods used to anticipate price action over the short term – including flow analysis, supply and demand analysis, seasonal analysis, and quantitative analysis. All of these techniques look at relative supply and demand from a slightly different perspective. Many are statistical in nature.

7.1 FLOW ANALYSIS

The key to anticipating market dynamics is to understand the motivations of the participants. Speculators are out to make money immediately; they get in and get out, all within a very short period of time. On the other hand, more long-term transactions are based on investors wishing to hold an asset or those hedging exposure generated from an underlying business. These trades are not unwound unless the fundamentals change. In short, if you know who is trading, then you can assess the likelihood of the position being reversed in the short term.

Flow analysis uses information about transactions to forecast future movements in bond prices. Flows are used to estimate how investors are positioned in the market – that is, whether they are becoming increasingly bearish/bullish, extending/reducing duration, or anticipating curve steepening/flattening. Flows are also used to identify speculative activity, predict mean reversion, and time flows.[1] Flows are particularly important for the price action in thin, illiquid markets.

> **The source of the flows tells you whether its noise or the signal (i.e. the time horizon).**

Flow analysis is consistent with technical analysis, which is based on the premise that the longer a trend lasts, the more people there are in the trend and the more speculative it becomes (see Chapter 6). The build up of short (or long) positions by speculators may portend a near-term reversal of these positions – having a predictable effect on bond prices. The idea is to profit from situations where many market participants may be forced to exit losing positions.

Flows might explain price movements when fundamentals do not – that is, actions linked to portfolio rebalancing, changes in investor risk tolerance or market sentiment, and liquidity or hedging needs. Flows are particularly important in the emerging markets (especially short-term price action), where liquidity is substantially less than in the developed markets.

There are proprietary, market and commercial sources of information on investor positions. A large number of commercial and investment banks track the transactions of their client base, using this as a proxy for behavior in the market overall. Exchanges and professional dealing authorities are market sources of flow data. A sample of market sources and commercial proxies include:

- *AMG Data Services*, which provide a weekly report on the flows and holdings of US mutual funds with a combined value of $6 trillion (www.amgdata.com). Similar information is

available on a monthly basis from the Investment Company Institute (www.ici.com). Flows are classified by type of fund.
- *Chicago Board of Trade* (CBOT), which provides daily volume and open interest data for every product traded on the exchange (www.cbot.com). The CBOT also reports the put-to-call ratio alongside historical data for easy comparison and provides charts on historical volatility.
- *Commodity Futures Trading Commission* (CFTC), which produces a weekly *Commitments of Traders* (COT) report[2] providing positions in all existing US futures contracts (www.cftc.gov). The report also categorizes the holders of futures positions, which is useful for determining the extent to which recent movements in futures have been driven by speculative or commercial activity. The COT is widely used by banks and traders and is discussed in more detail below.
- *Eurex*, which provides daily statistics on open interest and volume by contract for euro – denominated derivative instruments (www.eurexchange.com).
- *London International Financial Futures and Options Exchange* (LIFFE), which provides daily volume and open interest for all currently listed contracts (www.liffe.com).
- *Ried–Thunberg and Company*, which takes weekly surveys on short- and long-term sentiment, FOMC policy actions, duration, and cash allocations (available via Bloomberg and Reuters).
- *Stone and McCarthy Research Associates*, which takes a weekly money manager survey on duration exposure, asset allocation within the bond market, cash positions, and overall sentiment about market prospects (www.smra.com). Survey results are available to clients.
- *Tokyo International Financial Futures Exchange* (TIFFE), which provides monthly data on trading volume and open interest for the 3-month euroyen LIBOR contract (www.tiffe.or.jp).

Flow analysis is performed by comparing short-term flows to the spot price action, or by comparing medium-term flows to the medium-term price trend. The short-term flow picture may indicate selling, while the medium-term flow picture may indicate buying. Together they indicate the timing of a trend reversal (Henderson, 2002). Daily and weekly flow data are more relevant for speculative trading in the very short term or for timing an investment. Monthly and quarterly flow data are more relevant for investors with longer time horizons.

The Commitments of Traders Report

The COT report is very useful for knowing who is long and who is short in the market – commercial or non-commercial accounts. The "commercial" traders in bond futures are those using futures to hedge business activities, such as insurance companies and pension funds. The "non-commercial" accounts represent speculative activity. The assumption is that the speculative community's open position in bond futures is a rough reflection of what the position might be in these bonds in the larger interbank market.[3] Speculative flows dominate the short-term price dynamics, while non-speculative flows dominate the long-term price dynamics. In practice, it can be difficult to differentiate between speculative and non-speculative flows.

Clearing members, futures commission merchants, and foreign brokers file daily reports with the Commission. Those reports show the futures and option positions of traders that hold positions above specific reporting levels set by CFTC regulations. If, at the daily market close, a reporting firm has a trader with a position at or above the Commission's reporting level in any single futures month or option expiration, it reports that trader's entire position

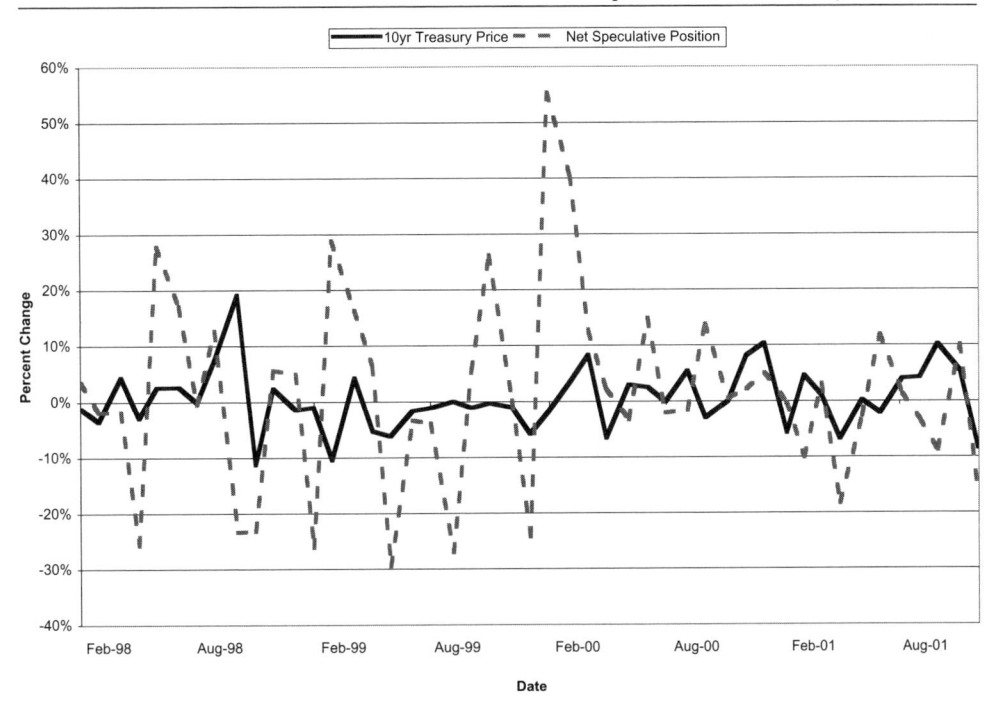

Figure 7.1 Speculative positions versus bond prices

Sources: COT and Federal Reserve.

in that commodity, regardless of size. The aggregate of all traders' positions reported to the Commission usually represents 70–90% of the total open interest in any given market.[4] The COT report includes data on:

- Open interest[5]
- Number of traders in each category
- Commercial and non-commercial holdings
- Spreading[6]
- Changes from the previous report
- Percent of open interest by category
- Concentration of positions held by the largest four and eight traders.

The COT report can be used to determine whether speculative positions have become "too large", signaling a near-term reversal.[7] This is done by comparing the net speculative position of the current week to previous periods and multi-year highs and lows. A comparison of changes in net speculative positions with the spot bond price action helps determine whether there has been a substantial build up of long or short positions. A comparison of positions and bond price trends provides an indication of their correlation – that is, the power of this proxy as an indicator of sentiment for the overall market. In other words, this proxy has no power if one observes that the closing out of big positions has no impact on the bond price. Figure 7.1 suggests that the speculative positions in the COT report have predictive power in some periods.

Strategy

Flow and fundamental data are reviewed to determine the ability of the prevailing trend to continue. Traders position themselves to take advantage of the reversal when it comes, while investors use this to guide exposure and time investments.

- A large net long speculative position in a bond future might portend the unwinding of these positions.
- The bond market's inability to rally even in the face of weak economic data could be the result of investor positions that remain long (i.e. "poor technicals").
- Proprietary flow data that identify a particular group of customers as the most persistent sellers might provide an indication or timetable for the group turning into buyers.
- Proprietary flow data might indicate that customers are positioned in bulleted strategies to take advantage of expected monetary easing and curve steepening. The unwinding of these positions will cause the curve to flatten.

7.2 SUPPLY AND DEMAND ANALYSIS

Supply and demand analysis is one method of anticipating short-term flows through the bond market. On the supply side, the focus is on issuance, redemptions, buybacks, and coupon/amortization payments. On the demand side, the focus is on the analysis of customer flows, interest in syndicated deals, and institutional research. The key question is whether the net inflows adequately sustain demand at particular maturity points on the yield curve. Supply and demand analysis is important for corporate bonds, particularly the high-yield market.

Supply Technicals

New issuance in the primary market is the source of the bond market. The dynamics of new issuance are understood by examining the issuance calendar. New issuance must be adjusted to account for the effect of redemptions, buybacks and coupon/amortization payments (Table 7.1). Refunding auctions replace old debts with new ones, usually to lower the interest costs paid by the issuer.

Table 7.1 Net supply

Inflows	Offsets
New bond issuance (including refunding)	Coupon and amortization payments Redemptions Buybacks

In the government sector, issuance is a function of the public sector's borrowing requirement (the size and growth of the budget deficit). When deficits are rising, new issuance is also on the rise. In the corporate sector, there are a number of motivations for issuing bonds (as opposed to equity) to finance investment – including governance and accounting issues, as well as the relative cost of finance.

Table 7.2 Factors affecting sovereign debt issuance and performance

	Budget financing requirement	Change in net bond issuance	Secondary bond market performance
Business cycle			
Recession	Rises	Increase	Underperformance
Growth	Falls	Decrease	Outperformance
Action			
Refunding		Increase	Underperformance
Buybacks		Decrease	Outperformance
Redemptions		Decrease	Outperformance
Coupon/Amortization payments		Decrease	Outperformance

New supply may or may not temporarily undermine performance in the secondary bond market. The impact depends on other factors in the market, especially the stage of the business cycle. For example, a very powerful global steepening environment would tend to underpin prices. New issues must compete with what is already available in the secondary market. As such, the coupon size and convexity exposure of the new issue may enhance (or detract from) the bond's appeal. Generally, less new issue in the sovereign debt market means less pressure on secondary market spreads (Table 7.2).

If, in the corporate sector, a new offering is well received, the issuer's spreads usually tighten. During some intervals in the investment grade corporate market, heavy supply often helps spreads as the new primary valuations validate and enhance secondary valuations. In effect, supply creates its own demand. However, this is not always the case, particularly during periods of concern about the state of the economy. At such times, a supply surge may be associated with spread weakness.

Demand Technicals

The dynamics of demand are very different from those of supply. Technical factors which affect demand in the short term might be associated with options expiry or the covering of short positions. Demand might also be related to supply. For example, Japanese bond indexes have been shortening because the maturing 10-year debt is being reissued at 2- and 5-year maturities as well as the traditional 10-year maturity. This shortening in the duration of the bond index has led to a corresponding increase in demand for short-dated bonds by investors forced to match the index.

Delays in the implementation of regulatory or accounting rules can also affect demand. For example, a delay in the implementation of the UK's accounting regulation FRS 17 (perhaps until 2005) led to a temporary reduction in the demand from pension funds.[8] The business cycle can also affect transitory demand. In a recessionary environment with plunging equity prices, regulatory solvency criteria for life insurers might lead to a forced liquidation of assets across all classes which would depress bond prices.

The availability of substitutes is also important. For example, demand is keen by financial institutions such as insurance companies or banks for high yielding securities of high quality. If their preferred investments, such as mortgages and commercial loans, are in short supply, they will turn to substitutes. To summarize, sources of technical demand include:

- Options expiry
- Short covering
- Index duration
- Regulatory/accounting changes
- Business cycle
- Substitutes

> *Tip:* **Use brokers that see the largest flows for insight on the transient supply/demand picture.**

7.3 SEASONAL ANALYSIS

Practitioners with shorter investment horizons might benefit from observed seasonal patterns in bond prices. It is important to note, however, that seasonality studies are prone to data mining risks. Moreover, the patterns may shift as the market takes advantage of these opportunities.

Annual Effects

- On average, credit spreads appear to peak in Q4 and fall during Q1, which is consistent with risk-taking capacity declining over the year and establishing positions for the new year (called the *January effect*). The global corporate asset class tends to outperform Treasuries during the first half of the year, particularly in Q1. A defensive shift regularly takes place across the entire credit quality spectrum in the corporate market during the second half of most years. In the investment grade sector, this phenomenon regularly shows up during Q4, while the high-yield market tends to react in Q3.[9]
- On average, the 10-year Treasury yield rises in the spring, peaking in early May; it then edges lower through the rest of the year. Monthly returns in Europe have historically, on average, been the highest in November and lowest in February. For example, 10-year German Bund yields tend to experience an increase from April through July, and a sharp fall in November (Ilmanen et al., 2001a, 2001c).

Month-, Quarter-, and Year-End Effects

- Secondary trading slows at month ends, more so at quarter ends, and the most at the conclusion of calendar years. This timing coincides with the period in which portfolio managers assess performance, prepare reports for clients, and chart strategy for the next period. Most dealers reduce exposure at year end in order to lock in their profits for the year.
- On average, Treasury yields fall faster around the end of the month, which may reflect the deployment of new cash or benchmark rebalancing. The 10-year Treasury yield falls an average 3 bps between the last three business days of the month and the first three business days of the month. The effect for the 10-year German Bund has been weaker.

Weekday Effects

- Anecdotal evidence points to the superiority of transacting mid-week. New corporate supply and origination are clustered on Tuesdays, Wednesdays, and Thursdays. Markets tend to trade more on Tuesdays.

Holiday Effects

- Major holidays dampen primary and secondary trading activity, especially at the year end. The peak summer vacation season in August also limits activity across the global market. Given the reduction in liquidity during these periods, it is best to transact prior to or after peak holiday periods.
- Ilmanen et al. (2001b) find that the Treasury curve has a clear post-holiday steepening bias, which is most pronounced around the Christmas/New Year period.[10] The bias may reflect new cash being parked into short-term Treasuries before being invested in riskier assets later in January. Alternatively, this may reflect the excessive richening of longer-dated Treasuries late in the year (from the November auction into the year end, the Treasury curve on average flattens). There is also the possibility of year-end "window dressing" where riskier assets and the year's losers are sold. Tax-based arguments are also consistent with this phenomenon.
- Note that the demand for emerging market debt in countries with current account deficits diminishes during European and US summer holidays.

Seasonal Financing Patterns

- The Treasury curve tends to steepen early in the month and flatten late in the month in sync with the regular auction cycle. Specifically, the 2s/10s spread widens by an average 2–3 bps in the fortnight between $T - 3$ and $T + 7$; and then gives it all back in the following fortnight. The Bund curve on average steepens during the first week and flattens thereafter.
- Long-dated Treasuries have tended to cheapen in the run up to their issuance. There is a quarterly refunding effect for Treasuries in early February, May, August, and November – when yields rise above the preceding and subsequent months' average yields.

Volatility Patterns

- Implied volatility (risk aversion) reaches a low during the summer. Within-week bond volatility tends to peak on Friday mornings.

7.4 QUANTITATIVE ANALYSIS

The quantitative analyst relies on sophisticated computer models to identify market relationships. These models are generally based on economic and/or price data and have a number of applications (Table 7.3). The more exotic analysis uses non-linear models, neural networks, genetic algorithms, and frequency models. Quantitative analysis is useful for creating a more disciplined investment approach – overcoming any emotional attachment to positions or an inability to process more than a few variables at a time. The key function of quantitative analysis is to assess relative value and measure (manage) risk.

Table 7.3 Applications of quantitative analysis

Application	Description
Active management	Predict bond/portfolio behavior given alternative interest rate scenarios.
Immunization	Create/maintain a portfolio that has an ensured return over a specified horizon, irrespective of interest rate change.
Passive management	Create/maintain a portfolio that will track the performance of a given index using a manageable set of securities.
Individual security analysis	Compare individual securities; analyze the term structure; and value bonds and options.
Other	Performance attribution; and risk analysis.

Note: This table is adapted from material in Fong (1997). These applications are discussed in further detail in Chapter 9.

Additional Risk Factors

The use of quantitative models introduces *model risk* – that is, the risk that the valuation model is misspecified, or that a "correct" model is misapplied. Over-fitted models have high predictive value on past data but little forecasting ability for future returns. Model risk stems from the reality that quantitative models only capture a portion of the market's dynamics. As such, investors must be vigilant about maintaining the relevance of their models.

Quantitative models used to identify mispricings are exposed to *correlation breakdown risk*. Correlation breakdown is the sudden change of historical relationships between corresponding variables. This tends to occur as a result of dramatic flight-to-quality events, such as a sovereign default or other economic crisis, that rapidly move interest rates, widen credit spreads, and dry up liquidity.

Mean Reversion

Mean reversion is the process by which prices, interest rates, or volatilities tend to return to some average – as complex or simple as you wish to define it – after reaching extreme levels. Mean reversion is a widely used concept – applied in simple "buy the dips and sell the rallies" strategies as well as more complex fixed income arbitrage strategies. For example, cheap issues or sectors (those with wider than average spreads) are purchased in anticipation that the spread will revert back to a "normal" level. Conversely, rich issues or sectors (e.g. those with narrower than average spreads) are sold in anticipation that the spread will widen (and prices will fall) in line with the historical trend.

Mean reversion as a concept is only applicable within a certain paradigm. Over the long term (e.g. beyond four years), credit curves are not mean reverting. There are five reasons that care should be taken when applying the concept of mean reversion:

1. The mean is highly dependent on the interval selected and there is no market consensus on the appropriate interval at which to judge relative value.[11]
2. It is uncertain why a somewhat arbitrary mean should exert a mysterious gravitational effect on current spreads in the near future (unless it is self-fulfilling).

3. The timing of supposed reversion is uncertain. In the absence of macroeconomic changes or sector/issuer-specific developments, spread persistence often rules. That is, rich sectors remain rich and cheap sectors remain cheap for long intervals.
4. There is the risk that anomalies will no longer mean-revert.
5. Inferences may be biased. Standard curve-fitting techniques assume a normal distribution (e.g. symmetrical and bell shaped with narrow tails), when in fact market distributions are skewed (e.g. the mean and the mode differ) and the tails are fat.

Relative Value Analysis

Relative value (RV) refers to the ranking of investments by sectors, structures, issuers, and issues in terms of expected performance during some future interval. Relative value measures include yield spreads, swap spreads, and rolling yields. Relative value analysis refers to methodologies used to generate such rankings of expected returns. The methodologies used might involve: historical relationships, credit or liquidity considerations, option-based analytical models, total return analysis, primary market (supply) analysis, and demand analysis.[12]

In the case of total return analysis, for example, expected returns for various scenarios are examined to produce relative value signals. Each scenario is assigned subjective probabilities, and the tolerance for loss relative to the liability is specified. Then the various outcomes are optimized for a suggested portfolio structure. Different scenarios might be: static spread, reversion of bond spreads to the 3-month average, or significant market volatility. The problem with total return analysis is its complexity. Moreover, two investors using the same framework can get different results due to different data sources and estimation techniques (Ilmanen, 1995b).

RV analysis is used to assess whether a bond, sector, or market is mispriced relative to some statistically determined norm. The idea is to sell the overvalued ("rich") security/sector and buy the undervalued ("cheap") security/sector, realizing profits when inefficiencies disappear and prices return to fair value.[13] The risk is that sectors/securities that are *theoretically* mispriced may not become fairly valued within the applicable investment horizon.

> **Hold cheap bonds until they become rich.**

Cheapness is evaluated by comparing current yields or valuations to either the historical mean or a model-based equilibrium value. Historical analysis relates to the evaluation of trends, changes in the relationships between different variables, and volatility. Model-based analysis might evaluate relationships in the term structure or credit spreads.

It is important that RV comparisons be evaluated in the context of supply and demand factors – some of which are temporary while others are effectively permanent over the investment horizon. For example, new issuance may cause temporary cheapness, or lower financing costs may cause temporary richness. Portions of the yield curve may also become dislocated as the result of investor preferences for certain issues or maturities. For example, many prefer to trade only benchmark issues because of their better liquidity. Also, certain bonds are preferred to cover short bond futures positions. On the other hand, bond richness may be the result of more permanent tax benefits or accounting regulations. As such, it is important to distinguish between the more flexible maturity *preferences* and the more inflexible *constraints* of key market participants.

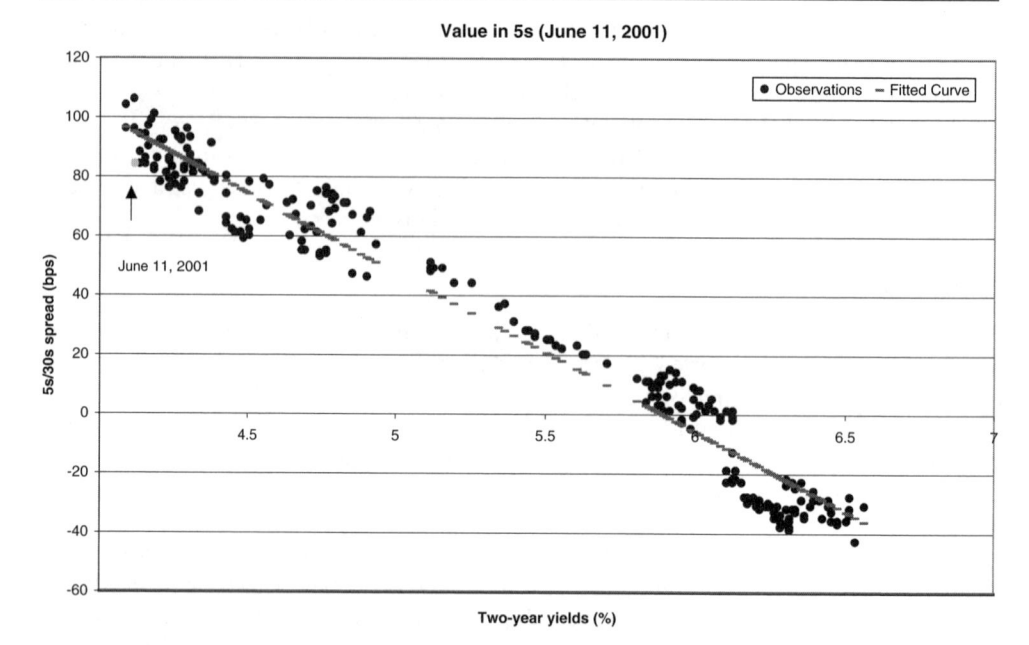

Figure 7.2 Evaluation of a 2s–5s–30s butterfly

RV analysis can be used to evaluate butterfly trades – that is, those that seek to capitalize on anticipated changes in the shape of the yield curve.[14] The basic idea is to determine how the current yield curve is positioned relative to the historical relationship. This can be evaluated in a number of ways, and two techniques are illustrated in the following examples.

Example 7.1 – Evaluation of a 2s–5s–30s butterfly
Consider the case where we are asked to determine whether a bullet of 5s is undervalued relative to the wings (a barbell of 2s and 30s). One technique is to plot daily observations in the spread between 5s and 30s against the 2-year yield over a 1-year interval and compare it to the fitted curve (Figure 7.2). The point representing the current relationship (e.g. June 11, 2001) is then identified relative to the fitted curve. Points below the fitted curve represent value (cheapness) in the 5-year sector, while points above the regression line represent richness. Based on the historical relationship in this example, one might expect the 5s/30s spread to widen (i.e. the curve to steepen) – that is, the price of 5-year bonds to rise relative to 30-year bonds. Hence, in this case one would find "value in intermediates".

Example 7.2 – Evaluation of a 2s–5s–10s butterfly
Consider the case where we are asked to determine whether a bullet of 5s is overvalued relative to the wings – in this case a barbell of 2s and 10s. Another valuation technique plots daily observations of the 2s/5s and 5s/10s spreads against the fitted curve over a 1-year interval (Figure 7.3). The point representing the current relationship (e.g. September 20, 2001) is then identified relative to the fitted curve. In this case, points above the fitted curve represent value (cheapness) in the 5-year sector, while points below the regression line represent richness. Based on the observed historical relationship in this example, one might expect the 5s/10s spread to narrow and the 2s/5s spread to widen – that is, the price of 5-year bonds to fall

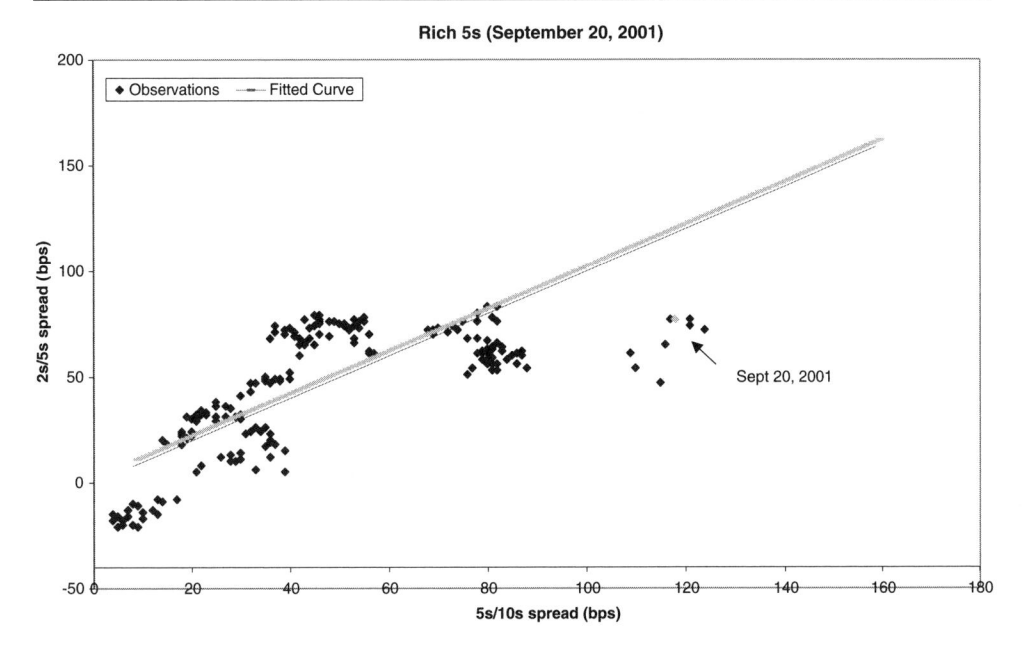

Figure 7.3 Evaluation of a 2s–5s–10s butterfly

relative to both 2s and 10s. Hence, a bullet of 5s would be considered expensive relative to this barbell of 2s and 10s.

This technique could also be used to choose between two butterfly trades, such as the 2s–5s–10s and the 2s–5s–30s. In this case, the current relationship is evaluated against the fitted curve for an indication of whether the spreads are historically attractive. The preferred trade is most likely the one that reverts more quickly to the mean. For bonds with longer maturities (beyond 10 years) and high coupons, however, the value of convexity will also need to be evaluated.

Caveat

Identifying bond mispricings and exploiting the implied profit opportunities are two different things. That is, the mistakes of others produce an extra source of risk as well as a potential profit opportunity. The risk here is related to the unpredictability of investor sentiment – including the possibility that a mispricing worsens before it disappears or that it still remains when the position must be liquidated. As with any investment, some risks are worth taking; others are not.

7.5 THE LIMITATIONS OF STATISTICAL METHODS

In this chapter, we examined a number of statistical techniques used to anticipate short-term market dynamics. The coverage is by no means comprehensive, as numerous commercial and proprietary tools also exist. Whatever the specific statistical technique, however, it will suffer from the limitations described below.

Complexity versus Predictive Power

Complex models tend to be very scenario specific, which limits their applicability. They can be used, but they must be employed intelligently.

Garbage In means Garbage Out

When one is focused solely on the elegant solutions to closed form equations there is the risk that one becomes distanced from the behavioral aspects that drive the model – human preferences determined under conditions of uncertainty. Moreover, even if we had the perfect model, the reality is that we must apply it imperfectly; that is, with imperfectly measured and uncertain (probability-based) inputs. By implication, the best analysts have not only the best methods, but also the best datasets.

It's Still Fortune-Telling

Models, no matter how complex, are fitted to old data. In other words, models explain the past. Hence, in a dynamic world there is a risk that models may not represent the future. In a world of rapid change, successful performance demands flexible thinking. By construction, however, models are generally inflexible. Hence, it is best to use several techniques, and this takes us to Chapter 8.

NOTES

1. Flows are timed by comparing short-term exposure (1 month) to medium-term exposure (6 months).
2. The report draws from the Chicago Board of Trade, Chicago Mercantile Exchange, New York Board of Trade, and other US exchanges. The CFTC also produces a weekly combined report on futures and options.
3. Interbank transactions take place between banks.
4. Source: CFTC.
5. Open interest is the total of all futures and/or option contracts entered into and not yet offset (by a transaction, delivery, exercise, etc.). The aggregate of all long open interest equals the aggregate of all short open interest. Open interest held or controlled by a trader is referred to as that trader's position.
6. Spreading measures the extent to which each non-commercial trader holds equal long and short futures positions.
7. Trades that have become "crowded" are associated with "consensus risk".
8. The UK's FRS 17 encourages pension funds to hold a higher percentage of sterling corporate bonds (as opposed to equities or Gilts).
9. Malvey (1997) found that in the period 1973–1995 a simple upgrade trade – out of Baa's and into A's by the start of Q4, and back into Baa's by the end of Q4 – produced 93 bps in incremental returns before transaction costs. During this 23-year period, this Q4 effect was evident in 14 years (and the Q1 effect was evident in 18 years). In all but one of the exception years, the effect occurred in Q3 – perhaps as greater market awareness of this seasonality contributed to its early arrival.
10. However, there is not a similar holiday effect for German Bunds.
11. A rule of thumb is to use shorter-based means for shorter dynamics. For example, compare the latest monthly observation with the average over the previous three months.
12. Applications of RV analysis are discussed in Chapter 9.
13. Cheap bonds enhance the risk/return characteristics of the portfolio in all scenarios, whereas rich bonds do so in only a few.
14. A butterfly trade involves the simultaneous purchase and sale of a bullet and barbell (or vice versa). Butterfly trades are discussed in more detail in Chapter 10.

8
An Integrated Approach to Bond Strategy

To a man with only a hammer, every problem looks like a nail.

PROVERB

We have now assembled a vast array of tools for use in constructing a view on fixed income market movements. The challenge at hand is to put these tools to their best use. This requires understanding their relevance and knowing how to resolve mixed signals. In other words, an overall framework is required.

8.1 AN INTERDISCIPLINARY MODEL

As we have seen thus far, individual models have both strengths and weaknesses. This reflects the fact that a model is constructed with a specific purpose in mind – such is the nature of the scientific process in the social sciences. As a result, models have a tendency to work during some periods but not during others. This is particularly the case for linear equilibrium models applied to processes with multiple feedback mechanisms – such as bond, currency, and equity markets.

In a similar vein, the disciplines of economics, politics, sociology, and psychology all analyze group behavior from a different perspective. Each discipline asks a different question and looks for the answer using a different framework. Effectively, each discipline focuses a flashlight into the darkness. Arguably, however, financial markets extend well beyond the light beam of each discipline's torch. For the practitioner attempting to earn a living in the dynamic environment of financial markets, multidisciplinary thinking is essential. In the absence of having "the true model", the best alternative is to have access to many models. Indeed, investment decisions are more likely to be correct when a number of models from different perspectives point to the same conclusion.

Consider the following model where price and fundamental value can differ. The market price of a bond (or any financial asset) is a function of four components: (1) economic fundamentals; (2) market sentiment; (3) technical factors (such as flows related to seasonal demand or bond issuance); and (4) random events (unforeseen news or "wildcards"). By construction, the bond might never be at fair value, though it may move toward it. The basic premise of this approach is to look for an alignment or consensus among these indicators to guide the market forecast; and to understand any misalignment by carefully examining the nature of the alternatives (the boundary conditions) and the strength of market sentiment (the energy entering the system).

The relative importance assigned to each of the four explanatory components depends on the time horizon and the market context. No component will dominate every period. In general, economic fundamentals determine the long-run trend, while sentiment, technical factors, and random news events determine prices from day to day. Trending or deep markets, such as these for Treasuries, Bunds, and JGBs, are more efficient than disorderly or thin markets found in some emerging debt markets.

Equation 8.1

Price = Fundamentals + Sentiment + Technical factors + Wildcards

---

This model is inspired in part by the fierce ongoing debate surrounding the efficient markets hypothesis (EMH). The essence of the EMH debate is whether or not asset price movements are predictable. The EMH view is that prices at all times discount all relevant information. Because news occurs randomly, the price movements that discount new information are also random. Hence, EMH allows for no over- or underreaction, no price trends, and no changes in prices without a change in news. In a world where market prices reflect their fundamental value, unexploited profit opportunities do not exist for long and investors cannot outperform the market without taking on more systemic risk than the market (Fama, 1970). Since a study of previous random events can not be used to predict the future, market forecasts are a waste of time. By implication, the best strategy is to passively index your portfolio.

Psychologically, EMH is difficult to accept for pattern-seeking humans. Even if markets do behave a lot like coin tosses, they produce interesting patterns. These patterns are difficult to ignore, and may even become self-fulfilling if the majority uses them as a cue. Although the research is still in its infancy, behavioral finance has produced evidence of bias and systemic errors that generate profit opportunities. Even without a behavioral bias, it has been shown that prices can persistently deviate from fundamentals as a result of the risk associated with arbitrage.

Each side of the EMH debate points to elegant theory and compelling empirical evidence. Proponents of EMH are focused on the research that confirms market movements to be random. Meanwhile, detractors are focused on EMH anomalies and psychological bias. In short, the tendency is to think of EMH in "either/or" terms.

Instead of saying that the world is *either* efficient *or* it is not, this model accommodates *both* views. Given that there is "clear" evidence supporting both sides, it seems evident that asset prices have "rational" as well as "irrational" characteristics. In other words, both fundamental and technical analyses are legitimate tools. Hence, the key point for practitioners is not *whether* markets are efficient (or efficient enough). Rather, the key is understanding *when* they are more efficient or more emotional.

Essential elements from the models discussed in Chapters 1 through 7 are presented below within the context of this interdisciplinary framework.

Economics

Economics helps to identify the long-term economic cycle. Long-term "buy and hold" investors will want to find the up-cycle and ride it until it ends. As economics provides the guideposts of equilibrium values, it helps short-term traders to distinguish between the noise and the signal. In other words, economics helps to locate our friend – the trend.

"Fundamental" bond price ← Interest rate, Coupon, Principal, Maturity

---

An Integrated Approach to Bond Strategy

The fundamental bond price is a negative function of the interest rate and maturity; and a positive function of the coupon and principal. The coupon, principal, and maturity are prespecified within the bond indenture. The interest rate is a positive function of money demand and a negative function of money supply.

> **Interest rate ← Money demand, Money supply**

Money demand is a positive function of consumption, investment, government spending, and net foreign demand. The government influences money demand directly through increases/decreases in government spending (net of tax and other revenue). The government can also influence money demand indirectly via changes in polices that effect consumption (taxes, subsidies, and grants), investment (taxes and regulation), and foreign demand (tariffs, quotas, and exchange rate).

> **Money demand ← Consumption, Investment, Government spending, Net foreign demand**

Politics

Political analysis is useful for providing insight into intermediate- and long-term trends – depending on the dynamics of predominant political influences or institutional reform. Politics affects the implementation of fiscal policy (taxes and spending) as well as monetary policy (money supply).

> **Money supply ← Budget deficits, Independence, Targets (price stability, growth, liquidity)**

Monetary policy is less expansionary when the central bank is independent of political influences, or when faced by an inflationary environment. Monetary policy is more expansionary when economic growth is fragile and inflation is expected to remain subdued. A crisis in liquidity which threatens the banking system would also result in a loosening of monetary policy.

Demographics

Demography is useful for identifying the very long-term trend. The interest rate is a positive function of spenders (money demand) and a negative function of savers (money supply). The spenders of the population tend to be those under the age of 40 and above the age of 70.

> **Interest rate ← Spenders, Savers**

Psychology

Market sentiment is important for short-term market dynamics. The sentimental component of risk-free government bond prices is a positive function of anxiety and the increased aversion to losses. A heightened level of anxiety – such as that associated with increased volatility – reduces risk appetite and, in extreme cases, produces a flight-to-quality (especially at the short end of the curve). Conversely, the sentimental component of corporate bonds is a negative function of anxiety (via an aversion to credit risk). The greater the anxiety (or fear), the greater is the tendency to follow the crowd and the more important is sentiment in the overall bond price.

> "Sentimental" bond price ← Anxiety, Salient history

The salience of history has, *a priori*, an indeterminate impact on bond prices. If the past seems less relevant, such as in a trendless market, then recent news which contradicts the past is given more weight and markets tend to overreact. If history is more salient, such as in a trending market, then recent news which contradicts the past is discounted and markets tend to underreact.

Technical Factors

Technical factors are important for short-term market dynamics. They can also be more apparent in less liquid markets. In contrast to most economic models which are based on a "generic" investor, technically-based analysis focuses on the motivations of different types of market participants. This serves to decipher the noise within a price movement.

> "Technical" bond price ← Transient supply/demand, Richness, Speculative flows

The technical component of a bond price is a negative function of supply and a positive function of demand. Even though fundamental factors might be supportive of bond prices over the long term, on any given day transient factors (such as bond issuance, options expiry, or seasonal trades) may be a countervailing influence. Alternatively, the bond may be perceived as too expensive relative to other investment opportunities, particularly if "everyone" in the market has overweighted the bond or sector.

As speculators seek immediate profits – by getting in and out of a position all within a very short period of time – speculative flows have no net effect on the trend; they only generate volatility (the 'noise' in the price action). (In contrast, non-speculative transactions are not unwound unless the fundamentals change.)

8.2 THE APPROPRIATE USE OF TOOLS

There are two criteria for selecting the appropriate analytical tool: the time horizon, and the market environment. For investors with a long time horizon (a year or more), the focus is on gauging the fundamentals and assessing the credit/macro trends. Long-term investors, however, should not ignore market sentiment completely as it has value for timing market entry and exit.

Table 8.1 Analytical tools and their best application

Model	Time horizon	Market context	Bias
Economic fundamentals	Long term	Especially deep, orderly[2] and efficient markets	Price = Fundamentals only
Political business cycles	Medium, long term	Especially inefficient and disorderly markets	Growth in run up to elections; inflation afterwards
Multiple central bank targets	Medium, long term	All	Inflationary if have growth, employment target
Central bank independence	Medium, long term	All	More inflationary, the less independent
Demographics	Long term	All	Depends on spending/saving of dominant generations
Technical analysis	Short term	Especially trending, inefficient, and orderly markets	Volatile forecasts in short run; extended trends in long run. Price = Sentiment only
Flows	Short term	Especially thin or small markets	None
Transient supply and demand	Short term	Especially thin or small markets	None
Seasonal factors	Short term	Especially thin or small markets	Over-fitting data (historical bias)

Moreover, sentiment should not be ignored when it becomes extreme, which can persist for long periods. For traders with a very short time horizon (a few days to several weeks), the focus is on flows and transitory shifts in relative demand or market psychology. Because of its reliance on real-time data, technical analysis is well suited for those requiring a hair trigger response.

For investors with a medium-term horizon (several months[1]), sentiment generally remains key. As such, technical factors will tend to have better explanatory power than fundamentals. Still, fundamentals are not irrelevant, even in the very short term, as near-term central bank actions are guided by them. When attempting to balance the roles of fundamentals and technicals, think of fundamentals as the compass heading. The actual path you take to get to your intended destination will not be a straight line. Depending on your compass skills, sense of direction, and the terrain, you might end up pointing in the wrong direction along the way.

It is important to note that the time horizon is a fluid concept. As already noted, a long horizon has a different meaning depending on whether you are a trader or an investor. Moreover, individual traders and investors will define the horizon differently. Even if one is invested solely on the basis of economic fundamentals, the relevant time horizon will depend on the speed with which the underlying fundamentals are changing. For a country that is in a state of economic and political flux (such as Brazil in 2002), one would have a shorter time horizon owing to the faster pace of fundamental change. On the other hand, for a country where the fundamentals are more stable and change more slowly (such as in the Euro area), one would have a longer time horizon. Even within a single country, there will be periods of relative stability and instability that necessitate an adjustment in the applicable time horizon. In this sense, the time horizon is related to the market environment.

The market environment is also relevant in the selection of the appropriate analytical tool. Deep and orderly markets – like those for Treasuries, Bunds and JGBs – are more efficient and generally less affected by normal swings in sentiment. On the other hand, thin and volatile markets – like those of many emerging markets – are less efficient and generally more affected by swings in sentiment. However, in extreme conditions, characterized by a flight-to-quality and a drying up of liquidity, market psychology can overwhelm fundamentals even in the deepest, most efficient markets.

Because of feedback effects, the distinction between sentimental and fundamental factors can become blurred. For example, an initial plunge in equity markets due to a plethora of grim corporate earnings reports can fuel market anxiety, which leads to more selling in the equity market (and more buying in the bond market). The anxious mood causes consumers to postpone big purchases and vacations, which in turn weighs on corporate earnings. Businesses scale back plans and shed labor, which then weighs on consumer confidence ... and so on – with sentiment and fundamentals continuing to feed on each other.

8.3 RESOLVING MIXED SIGNALS

Effective decision making requires acquiring the correct building blocks and giving them the correct weights. When all or most of the relevant models are pointing the practitioner in the same direction, weighting is not an issue. Inevitably, however, the signals will become crossed. When this happens, keep in mind that the simplest ways of combining information may give as good a long-run performance as fancy weighting schemes.

Conflicting signals may be a sign to: (1) remain on the sidelines until the picture is clearer (e.g. the risk is greater than the reward); or (2) take advantage of an opportunity (e.g. the reward outweighs the risk). The action chosen depends on supplementary analysis.

The first supplementary task is to evaluate the degree of conviction you have for the analytical results and the downside risks attached to each. It is also helpful to identify the reason for the mixed signals. For example, if the fundamentals look good but the chart looks bad, it may be that something has not yet appeared in the fundamentals due to differences in the frequency of the source data. Alternatively, perhaps seasonal factors or exceptional events are the culprits. Table 8.2 presents some rules of thumb from technical analysis for resolving mixed signals.

Note that the market may not necessarily react to news – even if it is particularly dramatic. A classic example is the lack of market response following the assassination of US President

Table 8.2 Maxims from technical analysis for resolving mixed signals

- When fundamentals and momentum clash (perhaps because a torrent of strong growth data sours bond market sentiment), value assessments lose out first.
- If the news is good, but the market can't go up, you need to be short.
- Market overshooting is more of a rule than an exception.

John F. Kennedy. If a market is fundamentally and technically poised to move higher, a news item will not cause it to reverse direction.

When conflicts persist, it may be time to re-examine your sources and methods. Perhaps a statistical methodology has changed. Perhaps markets are volatile within a trading range, when the technique is better suited for trending markets. Has something been overlooked? Is a subconscious bias getting in the way? In short, has the data, model, or inference become flawed? It may be time to find an innovative information source or even a new technique.

> **When in doubt, stay out.**

8.4 EVALUATING DOWNSIDE RISK

Evaluating downside risk requires anticipating all contingencies, including wildcard events. Predicting the financial equivalent of the 100-year flood is simply impossible. Nevertheless, there are a number of techniques which attempt to do just that – including 'what-if' scenarios, "Value-At-Risk" analysis, and Monte Carlo simulations.

A more basic method is to employ a "maximum pain" approach which identifies: (1) the worst possible events; (2) the worst possible time that they can occur; and (3) the most vulnerable market participants. When the downside risk is intolerable, there is always the option of waiting for a more palatable opportunity. If waiting is not an option, then the size of the position should be small enough such that a string of losses does not put you out of business (see Chapter 11).

8.5 SYSTEM CHECKS

It is important to make regular system checks. Your reputation and livelihood depend on it. The goal is to achieve unbiased critical analysis.

Logic Check

Put aside the data and mechanics and ask yourself: Does it make common sense? This is analogous to looking out the window before presenting a weather forecast. Just because the high tech models say that it should be sunny doesn't mean that it isn't raining!

As change is the nature of a dynamic marketplace, there are no prepackaged absolute answers. Hence, there is always the risk that one has wandered into uncharted territory. Analytical systems have to be monitored and adjusted using individual judgment.

Bias Check

Analytical systems require adjustment, and adjustment requires the use of judgment. However, judgment can be distorted by a number of psychological biases. Remember that part of the reason that the systems are in place is to counteract emotion. Hence, adjust systems with care – that is, be sure to evaluate the adjustment itself in terms of potential bias. To begin with, each person has a "comfort zone" which makes him or her predisposed to either a fundamental or a technical view.

Most of the analysis you read or advice you hear will have an implicit bias. For example, sell-side research may have a sales bias. The key is to *consciously* identify the bias to enable you to make a balanced judgment and apply the implications appropriately. Can you pinpoint the unspoken bias in the following advice to investors?

Example 8.1 – "Ignore the market"[3]
"Don't even try to guess market direction. Buy quality stocks at undervalued prices and hold on until those values are recognized".

Example 8.2 – "Never follow the crowd"[4]
Following the crowd means buying toward the top – because popularity is reflected in a high price. In the long run, the crowd is always wrong.

Example 8.1 makes the implicit assumption that markets are mean reverting. 'Buying cheap and selling rich' is a fundamentally based strategy that works best in uptrending markets. Example 8.2 is based on a long investment horizon and the contrarian belief that the crowd is always wrong about timing a reversal. The "long run" can be very long and may even extend beyond the relevant investment horizon of long-term investors. Moreover, if you bought the NASDAQ in January 1999 and sold in February 2000, you could have retired. So following the crowd is not always wrong. The key is knowing when to break rank with the crowd once you have joined. In short, timing is everything. Note that even if an argument is persuasive and without an implicit bias, it may not apply to your investment horizon.

Notes about Data

It is crucial to understand your data as much as your model. The best models are worthless if the data fed into them are flawed or misunderstood. As such, a failure to understand the strengths and weaknesses of your data is a prescription for faulty analysis. Note that the methodology and weaknesses of data sources published by statistical agencies are in a continual state of change; hence, a one-time assessment is insufficient.

Consider creating your own leading indicators and proxies. For example, investment banks utilize client surveys and proprietary transaction data as a barometer for risk appetite. One of my favorite proxies is taxi drivers because of their intimate perspective of the economy. Alternative (creative) sources are also useful for completing your logic check and they might give you an edge. So always be on the lookout for new sources and methods. This requires thinking "outside the box" and exposure to different experiences.

Finally, the periodicity of the data used for analysis should match the sensitivity of your investment decision. In other words, don't use long-term research for short-term trading. Instead, use daily data for daily or weekly trading. Use quarterly or annual data for long-term investment. If you have noisy data, you will need to use a bigger threshold for evaluating the changes in the data. For example, a single standard deviation from the mean is appropriate for hedging activity, whereas flow data require a threshold of two standard deviations.

Notes about Information Management

> *When you can only see trees and bushes it is all too easy to wander off course.*
> JON LEWIS (2002)

A focus on the news of the day reinforces the tendency to overemphasize the short term (Gallea and Patalon, 1998). This is fine if your investment horizon is very short term. Some market news is truly important to heed (such as a Fed or ECB change in interest rates), but a lot is transitory. Monthly economic data are volatile (even when adjusted for seasonality) and, in any case, most are revised several times. Headlines and sound-bites can give unwarranted importance to the latest economic number if you are investing over the long term.

Sometimes the same news event will have a different response in different markets. For one thing, news items may be given a different "spin" or a different priority.

Remember your investment time horizon, and use it as a reference point to filter information. I am not suggesting that you ignore any piece of news, but unless you are a day trader, consider allowing more pieces of news to accumulate in your "in box" before revisiting your analysis. That pile in your inbox will give you some perspective by which to evaluate the "big picture". Procrastinators, rejoice!

> **Just because the market changes its view every day, doesn't mean that you should.**

Don't give more importance to the single argument conveyed via 20 separate reports than to the argument conveyed in a single story. The value of the argument should be judged not by the number of times you hear it but on the case it makes. In other words, concurring opinions should be treated as a *single* opinion.

It is important to focus your efforts where there is the most potential for reward. For example, if 80% of the risk of a given bond is predominantly a function of market and sector risk, then focus 80% of your research time on the market and sector.

Finally, do your homework and take a closer look at those "expert" arguments. Remember the recent US "productivity miracle" that "everyone" was talking about? A close examination of US productivity data shows a *5-year* phenomenon of above-average performance during 1996–2000.[5] Moreover, this "above-average performance" is not at all profound by historical standards. You don't need to reinvent the wheel, but you must rely on your own critical thinking and reach independent conclusions. That means investigating original sources and drilling down through the key aspects of the analysis.

8.6 A TEMPLATE FOR CONSTRUCTING A VIEW ON WHICH TO TRADE

The template shown in Table 8.3 can be used to build a case that answers the key questions faced by a fixed income practitioner:

1. *Market direction:* Up or down?
2. *Yield curve:* Flattening or steepening?
3. *Yield spreads:* Widening or narrowing?
4. *Volatility:* Rising or falling?
5. *Turning points:* Imminent or not?

Perhaps it goes without saying, but the best scenario is a golden triangle – that is, when fundamentals, technicals, and market psychology are all in alignment. In emerging markets, however, the political signal is critical. A further note of caution: "Alignment" should not be inferred from the consistency of one fundamental, technical, and sentiment indicator, but rather from a *number* of indicators of each type.

Table 8.3 The strategy template

Indicator	Independent forecast (action and timing)
Fundamentals Growth (direction, pace) Inflation (pace, variability) Demographics (trend)	
Politics Monetary policy changes Fiscal policy changes Geopolitical considerations	
Behavior Risk appetite (volatility) Sentiment Momentum	
Technical factors Flows (market position) Seasonals Issuance vs transient demand	
Quantitative indicators Rich versus cheap Extreme vs normal valuations	
Wildcards (downside risks)	
	EVALUATION
View *Risk versus reward* *Price targets*	What is the strength of your conviction? Are you in or out? Is the trade crowded? Entry and exit points (stop loss, take profit)

Once an independent forecast is made, it must be compared to the market's consensus expectation in order to derive the strategy implications. A difference between your independent forecast and the market consensus represents a possible trading opportunity. The difference may be due to the data forecast, an emphasis on different variables, or the timing of the response. As sentiment or the fundamentals change, so too will your forecast (and potentially your strategy). The market responds to news in a knee-jerk fashion. Your response, however, will depend on your time horizon.

Market Expectations

The most relevant question for practitioners is whether their view differs from the market consensus. If your forecast is already discounted or "priced in" to the market (when market expectations are the same or "close enough"), bond prices are considered to be fairly valued. As such, a comparison of the two sets of expectations – that of the practitioner and that of the market – determines whether there are profit opportunities to exploit. In short, this assessment determines whether you close a position or open a new one.

An Integrated Approach to Bond Strategy

Table 8.4 US interest rate expectations as of August 2002

	Investor forecast		Market forecast	
	Level (%)	Change (bps)	Level (%)	Change (bps)
One-month (Sep. 2002)	1.75	0	1.7500[7]	0
Three-month (Nov. 2002)	1.75	0	1.5625	$-18.75 (= 25 \times 0.75)$
Six-month (Mar. 2003)	1.5625	-18.75	1.5625	0
One-year (Aug. 2003)	1.5625	0	1.5625	0

Interest rate futures are used to proxy the market's view. For example, Fed Funds or Eurodollar futures can be used to infer market expectations about US interest rate risk.[6] Table 8.4 presents a hypothetical forecast of US interest rates over a 12-month period alongside a set of rates implied by Eurodollar futures observed in the market. By comparing the difference between the investor forecast and Eurodollar futures, we determine that the market appears to be discounting about a 75% probability of a 25 bps rate cut by the FOMC by November.[7] Beyond March, however, the market's evaluation of interest rate risk is consistent with the investor's – in which case, the investor would be advised to maintain a neutral position from that point until new profit opportunities present themselves.

8.7 LIMITATIONS OF THE INTERDISCIPLINARY APPROACH

Order cannot be created where there is none.

Unlike most approaches, this model has the advantage of flexible thinking. However, just like any other model it can lull you into a false sense of security. In other words, it can lead you to believe that you actually *can* predict the future. The reality is that random events occur on a regular basis. As a result, bond prices will diverge more from expectations than you think they should. The appropriate response is to learn from your mistakes and to engage in a proactive search for new sources and methods.

NOTES

1. A 1- to 3-month horizon is considered "short" for investors and "long" for traders.
2. In an orderly market there is two-way risk; in a disorderly market, the bet is one way.
3. John Templeton, as quoted in Lifson and Geist (1999: 163).
4. Bernard Baruch, as quoted in Lifson and Geist (1999: 165).
5. US non-farm output per hour averaged 2.5% during 1996–2000 compared with 2.2% for the period 1949–2000; 3.8% during 1962–1966; and 3.4% during 1949–1953 (*Source:* US Bureau of Labor Statistics).
6. Use Euribor futures for the Euro area; Short Sterling futures for the United Kingdom; and Euroyen futures for Japan. Information on Euribor and Short Sterling futures is available from EUREX and LIFFE, respectively. Information on Euroyen futures is available from TIFFE. The CME has data on Eurodollar futures, while the CBOT has data on Fed Fund futures.

7. A Eurodollar futures price of 98.25 implies an interest rate of 1.75% (100 − 98.25). Eurodollar futures are more liquid than Fed Funds futures. Other methods of measuring market expectations include an adjustment for liquidity risk, an adjustment of about 10–15 bps.

RECOMMENDED READING

Hagstrom, R.G. (2000). *Investing: The Last Liberal Art*. New York: Texere.

Part III
Implementing Your View

Part I gave us a clear understanding of the nature of fixed income risk and the way this risk is influenced by economic forces. Part II provided a tool kit of techniques that allows us to construct a forecast independent from the market consensus. This independent view, when contrasted to the market consensus, identifies the risks that a particular investor might wish to take on. Part III now shows us how to put our analysis into action and generate returns.

Chapter 9 examines the investment alternatives. Because different investors and traders have different objectives and risk appetite, the selected instruments and strategy will vary. Chapter 10 shows how to structure trades to achieve a particular risk exposure. Chapter 11 considers a number of other decisions relevant for implementation – including asset allocation within fixed income and risk management. Chapter 12 presents six pearls of wisdom for the financial battlefield.

9
Fixed Income Instruments, Investors and Portfolio Management Styles

This chapter lays the groundwork for establishing specific fixed income trades, discussed in Chapter 10. The implementation of a fixed income strategy begins by evaluating different investment alternatives – both in terms of fixed income instruments as well as portfolio management styles. As individual investors have different objectives and constraints, specific choices will vary. In general, investors with longer time horizons will be able to tolerate more risk than investors with shorter time horizons.

The first part of the chapter discusses the nuances of different instruments available to fixed income investors. The second part examines the motivations and constraints that different investors bring to the market. The final section describes alternative portfolio management styles (passive, structured, or active) – the choice of which is ultimately framed by the risk tolerance of the investor. Within active portfolio management, directional as well as market-neutral strategies are available – the choice of which is framed by the opportunities identified by the investor.

9.1 THE FIXED INCOME UNIVERSE

At year-end 2001 the nominal value outstanding of the debt traded in the global bond market totaled US$37.2 trillion – roughly 3.7 times larger than annual US GDP. The US accounts for 48% of this debt, followed by the countries of the Euro area (21%) and Japan (16%). Domestically issued government debt accounts for half of the volume in the global bond market. Financial institutions (21%), corporations (11%), and debt issued in international markets (18%) account for the remainder. Within the US debt market, the mortgage-backed sector is the largest with 22%, followed by Treasuries with a 16% share.

There are a number of ways, aside from the issuer, to delineate sectors within fixed income:

- Tax status – taxable or tax-exempt
- Structure – with or without embedded options
- Quality – investment grade, non-investment grade, emerging markets
- Maturity – short, intermediate, or long term
- Coupon – current, indexed, zero, step-up, floating or deferred
- Currency.

A specific fixed income security often falls into a number of different classifications. For example, agencies issue mortgage-backed securities with call provisions. In short, fixed income investors have a wide selection of assets from which to choose. The various sectors are highlighted below.

Other
15%

Japan
16%

US
48%

Euro area
21%

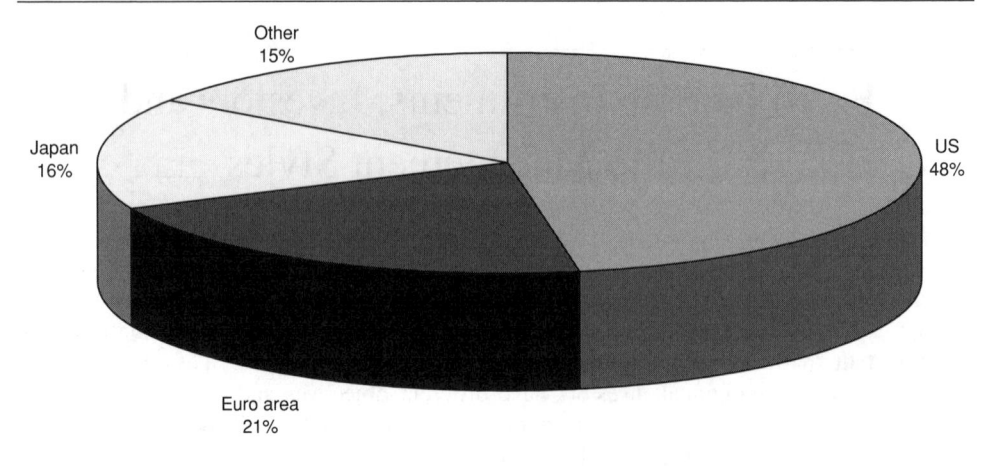

Source: Bank for International Settements.

Figure 9.1 Composition of the world bond market

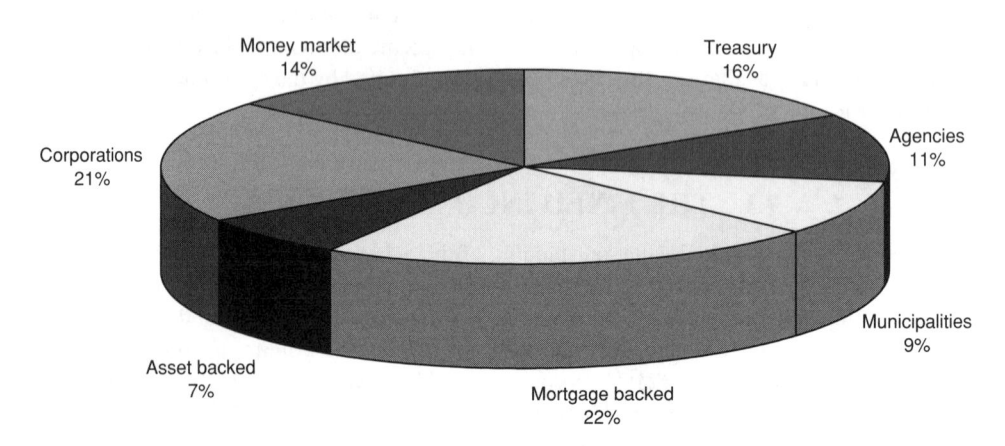

Money market
14%

Treasury
16%

Corporations
21%

Agencies
11%

Municipalities
9%

Asset backed
7%

Mortgage backed
22%

Source: The Bond Market Association.

Figure 9.2 Composition of the US debt market

9.1.1 Government Securities

Government Bonds

Securities issued by the US government (Treasuries) have virtually no credit risk as they are backed by the full faith and credit of the US government, and are the most liquid government securities in the global government bond market. As such, Treasuries serve as the benchmark for debt issued around the world. The debt of other developed market governments (UK Gilts, German Bunds, etc.) is also considered virtually free of credit risk. Within government bonds, a distinction is made between on-the-run (the most recent issue) and off-the-run (older issues) securities. The major difference between on-the-run and off-the-run securities is liquidity. Further distinctions within the government sector include:

Inflation-indexed bonds

These government securities offer the investor protection against inflation. Examples include US TIPS (Treasury Inflation Protection Securities), UK "linkers" and French OATi and OATei. In the case of TIPS, the interest paid is based on the principal, which is adjusted for inflation, protecting the real yield.[1] If inflation were to fall, the bond would be redeemed at the higher of the original par value and the inflation-adjusted principal. Changes in the yields of inflation-indexed bonds reflect changes in real yields, whereas changes in conventional nominal bond yields reflect the combination of changes in real yields and inflation expectations. Holders of US TIPS or UK linkers profit from a decline in the real yield or from an increase in the market's inflation forecast. TIPS prices are also affected by the liquidity preferences of bond holders.[2]

In an inflationary environment, TIPS yields should be lower than nominal yields by an amount equal to investors' inflation expectations. The break-even inflation rate – that is, the inflation rate at which a bond buyer would be indifferent between TIPS and nominal Treasuries – is equal to the nominal Treasury yield less the TIPS yield for a comparable maturity.[3] If the break-even inflation rate is less than the forecasted inflation rate, then the index-linked bond is considered cheap relative to its conventional counterpart. Pension funds and other asset-liability managers are big fans of inflation-linked bonds. Note that US federal income taxes must be paid on the inflation-adjusted principal (in addition to the coupon income) even though this income is not received until the bonds are sold or mature.

Government Agency Securities

In the US, agencies include securities issued by federally-related institutions and government-sponsored enterprises (GSE). Federally-related institutions are arms of the federal government, and, in most cases, these securities are backed by the full faith and credit of the US government. Examples of such debt include the Government National Mortgage Association (GNMA or Ginnie Mae) and the Tennessee Valley Authority (TVA). On the other hand, GSEs are privately owned, publicly chartered entities that are generally *not* backed by the full faith and credit of the US government. Examples of GSE debt include the Federal National Mortgage Association (FNMA or Fannie Mae), the Federal Home Loan Mortgage Corporation (Freddie Mac), and the Student Loan Marketing Association (Sallie Mae).

The yield spread between US agencies and Treasuries of comparable maturity reflects differences in liquidity and perceived credit risk – that associated with the financial problems of the issuing entity and the likelihood that the federal government will allow the entity to default. In the European debt market, the bonds issued by Kreditanstalt fuer Wiederaufbau (KfW) are guaranteed by the German government.

Municipal Bonds

These are debt securities issued by state and local governments, generally current coupon securities with 10 years of call protection. There are general obligation (GO) bonds (which are backed by tax revenues) and revenue bonds (which are serviced by the revenue arising from specific public works, with no legal obligation for the issuer to make up for a shortfall in revenue). In the US, interest income on municipal bonds is usually exempt from US federal income tax. In some cases interest on in-state bonds is also exempt from state and local income taxes. Investors in the municipal bond market tend to be those that benefit from tax exemption[4]; hence, demand tends to shift with the tax code. Investors in municipal bonds are exposed to tax risk – specifically, (1) the risk that federal income tax will be reduced (since the higher the marginal tax rate, the greater the value of the tax exemption feature); and (2) the risk that the issue will be declared taxable. Because of the tax exemption, the yield on high-quality municipal bonds is less than that on Treasuries with the same maturity. Yield spreads within the municipal bond market for the same maturity are attributable to differences between different sectors within the revenue market and between credit ratings. For example, a temporary oversupply of high-grade state general obligation (tax backed) bonds may cause the spread with lower-grade revenue bonds to narrow.[5] The appropriate benchmark curve for this market is a nebulous issue. Although municipal bonds are government securities, they are considered more comparable to corporate securities.[6]

9.1.2 Corporate Securities

High-Grade Corporate Debt

These securities are classified by the credit rating agencies as investment grade, with creditworthiness ranging from lower-medium (BBB$^-$) to high (AAA).[7] Corporate bonds typically have semi-annual coupons, sinking funds, maturities of 5–40 years, and deferred call provisions. The major sectors within this market include utilities, industrials, transportation, and finance. Debt is issued by thousands of corporations with different credit stories, the analysis of which requires an intensive review of the issuer – including the scrutiny of accounting practices, debt structure, and corporate management – which is beyond the scope of this book. Yield spreads within the corporate bond market for the same maturity are attributable to differences between credit ratings, corporate sector, and liquidity. Investment houses are increasingly moving to create high-grade benchmarks to: 1) measure relative returns, and 2) create hedging vehicles against portfolios of individual bonds.

High-Yield (or 'Junk') Bonds

These are non-investment grade securities (below BBB$^-$) as well as unrated securities of similar quality. Non-investment grade securities include the debt of companies with low creditworthiness, considered to be speculative, or facing substantial risk of default. In terms of risk, high-yield bonds are comparable to equities and emerging market debt. Investors in this market are seeking high current yield and capital appreciation through credit improvement. In addition to an intensive review of the issuer, investors should carefully examine the issue's structure (e.g. the indenture covenants, call/put characteristics, exchange/sinking fund provisions, and interest rate resets) as well as the underwriter, which plays a significant role in the success of high-yield issues.[8] In the high-yield market callables remain the structure of choice as many issuers hope to refinance prior to maturity at lower interest rates.

Distressed Debt

These are the debt securities of bankrupt and distressed companies. In case of liquidation, US corporate debt has priority over common and preferred stock (Chapter 7 of the US Bankruptcy Act). Investors should be aware, however, that the absolute priority rule does not apply to a company in reorganization (Chapter 11 of the US Bankruptcy Act).

9.1.3 Structured Securities

Callable Bonds

These securities have uncertain cash flows which make them subject to prepayment risk. A call provision allows the issuer to retire all or part of the debt before maturity (typically after a 5- or 10-year wait). Because call provisions are a disadvantage to the investor, call prices are usually set at a premium to par and decline linearly to par 5 to 10 years prior to scheduled maturity. In a declining/rising interest rate environment callable bonds will underperform/outperform non-callable bonds (called straight or bullet bonds). Falling interest rates and heavy corporate refunding tend to reduce investor demand for corporate callable bonds. The yield spread with straight bonds widens when interest rates are falling.

Putable Bonds

These securities transfer the risk of prepayment to the issuer. A put provision allows the investor to redeem the bond at par before maturity, typically after a 5- or 10-year wait. A put structure provides investors with a partial defense against sharp increases in interest rates as the price of a putable bond cannot fall as quickly or as far below par as a comparable straight bond, given that the investor can return the security to the issuer at par on the put date. In an environment of rising interest rates, issuers may shy away from issuing bonds with put options – preferring instead to pay an extra 10–20 bps in coupon yield for a longer-term straight bond, rather than run the risk of refunding the put bond in 5 or 10 years at a higher cost. Yield spreads with comparable straight bonds widen when interest rates are rising.

Convertible or Exchangeable Bonds

These securities are essentially corporate bonds with an option to buy common stock. For convertible bonds investors can exchange the bond for a prespecified amount of common stock in the issuing firm. For exchangeable bonds the exchange is for the stock of a firm that is not the bond issuer. Most convertible bonds have call provisions (although some have put provisions) so they are subject to call risk. When the stock price is low, the convertible bond trades much like a straight bond – that is, it is more sensitive to interest rate risk. Conversely, when the stock price is high, the bond trades much like an equity – that is, it is more sensitive to equity risk. In between, the convertible bond has characteristics of both bonds and equities.

The yield spread between convertible and straight bonds of the same maturity and liquidity is a function of equity and volatility risk. Specifically, the value of conversion is reduced by future down moves in the equity price, lower equity price volatility, and lower interest rate volatility. Hence, a long position in an "undervalued" convertible bond potentially benefits from: (1) a capital gain when the bond price rises toward "fair" value; (2) coupon income; (3) an increase in stock price volatility, which increases the value of the conversion option and produces a larger capital gain in the bond; (4) an increase in interest rate volatility, which increases the value of the conversion option; and (5) an increase in the stock price, which increases the value of the conversion option.

Equity-oriented investors in convertible bonds seek equity-like returns with less downside risk,[9] while more fixed income-oriented investors are attracted to "busted" convertibles – those purchased at a discount to fair value.[10] Hedge funds (particularly during volatile periods) like to take advantage of the pricing inefficiencies of these complex securities.

Bonds Issued with Attached Warrants

These securities are similar to convertible bonds with one important exception. Whereas investors in convertible bonds must give up the bond in order to hold the shares, investors in bonds with warrants may hold both bond and shares simultaneously. A warrant provides the bond investor with the option of purchasing from the issuer a prespecified amount of common stock at a prespecified price. Bonds with attached warrants represent a large part of the Eurobond market. The pricing of bonds with attached warrants is similar to that of convertible bonds.

Mortgage-Backed Securities (MBS)

These securities have cash flows that are dependent upon the cash flows of an underlying pool of mortgages. Because borrowers in the US are allowed to prepay part (or all) of the mortgage in advance of the planned timetable, MBS are subject to prepayment risk. Prepayment tends to be a function of the prevailing mortgage rate, characteristics of the underlying mortgage pool, seasonal factors, and general economic activity. Although backed by collateral, MBS are also subject to default risk because the collateral does not cover all the costs associated with default. Types of MBS include mortgage pass-through securities (Ginnie Mae, Freddie Mac, and Fannie Mae), collateralized mortgage obligations (CMO), and stripped mortgage-backed securities. Ginnie Maes are guaranteed by the full faith and credit of the US government, while Freddie Macs and Fannie Maes are not. CMO and stripped MBS are derivative products based on the repackaging of cash flows from other mortgage-backed securities.

Asset-Backed Securities (ABS)

In the US, these securities are collateralized by assets that are not first-lien mortgage loans. Outside the US, however, ABS generally includes all types of securitized loans. The four most common types of ABS in the US are those backed by credit card receivables, home equity loans, manufactured home loans, and auto loans. Investors in ABS are exposed to credit and prepayment risk (in addition to the other basic risks associated with fixed income).

Floating or Adjustable Rate Debt Securities

These are corporate securities with coupons that reset over periodic intervals at some specified spread over a reference rate (such as LIBOR). Although the income from these securities is not "fixed", floaters are considered part of the fixed income asset class. Investors in floaters benefit from rising short-term interest rates which increase the coupon paid, while issuers of floaters prefer not to lock in comparatively high fixed rates.[11] Hence, periods of rising short-term interest rates tend to be associated with larger demand for, and smaller supply of, floaters. Investors in floaters tend to be banks engaged in asset swaps. Through the asset swap market, floater demand has contributed to tremendous spread compression at the front end of the fixed rate corporate curve (Malvey, 1997). The floater market is hypersensitive to credit risk.

9.1.4 Fixed Income Derivatives[12]

Interest Rate Futures

These exchange-traded instruments allow investors to adjust the interest rate sensitivity of a bond portfolio without purchasing or selling an actual bond. Interest rate futures can also be used to speculate on future movements in interest rates or to create synthetic securities that enhance yield. The seller of a Bund future, for example, agrees to deliver to the buyer at the settlement date a Bund with a prespecified period remaining to maturity. The specific Bund that is delivered is chosen by the seller of the futures contract and hence is the issue that is the cheapest to deliver (CTD).[13] The investor that is long the futures contract realizes a profit if the price of the underlying bond rises.

Interest Rate Options

These securities can be written on cash instruments ("options on physicals"), futures ("futures options"), or swaps ("swaptions"). Like futures, options can be used to speculate, hedge, or create synthetic securities. The options market is also used to buy and sell volatility. There are exchange-traded as well as over-the-counter (OTC) options. Options traded OTC typically are purchased by institutional investors who want to hedge the market risk associated with a specific security. There are also OTC options available to investors who wish to hedge yield curve risk.[14] Futures options on fixed income securities are preferred over options on physicals because: (1) payments for accrued interest are not required (unlike options on physicals); (2) delivery squeezes are less likely with futures; and (3) current futures prices are more readily available than current bond prices – a necessity with option pricing.

Interest Rate Swaps

These instruments can be used by investors to manage interest rate risk and to alter the nature or timing of cash flows, such as from a fixed to a floating basis or vice versa. Bond issuers can use swaps to reduce borrowing costs (either through credit arbitrage or by borrowing in markets where there is good investor appetite for the issuer's bonds) and to diversify their sources of funds. Each party in a swap agreement takes on counterparty risk – default risk on the exchange of interest payments – as opposed to default risk on the principal. Even though the risk and return characteristics of an interest rate swap can be replicated by a package of forward or futures contracts, such a package is not as liquid as a swap and is not as economical. Swaps are used by banks, corporations, governments, and supranationals.

9.1.5 Structured Products

Structured products enable investors to obtain exposures to securities (such as credit derivatives) that they might not be permitted to obtain directly. A structured product consists of a combination of instruments, usually including one or more derivative products, with the risk of the final product being transformed from the component risks. Unlike the fixed income instruments discussed so far, the risks faced by the investor and structurer are not the mirror image of each other. For example, the Bank for International Settlements offers its clients a Medium Term Instrument (MTI). An investor in a US MTI effectively holds a Treasury (with market risk exposure) but earns a yield that behaves like the swap rate (with credit risk exposure).

On the one hand, structured products give investors access to OTC markets and provide further opportunities to diversify assets and risks. On the other hand, structured products have more restricted secondary markets and greater risk in that risks are less evident and more difficult to measure. Fundamental to investing in structured products is being able to: (1) separate the structure into its components; and (2) identify the yield curve used to value the structure. Only then can an investor judge whether the structure conforms to his or her own future expectations and whether the structure's price replicates its components. In general, simplicity is the investor's best friend, while complexity is the structurer's best friend.

9.1.6 Country and Currency Considerations

In addition to the securities discussed above, a further distinction is made between local and foreign currency-denominated debt. Although a sovereign has the ability to meet local currency debt obligations through taxation or printing money, there is less ability to control the price of foreign exchange, which must be purchased to repay debt obligations denominated in another currency. Moreover, a government may give priority to domestic as opposed to foreign bond holders – requiring investors to distinguish between the ability to pay (economic risk) and the willingness to pay (political risk). Hence, default risk tends to be larger for foreign currency-denominated debt.

There is also supranational debt which is issued by international organizations (such as the World Bank, European Investment Bank, and Inter-American Development Bank) and global debt which is underwritten simultaneously in American, European and/or Asian capital markets. Eurobonds are offered to investors internationally by international syndicates and are not subject to the jurisdiction of one particular country.

Another asset class is emerging market (EM) debt. Investors often view EM debt, high-yield debt, and equities as competing asset classes. Although they have similar credit ratings, emerging market spreads have been wider and more volatile than US high-yield spreads. The principal sectors of EM debt are Brady bonds, Eurobonds, and local debt products.

Investors considering foreign currency debt will need to decide whether to hedge all or part of the added currency exposure.[15] A complete currency hedge locks in the coupon income and currency gain (or loss), leaving the local price change in the foreign bond (foreign interest rate risk) as the only unknown. The simplest way to hedge currency exposure is to use currency forwards or futures. For example, a long bond position combined with a short forward (or future) in the underlying currency would strip away the currency risk, leaving only foreign bond market exposure (Equation 9.1).

Equation 9.1
Total position = Capital gain + Accrued interest − FX hedging cost

The hedging decision (currency risk exposure) should be separated from the bond decision (interest rate exposure) because factors that influence bond markets often influence currencies differently. For example, bonds tend to respond to the business cycle – increasing/decreasing in value as economic growth and inflation decline/rise. On the other hand, currencies tend to be influenced more by relative purchasing power, short-term yield levels, and technical factors.[16] In addition to the usual considerations of interest rate movements, liquidity, and credit risk – the foreign bond investor must also assess the added return-for-risk from the foreign sovereign, net of withholding taxes and other fees.

A currency overlay can account for roughly 90% of total fixed income returns, depending on the time horizon and base currency of the investor.[17] Also, the currency adds significantly to the volatility of returns, particularly for shorter time periods. Most research on currency hedging for US dollar-based investors suggests that a partially hedged benchmark offers superior risk-adjusted returns compared with either a fully hedged or unhedged benchmark.[18]

Alternative Fixed Income Instruments and Strategy Structures 149

Table 9.1 Examples of fixed income securities

Issuer/type	Security (currency)
Supranational bonds	World Bank, EIB, IADB (in a variety of currencies)
Government bonds (Conventional)	Gilts (£), Bunds (€), OATs (€), JGBs (¥), Treasuries ($)
Government bonds (Index-linked)	Gilts (£), OATi (€), OATie (€), TIPS ($)
Agency/State bonds	Fannie Mae ($), Freddie Mac ($), KfW (€)
Municipal bonds	Los Angeles ($)
Investment grade bonds	Deutsche Telekom (€), BMW (€), Halifax (£), Boots (£), Sony (¥), Nippon Telegraph (¥), American Express ($), Boeing ($)
High-yield bonds	Enron (€, $, ¥), British Airways (£), Lucent Technologies ($)
Interest rate futures	Short sterling, Euribor, Euroyen, Eurodollar

9.2 INVESTOR TYPES

Investors are not a homogeneous group. In fact there are a variety of motivations that bring different investors to the market. There are also a variety of constraints placed on investors (Table 9.2). Aside from the obvious objective of earning profits, some investors are in the market to hedge risks generated from the course of doing business. Some are in for the long term; others are looking for quick profits. As for the constraints, these are largely prescribed by risk tolerance and investment time horizon. Moreover, investors have varying liquidity needs (some needing to convert investments into cash at short notice) and they face different legal, regulatory, and tax issues. Understanding the motivations and constraints of different investor types provides insight on the market flows and structural demand at various sections of the yield curve.

The investor's investment objective and time horizon are directly linked to the ability and willingness to absorb risk. For example, if capital preservation is the objective or the time horizon is short, investments will need to be "less risky" (subject to less variability). On the other hand, if capital appreciation is the objective or the time horizon is long, investments can be "more risky" (subject to more variability).

A portfolio set up to minimize the variability in its market value will, however, maximize the risk to income. In other words, there is no free lunch. Larger income requires investors to take larger risk, while greater certainty requires investors to sacrifice income. Individual investors assess this trade-off differently. Some prefer to aggressively pursue anticipated gains, others prefer to conservatively avoid anticipated losses. Hence, different fixed income investments are more or less relevant depending on the characteristics of the investor.

Table 9.2 Investor objectives and constraints

Objectives	Constraints
Maximum returns	Investment horizon
	Risk tolerance

Figure 9.3 classifies investors by the degree of risk aversion. At one end of the spectrum are the most risk-averse investors in search of current income – typically endowments that are limited to high-quality cash instruments. At the other extreme are the most aggressive investors in search of capital gains – typically proprietary traders and hedge funds making full use of the available range of fixed income instruments. In between are banks, corporations, insurers, and pension funds – looking to balance income and growth, manage liquidity and liabilities, and transfer away unwanted risk. These divisions, however, are becoming increasingly blurred.

Low Risk → High Risk
Endowments → Insurers, Pension funds, Banks, Corporations → Hedge funds, Proprietary traders

Figure 9.3 The risk aversion spectrum

Endowment Funds and Foundations

Endowment funds help to support institutions such as colleges, hospitals, museums, and charities. Because investment income is used to finance the current and future spending of the institution being supported, endowment funds need to produce current income as well as maintain the value of the endowment in real terms – that is, preserve capital. A portfolio of long-term bonds is preferred for income stability and durability, but is susceptible to inflation risk. As a result, many endowments target total returns, based on income and capital appreciation.

Risk tolerance varies. Where an institution relies almost exclusively on the endowment for funds, little risk can be taken. On the other hand, if the institution has income from other sources, an endowment can afford larger fluctuations in income levels. Liquidity is relatively unimportant for most endowments due to the long-term nature of their objectives. Most endowments are not subject to taxation.

Central Banks

Central banks are concerned with managing their foreign exchange reserves. Liquidity is important, so investments are low risk and tend to be concentrated in the money market. Central banks often diversify reserves into liquid fixed income instruments in order to: (1) add total return; (2) match assets and liabilities; and (3) provide a liquid source of currency intervention when needed. The US dollar's weakness in 2002–2003 is a good example of a currency/asset allocation switch by central banks seeking to increase their reserve weightings in Euro. In this case, central bank activity has been both the cause and effect of the dollar's move.

Non-Life Insurance Companies

Non-life insurance companies earn revenue from the collection and investment of insurance premiums. Insurance claims are paid out of investment income, or the regulatory surplus if current investment income is insufficient. High investment returns enable a company to add to its surplus, lower premiums, and increase business. As a result, there is a low tolerance for capital losses and falling investment income. The cash flows of non-life (e.g. property and casualty) insurers are highly volatile due to the unpredictable nature of many of their risks. Hence, liquidity is a priority and the investment time horizon is relatively short. Bonds constitute the lion's share of non-life insurers' investment portfolios. These investors hold most types of bonds, but tend to favor high-quality liquid bonds – that is, government bonds.

Pension Funds

For defined benefit pensions, the key investment objective is to meet the actuarial rate of return which will finance the fund's long-term liabilities. In order to neutralize interest rate risk, most pension funds match their long-term liabilities with long-term investments. In a defined benefit pension, the risk of inflation and poor investment performance is assumed by the employer, who will need to increase contributions to compensate for any deficiency of assets. For underfunded plans, the investment approach will need to be relatively conservative – that is, focused on yield – to ensure that the assets of the scheme grow to meet liabilities. For overfunded plans, the investment approach can be more aggressive – that is, focused on total return. Liquidity is less of a concern due to the receipt of regular pension contributions and the long-term nature of liabilities.

Pension funds tend to hold long-term investment grade corporate debt because of its higher yield. Regulatory requirements usually prevent pension funds from purchasing low-quality corporate securities.[19] Pension funds also hold government bonds for security and liquidity, particularly inflation-linked bonds. Prepayment risk makes pass-through securities unattractive, as pension funds want to satisfy long-term liabilities by locking in prevailing interest rates. Rather than managing all funds actively, many pension funds use low-risk index-tracking funds for the core of the fund and active strategies for the remainder.

Municipal Treasuries

Like pension funds, municipal treasuries seek to finance pension liabilities. However, some municipalities are prohibited by law from investing in certain types of securities. For example, state law prohibits California County and City Treasuries from investing in equities or corporate bonds.

Life Insurance Companies

Life insurance companies generally seek to neutralize market risk by matching the duration of their assets and liabilities. However, this matching can be complicated by regulatory accounting rules.[20] The investment decision is further complicated by the wide range of insurance products offered, including policies that pay out on death as well as policies that provide a means of saving and investment.

Funds associated with shareholder reserves tend to be invested in relatively low-risk assets, while funds associated with the statutory surplus[21] tend to be invested in higher risk assets. In the past, insurance companies had low liquidity requirements due to the long-term nature of their business, and could thus concentrate almost exclusively on long-term investing. However, the recent development of short-term insurance products, such as guaranteed investment contracts GICs, and the early termination of longer term products have made liquidity more important.

The advent of GICs has led to segmented portfolios in order to match assets and liabilities more precisely, and has caused the average investment time horizon to fall. Previously, the time horizon of insurance companies had been very long (up to 20 or 40 years), which led to an emphasis on long-term bonds and mortgages. Insurance companies typically hold corporate debt for its higher yield to fund projected long-term liabilities as well as some government bonds for security and liquidity. In some cases, regulatory requirements restrict investment in foreign and high-yield corporate bonds.

Mutual Funds

Mutual funds raise cash from investors, pool these monies and invest in a range of investments. Since mutual funds pursue varying objectives, they hold a wide range of bonds. Although mutual funds tend to have a "yield first" (low-risk) focus, high-yield bonds might also be included in the portfolio. Corporate debt is often used in an attempt to maximize both yield and total return. Some mutual funds actively trade bonds, while others pursue a more passive 'buy and hold' approach. Legal (or self-imposed investment constraints) have prohibited mutual funds from taking short positions and transacting in derivatives. Many mutual funds have maturity constraints. Some are required to hold bonds with maturities of no more than 10 years.

Asset Managers

Asset managers manage funds on behalf of institutions – such as an endowment or pension fund. The distinguishing feature about asset managers is their focus on the target benchmark. That is, performance and risk exposure are assessed on a relative as opposed to an absolute basis – that is, the focus is on relative return and tracking error.

Corporations

Although many large corporations are on the supply side of the fixed income market, corporates are also a source of demand. Corporations tend to be concerned with asset–liability matching and limiting the currency and interest rate exposures generated from their underlying business. The investment horizon tends to be short term and linked to free cash flow. Although swaps are often used to hedge interest rate risk or exploit credit arbitrage opportunities, most corporates are traditional "real money" investors – holding long bond positions. Some corporate treasuries pursue explicitly speculative strategies – where positions have no link to the underlying business – with the intention of boosting profits.

Commercial Banks

Commercial bank profits are determined by the spread between the cost of funds (raised on a variable short-term basis) and the yield earned from lending funds and investing in securities. Commercial banks prefer stable and predictable earnings, and this is achieved by matching assets and liabilities – both in terms of maturity and interest rate variability. Some banks will also take positions on interest rates – for example, increasing the level of floating rate assets relative to floating rate liabilities when rates are expected to rise. Asset swaps are quite useful for all of these ends. Without asset swaps, many commercial banks would be unable to invest in fixed income securities due to the floating nature of their liabilities.

Commercial banks require liquid investments to maintain capital adequacy ratios, meet withdrawal requirements of depositors, and provide loans to customers. Moreover, banks are generally unwilling to issue CDs with maturities longer than five years due to the volatility of interest rates and loan demand. As a result, the investment horizon is relatively short.

Commercial banks invest primarily in government issues due to their low-risk and liquid nature, and are an important source of demand for corporate floating rate notes. Pass-through securities are generally avoided due to their prepayment risk.

Hedge Funds

Although the hedge fund universe is quite diverse, hedge funds typically have three aspects in common: (1) the use of leverage; (2) the use of short positions; and (3) the focus on total return. Hedge funds actively invest in a variety of asset classes, and pursue directional as well as market-neutral strategies. The time horizon is a function of the strategy pursued, but generally is short to medium term. In contrast to asset managers concerned with asset allocation and relative return, the key determinants for hedge funds executing a trading strategy are funding cost and total return.

Proprietary Traders

Traders are purely speculators. The objective of traders is to earn excess returns by taking on the risk that others in the market do not want or are not allowed to take. In other words, traders buy/sell when investors are selling/buying. Traders have no constraints – outside of those imposed by their employer and creditors – in terms of the use of derivatives, shorting, or leverage. The time horizon is very short, with some positions held for a matter of weeks, days, or even hours.

* * *

The investment process begins by examining the objectives and constraints of the investor. The results of this examination are then used to determine the investor's position in the trade-off between risk and reward. Armed with an understanding of where the investor stands in this trade-off, one can begin to form an investment strategy. We now turn our focus to the different frameworks used to construct individual portfolios.

9.3 PORTFOLIO MANAGEMENT

The overall strategy for the portfolio is one of the mechanisms used to translate the investor's risk tolerance into practical parameters. The structuring of specific trades is the other mechanism. At the heart of a portfolio strategy is the decision to engage in passive, structured, or active management. A passive portfolio strategy targets market performance, represented by a preselected benchmark index.[22] Passive management (also called indexing) offers the lowest risk and the lowest expected return of the three management styles. A structured portfolio strategy (also called asset–liability management or ALM) targets income – at an amount sufficient to meet future obligations. Active management – generally through the anticipation of interest rate or spread changes – targets total return but at greater risk. Elements of these three approaches can also be combined, providing a spectrum of possibilities.

The choice between passive, structural and active portfolio management depends on the nature of your liabilities and whether you believe markets are efficient (or that market inefficiencies are not exploitable). Passive indexing can be used to obtain the desired breadth of security diversification while minimizing transaction costs and management fees. For a pension fund or life insurance company with a future liability stream which needs to be satisfied, a structured strategy may be more appropriate than passive indexing – as market returns may

154   Fixed Income Strategy

Table 9.3 Portfolio strategies and investor types

Investor type	Portfolio strategy	Return objective	Curve bias
Mutual funds (some)	Passive	Relative return (with respect to a benchmark)	Long end
Life insurers, Pension funds	Structural (ALM)	Income (a focus on yield)	Long end
Commercial banks	Structural (ALM)	Positive spread between lending and financing	Short end
Hedge funds, Traders	Active	Absolute, total return (a focus on capital gain)	No bias

not be sufficient to satisfy future liabilities. For the investor that believes in market efficiency – that is, that portfolio managers are unable to outperform the market – passive management might be more appropriate.

Although research strongly indicates that active investment managers are, on average, unable to outperform the market after fees over extended periods, an investor may prefer active portfolio management. During bear markets active management is particularly palatable. Moreover, exploitable market imperfections (though transient) and managers with superior analytical skills (though difficult to identify) do exist, and managers have outperformed the market after fees (sometimes spectacularly) for periods of time. The distribution of hedge fund returns, for example, is positively skewed, which suggests that mispricing opportunities *are* being identified and exploited (Lavinio, 2000).

9.3.1 Passive Portfolio Management

Passive fixed income portfolio strategies target benchmark performance by mirroring the duration of a preselected market index. Other benchmark risk factors may be matched exactly or allow for minor mismatches. Trades produced by passive portfolios are the result of portfolio rebalancing – required because of duration changes that result simply from the passage of time – and have nothing to do with mispricing opportunities.[23] Rebalancing is most frequent when market volatility is high.

Passive strategies involve taking long positions in the bond. In other words, there are no short positions and derivatives are not used. Reasons to take a long position in a particular bond include: greater liquidity, larger convexity, price advantage, lower risk premium, high return prospects, and best risk–reward.

Some of the largest pension funds, endowments, and insurance companies have placed a significant portion, if not all, of their fixed income assets in index-tracking funds. Investors have turned to indexes for higher long-term returns, more consistent performance, lower management fees, fewer transactions, and more control over the investment decision.[24] Indexing and enhanced indexing are two methods used to passively manage a portfolio.

Indexing

Indexing involves the full replication of a benchmark (buying all the bonds in the proper proportions). In practice, this is very difficult and costly to accomplish. For example, the

Lehman Aggregate Index is based on over 5,000 bonds – many of which are illiquid. Instead of buying all the bonds in an index, securities can be selected that replicate different characteristics of the index – such as duration, coupon, maturity, sector, credit rating, or call features. Research indicates that a desired target can be replicated with less than 40 securities (Evans and Archer, 1968; McEnally and Boardman, 1979).

Any discrepancy in the performance of the portfolio versus the benchmark is reported as the tracking error. Tracking error is the result of transaction costs in constructing the portfolio, differences in composition between the index and portfolio (in terms of duration, curve, and sector allocations), and pricing discrepancies (since the execution price of a trade may differ from the price used to compile the index).

One way to enhance passive investment returns is to intelligently manage the necessary transactions when indexes change their constituents or weightings. The disadvantage of indexing is the poor performance during periods of rising interest rates and the incremental returns foregone by not investing in high-performance instruments outside the benchmark. This opportunity cost can be high as many fixed income sectors are excluded from the broad market benchmarks. Enhanced indexing addresses these problems.

Enhanced Indexing

Enhanced indexing is a hybrid of passive indexing and active management with the objective of outperforming benchmark targets (by 50 to 300 bps) while still maintaining a low-risk profile. One technique is to match duration but allow small and controlled deviations from the benchmark in terms of cash flow, sector, quality, and call features. Another technique is to passively index the core of the portfolio and allow active management in the remaining periphery with a certain degree of prescribed latitude.

The enhanced performance achieved from the active management component depends on the risk associated with the benchmark, the strategies employed, the latitude given to deviate from the benchmark, and the level of volatility in interest rates and spreads. Although greater latitude means greater potential to enhance returns, it also means greater risk of underperforming the benchmark. Investors unwilling to accept interim underperformance and higher fees should not choose enhanced indexing.

9.3.2 Structured Portfolio Management (Asset–Liability Management or ALM)

In contrast with passive strategies that target market performance, a structured portfolio strategy targets liabilities – or rather, a level of income sufficient to meet future obligations. For pension funds and insurance companies, the income target would be linked to future retirement obligations and insurance claims. For endowments, the income target would be linked to required expenditures. Structured strategies are also appropriate for banks.

Much like enhanced indexing, structured strategies target duration while allowing for some enhancement of returns via active management. In this case, however, the targeted duration is with respect to future liabilities (as opposed to the duration of a benchmark index). Without this matching of assets and liabilities, investors would be fully exposed to interest rate risk. Hence, the essence of a structured strategy is to lock in a prevailing market return while at the same time controlling interest rate risk.[25]

Immunization and dedication are two types of structured portfolio strategies. Immunization protects investors from small parallel shifts in the yield curve, while dedication protects investors from non-parallel shifts. Both strategies use portfolio optimization techniques and are based on linear models to forecast risk. More recently, modern asset liability management (MALM) has shifted to the use of non-linear risk forecasting models, such as VAR and Monte Carlo simulation. These non-linear models take direct account of volatilities and correlations among instruments (Gibson, 1997).

Immunization

An immunization strategy constructs a portfolio which matches the average modified duration of future cash flows such that the fixed income returns on the portfolio fund future payouts. By replicating the modified duration of liabilities, the portfolio assets neutralize the investor's exposure to small parallel shifts in the yield curve. However, the investor still remains exposed to non-parallel shifts in the yield curve.

The continuous matching of the duration of assets and liabilities requires frequent rebalancing due to market volatility and the passage of time (since asset and liability durations decay at different rates). These rebalancing transactions can create quite unpredictable realized capital gains/losses that may not be appropriate for the investor. However, rebalancing affords a chance to benefit from mispricing opportunities which can add incremental value. Alternatively, futures contracts can be used to match the duration of liabilities, allowing a portfolio to be selected without regard for duration.

Consider a one-period immunization that requires funding a liability 5 years from today. The purchase of a 5-year zero coupon bond maturing on the liability payment date, however, is not a sufficient condition for immunization, as two other conditions must also be satisfied: (1) the market value of assets must be greater than or equal to the present value of the liabilities in order to ensure that the assets will grow to equal or exceed the future value of the targeted income; and (2) the dispersion of assets (the degree of barbelling) must be greater than or equal to the dispersion of liabilities.[26]

Dedication

A dedicated bond portfolio targets the key rate duration of future cash flows. Specifically, this strategy matches monthly cash flows from a portfolio of bonds to a prespecified set of monthly cash liabilities. By replicating the key rate durations of the cash flows, the portfolio avoids exposure to market and yield curve risk – that is, both parallel and non-parallel shifts in the yield curve.[27]

Trades produced by dedicated portfolios are the result of rebalancing required by changes in key rate durations as well as mispricing opportunities. Rebalancing dedicated portfolios is less of a problem than with immunized portfolios because key rate matching requires fewer transactions (Christensen and Fabozzi, 1997). Although dedicated portfolios protect investors from all types of yield curve shifts, they are more expensive to implement than immunized portfolios.

9.3.3 Active Portfolio Management

An active portfolio strategy targets performance that exceeds the benchmark. Active portfolio managers must produce a return in excess of transaction costs and their higher management fees in order to add value. To generate such returns, positions must be taken that differ from the market consensus. The latitude given to managers to take positions that deviate from the benchmark depends on the investor's risk tolerance. Active strategies may be anticipatory or responsive.

Directional Strategies

Directional (or market timing) strategies seek to profit from correctly anticipating directional changes in market interest rates – not necessarily due to market inefficiencies, but due to slow information flow, emotions, or errors that cause prices to deviate from forecasted equilibrium levels. As success depends upon the ability to predict market moves and identify mispricing opportunities (i.e. access to better information and exceptionally skilled analysis), market timing strategies are heavily exposed to model and event risk.

Market timing strategies – which involve long (and/or short) positions in bonds – are most successful in inefficient markets. If desired, interest rate risk can be hedged by combining long and short bond positions. A "long/short" strategy that retains a long bias invests in a core holding of assets and then partially hedges the long position with short sales of other bonds or bond derivatives.[28] Ideally, returns resemble that of a call option with full/partial participation in bull markets and protection against losses in bear markets. The short position adds value by: (1) capitalizing on the spread earned between the long and short position; and (2) hedging market risk (with profits from buying back the borrowed security at a lower price in a bear market). Short selling exposes the investor to the risk of short squeezes that cause a sudden increase in demand and price of the borrowed asset. The key driver of performance with the "long/short" strategy is security selection.

Relative Value Strategies

In contrast to market timing strategies which seek to capitalize on anticipated changes in market direction, relative value (RV) strategies seek to capitalize on anticipated changes in bond spreads of related securities and their derivatives. Specifically, RV strategies anticipate that the price difference of two bonds reverts back to some "normal" level after moving apart from each other. This is essentially a mean reversion strategy.

Market-neutral RV strategies seek to generate returns in both bull and bear markets by neutralizing exposure to interest rate risk. A market-neutral strategy is implemented by establishing simultaneously a long position in an undervalued security and an equal short position in an overvalued security (i.e. fixed income arbitrage[29]). Another market-neutral strategy is to buy value and strength (focus on the very best bonds), essentially a "buy high and sell higher" technique. Specific market-neutral spread strategies include:

- *Arbitrage between similar bonds* – such as a long position in an underpriced 7-year duration UK Gilt and a short position in an overpriced UK Gilt of the same duration (duration neutral arbitrage). This often involves cheapest-to-deliver bonds underlying a futures contract on the bond, or on-the-run versus off-the-run issues (short the latest issue of 10-year Gilts and long the second most recent issue).
- *Arbitrage along the yield curve (butterfly trades)* – such as a long position in "cheap" 7- and 9-year bonds and a short position in "rich" 8-year bonds. Relative mispricings along the yield curve often occur due to high institutional demand for certain maturity bonds.
- *Arbitrage between physical securities and their futures (basis trades)* – such as a long position in an underpriced German 10-year Bund and a short position in an overpriced German

10-year Bund future. Bond futures have a delivery option and a wild card option, which can generate arbitrage opportunities.
- *Convertible bond arbitrage* is based on inefficient pricing in the relationship between the bond and stock option (particularly during volatile periods). The strategy involves taking long positions in "cheap" convertible securities and hedging the equity risk (by selling short the corresponding stock, stock option, stock index future, or stock index option). A long position in a convertible bond is long stock price volatility. When the convertible bond price reaches its "fair" value, the position is cashed out. The optimal trade involves credit healthy companies with overvalued stocks (Jaeger, 2002). In addition to the normal arbitrage risks (discussed below), convertible bond arbitrage is subject to equity and volatility risk.
- *TED spread trades* anticipate a change in the TED spread. A basic form of the TED spread trade involves a long position in Treasury bill futures and an equal short position in Eurodollar futures with the same expiration month (or vice versa).[30] Eurodollar time deposits, which are not backed by the full faith and credit of the US government, offer higher rates of return than Treasury bills to reflect their additional credit risk. Hence, the TED spread can be thought of as the risk premium associated with investing in uninsured bank debt as opposed to riskless Treasuries. As such, the Treasury bill–Eurodollar spread is generally traded as an option on "flight-to-quality". The TED spread widens in response to global financial or political crises as investors flock to the traditional safe haven, short-term US Treasuries. High interest rates, bear equity markets, and a severe global recession are also associated with a wide TED spread. On the other hand, low interest rates and economic recovery usually decrease the probability of defaults on bank loans and reduce funding problems for the banking sector, narrowing the TED spread. When the TED spread is tight, the TED spread trade is a cheap bet on general credit deterioration or economic uncertainty with limited downside.

Non-market-neutral RV strategies seek to benefit from changes in interest rates as well as changes in spreads. Examples include:

- *Yield curve spread trading (yield curve arbitrage)* is based on a particular forecast on the future shape of the yield curve with exposure to duration and convexity risk. For example, going long the short end of the curve and going short the long-end of the curve in anticipation of curve steepening.
- *Credit spread trading (credit arbitrage)* is based on the identification of yield curve differentials for securities with different, but closely related, credit qualities. For example, going long a AA-rated bond with a spread to Treasuries of 80 bps and going short a AAA-rated bond with a spread to Treasuries of 50 bps. Alternatively, investors unable to take short positions could hold a "credit barbell", where credit risk in shorter maturities is offset by safe government issues in longer maturities.
- *Other spread trading* opportunities include: (1) corporate versus government bond yield spreads; (2) municipal versus government bond yield spreads; (3) cash versus futures; and (4) on-the-run versus off-the-run bonds.

Profits are realized on RV strategies when mispricings disappear and prices return to fair value. The mispricing of bonds might be the result of sudden market events, exogenous shocks to supply or demand, maturity preferences of investors, restrictions on investors (to certain credit ratings or maturities), unanticipated credit downgrades, complex options features, deliverable characteristics for a futures contract, and complex cash flow properties. RV investors are often long and short in equal amounts of securities with similar but unequal liquidity and credit quality. Hence, a spread is earned for holding less liquid or lower credit quality instruments. RV strategies with a positive financing spread (positive carry) make profits even if the mispricing persists. Relative value strategies involve a number of risks, including:

- *Model risk* – The complex interactions of fixed income instruments (including yield curves, volatility, credit spreads, expected cash flows, and option features) may be misspecified or misapplied, generating false valuation signals.
- *Event risk* – Market stress situations, particularly extreme flight-to-quality events often trigger a breakdown in the historical correlation between corresponding instruments. Even under normal conditions, mispricings may persist for extended periods.
- *Liquidity risk* – Often fixed income arbitrageurs are short liquidity. In other words, they hold a long position on a comparatively illiquid security and an offsetting short position on a relatively liquid asset, thereby earning a liquidity premium. Short positions are susceptible to short squeezes, and leveraged positions are vulnerable to larger haircuts.[31]
- *Credit risk* – RV strategies by definition involve holding securities with wider spreads (lower credit quality). Some of the credit risk is hedged by the corresponding short position.
- *Interest rate risk* – Some market neutral strategies are contingent on low financing costs and are therefore affected by higher financing costs from rising interest rates.
- *Legal/tax risks* – Changes in taxes and regulations can cause a stable relationship between two instruments to dissolve.

Relative value strategies perform well during times when there is a low likelihood of financial distress and in markets with constant (or slowly changing) volatility and correlation between fixed income instruments. However, these strategies are exposed to potentially large losses in times of severe financial distress.

Reactive Strategies

Non-expectational strategies respond to – rather than forecast – changes in interest rates and yield spreads. In other words, reactive strategies ride with the market, rather than fight it (Fong, 1997). Momentum and duration-based mean reversion are two types of reactive strategies.

Momentum

A momentum strategy follows a trend, buying in an uptrend and selling in a downtrend. The trend-following tactic is to stay in markets with major trends and get out once the trend changes. With this strategy, one can never buy a market too high or sell a market too low. The most critical factor is not the *timing* of the trade, but rather how much to trade over the course of the trend. Trend-following involves the identification of short-term trends (using statistical methods) and is implemented by opportunistically switching between long- and short-term bond instruments. Alternatively, a synthetic call option can be created on the best performing maturity sector.

Duration-Based Mean Reversion

This strategy assumes mean reversion in interest rates. Constant duration strategies maintain a fixed duration over a complete interest rate cycle. Duration-averaging strategies extend duration as interest rates rise and shorten duration as interest rates fall.

Table 9.4 Portfolio management summary

Portfolio strategy	Position description
Passive	Buy and hold (long only position)
Structural (ALM)	Buy and hold (long only position)
Active: Directional	Long, short, or long/short positions
Active: Relative value	Long/short combinations
Active: Momentum	Series of longs or shorts depending on the direction of the trend; buy in a uptrend and sell in a downtrend
Active: Mean reversion	Buy the dips and sell the rallies

Our view of the world relative to market expectations tells us where the yield curve is most likely headed, while our objectives and constraints dictate our capacity to take risk and the relevant portfolio strategy. The next task is to construct transactions that achieve the desired risk exposure. We discuss this in the next chapter.

NOTES

1. The specific measure used in the inflation adjustment is CPI-U, the non-seasonally adjusted index of urban consumer price inflation published by the US Bureau of Labor Statistics.
2. TIPS are not as actively traded as conventional Treasuries, which could make them more difficult to sell if they are not held until maturity.
3. An unrealistically small rate of implied break-even inflation for the term of a bond would indicate the effect of liquidity preferences.
4. Individual investors (via mutual funds) dominate the municipal bond market, showing a preference for the long end of the curve. Pension funds, commercial banks and property/casualty insurance companies occasionally cross over into this market (and with big effect) when valuations relative to taxable bonds become cheap.
5. High-grade municipal issuers can come to market with relative ease in a weak market environment.
6. For a history of defaults on municipal bonds, see Chapter 2 in Sylvan G. Feldstein and Frank J. Fabozzi, *The Dow Jones-Irwin Guide to Municipal Bonds* (Homewood, IL: Dow Jones-Irwin, 1987). For more information on managing municipal bond portfolios, see Slater, Jeffrey D. (1997). "Managing Municipal Bond Portfolios." In F. Fabozzi (ed.), *Managing Fixed Income Portfolios*. New Hope, Pennsylvannia: Frank J. Fabozzi Associates.
7. Based on Standard & Poor's rating scale.
8. For more information on managing a high-yield bond portfolio, see Madden, J.T. and Balestrino, J. (1997). "Management of a High-Yield Bond Portfolio." In F. Fabozzi (ed.), *Managing Fixed Income Portfolios*. New Hope, Pennsylvannia: Frank J. Fabozzi Associates.
9. The advantage of owning a convertible bond as opposed to the equity is that downside equity risk is reduced by the coupon income from the bond. The premium paid to own the convertible bond, however, curtails the investor's upside potential from increases in the value of the equity.
10. When a declining stock price pulls down the value of the bond, the convertible is "busted". For more information about the advantages of investing in busted convertible bonds, see Leach, W.R. (1997). "Using Busted Convertibles to Enhance Performance." In F. Fabozzi (ed.), *Managing Fixed Income Portfolios*. New Hope, Pennsylvannia: Frank J. Fabozzi Associates.
11. Conversely, inverse floaters pay lower coupon rates when interest rates rise. Hence, investors in inverse floaters benefit from falling interest rates.
12. Derivatives are discussed in more detail in Chapter 1.
13. The specific bonds that the seller can deliver to satisfy the futures contract are published by the futures exchange prior to the initial trading of the contract.

14. Goldman Sachs offers an option on the slope of the yield curve, called SYCURVE. The call/put option represents the right to buy/sell specific segments of the yield curve.
15. For a broad overview of the currency hedging debate, see Gary L. Gastineau, "The Currency Hedging Decision: A Search for Synthesis in Asset Allocation." *Financial Analysts Journal* (May–June 1995), pp. 8–17.
16. For assistance with developing a currency strategy, see Callum Henderson's *Currency Strategy: The Practitioner's Guide to Currency Investing, Hedging and Forecasting.* New York: John Wiley & Sons (2002).
17. The annual average contribution of currency movements to the total return of the Salomon Brothers Non-US Dollar World Government Bond Index for the period 1985–1995 was 92% – ranging from a low of 85% to a high of 103%. The annual average contribution of currency movements to the total return of Salomon Brothers World Bond Market Performance Index for the period 1978–1995 was also 92%. Currency becomes even more important as the time period is shortened. (Calculations based on data presented in Steward and Greshin (1997a, 1997b).)
18. Contrary to the generally accepted belief that diversification into foreign bonds provides significant risk reduction, Rosenberg (1997) finds only a fairly modest reduction on an unhedged basis with a passively managed portfolio. Moreover, on a hedged basis, international diversification may even be more expensive (allowing for hedging costs) than not hedging currency risk at all.
19. Some pension funds also have limitations on MTNs and foreign corporate debt.
20. For example, US accounting rules require one side of the balance sheet to be carried at market value and the other side of the balance sheet to be carried at book value. As a result, there is an inability to liquidate portfolios without impairing the statutory surplus in an environment of rising interest rates.
21. By law, insurers must have reserves to pay the actuarially estimated cost of future claims. This surplus affects an insurance company's ability to write new business as well as its financial position/rating (which affects its ability to attract new business).
22. Risk exposure may be high or low depending on the benchmark chosen.
23. The durations of the benchmark and the portfolio held to mimic the benchmark decay at different rates.
24. Mossavar-Rahmani (1997) notes that index fund fees average 5–17 bps. Management of a customized benchmark might run 20 bps, while managed funds in excess of $1 billion might run 1–2 bps. In contrast, active management fees average 30–75 bps.
25. Only simply structured bonds (those without variable cash flows) are relevant for structured portfolios.
26. This is discussed in more detail in the Appendix to Chapter 10.
27. Matching key rate duration ensures that the portfolio has the same convexity as the liabilities (see Chapter 1).
28. A strategy which retains a short bias can be implemented by partially hedging short sales with long positions or out-of-the-money call options.
29. Arbitrage in this sense is not to be mistaken for 'risk-free' profits. A fixed income arbitrage strategy earns a spread by taking on risk.
30. The TED spread is defined as the Treasury bill futures price less the Eurodollar futures price. This is equivalent to the implied Eurodollar rate less the implied Treasury bill rate.
31. A "short squeeze" occurs when there is an insufficient supply of bonds (relative to demand) to deliver on short positions (i.e. shorting risk). A "haircut" is the amount of collateral required for margin accounts.

RECOMMENDED READING

Jaeger, L. (2002). *Managing Risk in Alternative Investment Strategies: Successful Investing in Hedge Funds and Managed Futures.* London: FT Prentice Hall.

Fabozzi, F. (1997). *The Handbook of Fixed Income Securities* (5th edn). New York: McGraw-Hill.

10
Fixed Income Trading

Active managers must justify their fees by generating returns that sufficiently exceed the target benchmark. This means taking on additional risk. That is, taking positions that differ from the benchmark. We know from Chapters 1 and 2 that the primary sources of risk for a fixed income investor stem from the uncertainty surrounding changes in the interest rate, yield curve, credit spread, and volatility, and with the benefit of Chapters 3–8 we can carefully craft forecasts on these factors. We also know from Chapter 9 what risks to take on, depending on what type of investor we are. How to manage the excess exposure taken against the benchmark – that is, how to place bets that the market is wrong – is the focus of this chapter.

The chapter is organized by risk exposure (see Table 10.1). We first consider "duration" trades, which are bets on market direction alone. Recall from Chapter 1 that duration accounts for only small parallel shifts in the yield curve. Next, we examine "curve" trades, which are bets on changes in the slope of the yield curve, as well as "combination" trades, which bet on changes in direction and slope together. Finally, we consider "spread" and "volatility" trades. Spread trades handle cross-market bets (between two yield curves), while volatility trades address convexity exposure.

Table 10.1 Targeted risk exposure and forecast scenarios

Risk exposure	Type of bet	Forecast scenario
Duration	Market direction	Bull, bear
Curve	Slope	Steepen, flatten
Combination	Direction + Slope	Bull[1]/bear steepener
Combination	Direction + Slope	Bull/bear flattener
Spread	Country/credit	Widen, narrow
Volatility	Convexity	High, low

Within each classification of trades, a number of scenarios – representing different forecasts and investor types – are considered. The risk preferences of the different investor types are represented by three different trades: (1) the basic trade, representing more risk-neutral investors (such as pension funds, insurance companies and commercial banks) with total return objectives; (2) a more conservative trade addressed to handle more of the downside risk, representing more risk-averse investors (such as endowments) with income objectives; and (3) a more aggressive trade designed to take more advantage of the upside potential, representing more risk-seeking investors (such as hedge funds and proprietary traders) with capital gains objectives.

10.1 MARKET DIRECTIONAL BETS

This section considers *market direction trades* with a *neutral curve shape* view (Table 10.2). A market direction bet is either bearish or bullish. Investors are bearish/bullish if they, relative to what is priced into the market, anticipate a rate increase/decrease. Market direction bets

Table 10.2 Trades that execute market directional bets

Investor's expectation (in contrast with the market consensus)	Trade
Interest rates expected to fall	Extend duration
Interest rates expected to rise	Shorten duration

are based on an anticipated parallel shift in the yield curve. As such, market direction bets are implemented by taking duration positions that deviate from the benchmark. Pure market direction trades are most effective when changes in the shape of the yield curve are likely to be insignificant.

A position that is long/short duration means that the duration of the portfolio is larger/smaller than that of the benchmark. Duration is increased/decreased when interest rates are expected to fall/rise as a portfolio with longer/shorter duration outperforms the benchmark during market rallies/contractions. There are a number of ways to alter the duration of a portfolio including: (1) selling or buying bonds; (2) using interest rate swaps; and (3) buying or selling interest rate futures.

Scenario 10.1

The investor expects the ECB at its next policy meeting to cut interest rates by more than the market is currently discounting. The investor believes that the shape of the yield curve will remain largely intact after the move. The investor is cash constrained in that purchases must be financed by sales of other assets.

- *The basic strategy* is to execute a cash-neutral duration extension – that is, sell at the short end of the curve (such as 1s or cash) and buy at the long end of the curve (such as 20s).[2] Extending duration increases the bond price response to a cut in interest rates via positive convexity. In a normal environment where the yield curve is upward sloping, the trade also benefits from positive carry and a roll-down advantage which provides a cushion against downside risk if rates should happen to rise or be left unchanged. The steeper the curve, the larger the cushion. Note that curve flattening and an increase in expected volatility also enhance the profitability of this trade (Table 10.3).
- *A more conservative trade* would temper the extension in duration. That is, sell 1s and buy 10s.
- *A more aggressive trade* would use leverage. That is, extend duration through the purchase of interest rate futures on margin. Alternatively, use derivatives to extend duration beyond what can be achieved in the bond market.

Table 10.3 Cash-neutral duration extension trade

Profit:	↓ interest rates, positive carry, roll (also curve flattening and ↑ volatility)		
Loss:	↑ interest rates (enough to offset carry and roll)		

Position	Structure	Weight	Matching
Long	Long end (20s)	+100%	Cash
Short	Short end (1s or cash)	−100%	Cash

Conversely, if the investor expects the ECB to raise rates more aggressively during the investment horizon (in contrast to market expectations of more subdued increases), then to capitalize on an anticipated bond market sell-off which leaves the shape of the yield curve intact, the investor would execute a cash-neutral duration shortener – that is, sell long-duration bonds (such as 20s) and buy shorter duration bonds (such as 2s). By shortening duration, investors reduce the sensitivity of the portfolio to interest rate risk – that is, smaller capital losses are incurred when the bond market sells off across the curve. This trade also benefits from curve steepening and a reduction in expected volatility. Since this trade has negative carry in a normal curve environments, there is the potential to lose money even if the increase in interest rates is correctly anticipated (Table 10.4).

Table 10.4 Cash-neutral duration shortener trade

Reduced losses: ↑ interest rates (also curve steepening and ↓ volatility)
Loss: ↓ interest rates, negative carry in normal yield curve environment

Position	Structure	Weight	Matching
Long	Short end (2s)	+100%	Cash
Short	Long end (20s)	−100%	Cash

10.2 YIELD CURVE BETS: STEEPENERS AND FLATTENERS

This section considers *yield curve trades* with a *neutral duration* view. Yield curve bets anticipate changes in the slope of the yield curve and, as such, involve allocating securities across the maturity spectrum different from that of the benchmark. One type of yield curve bet capitalizes on anticipated steepening or flattening in the yield curve over a particular maturity range. A curve steepens/flattens when the yield spread between the long and short end of the curve widens/narrows. Another type of yield curve bet capitalizes on changes in curvature.

Pure curve bets (Table 10.5) involve selecting a maturity allocation which is different from the maturity allocation of the benchmark while at the same time replicating the duration of the benchmark. The maturity allocation of a portfolio is altered using different combinations of bullet and barbell structures.[3] Distributional differences are important when the yield curve changes shape frequently and/or when changes in shape are of substantial magnitude.

Pure yield curve trades are useful for those investors that may wish, or be required, to match the duration of a benchmark. Neutral market exposure is also recommended when: (1) there is a lack of clarity with respect to the timing and/or direction of future curve shifts; (2) directional

Table 10.5 Trades that execute pure yield curve bets

Investor's expectation (in contrast with the market consensus)	Trade
Yield curve expected to steepen	Duration-neutral steepener
Yield curve expected to flatten	Duration-neutral flattener
Curvature expected to rise/fall	Duration-neutral butterfly

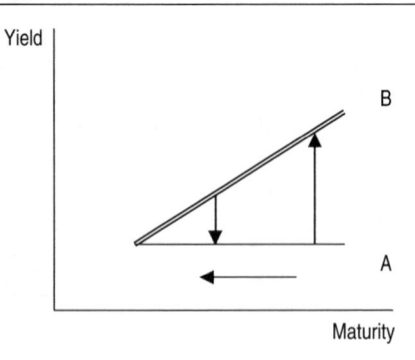

Figure 10.1 Curve steepener

expectations are in line with the market consensus; or (3) overall direction is expected to remain range bound (close to current levels).

Scenario 10.2

The investor expects that the UK Gilt curve will steepen over the investment horizon, with no overall bias on whether market direction will be up or down (Figure 10.1).

- *The basic strategy* is executed using a duration-neutral curve steepener – that is, sell a longer term bond (such as 20s) and buy a duration-matched amount of shorter dated bonds (such as 2s). This trade is long the short end of the curve and short the long end of the curve. The cash generated from the sale of the longer bullet will be insufficient to purchase the duration-matched amount of the shorter bullet. Hence, the trade requires drawing down cash balances or borrowing, which is a problem for the cash-constrained investor. Note that an unexpected decrease in volatility will enhance the performance of this trade. Still, the trade suffers from a roll-down disadvantage and has the potential for negative carry[4] if the yield curve is upward sloping – which puts the trade in the red from the beginning. In order to generate a profit on this trade, the capital gain earned from curve steepening must at least offset the roll-down disadvantage and negative carry. This trade is even more unattractive if the required change in yield is historically large. Hence, this trade requires a strong view about curve steepening – not just a firm belief that the curve will steepen, but also that the magnitude of the change in the curve will be large enough to generate a profit (Table 10.6).
- *A more conservative trade* would narrow the maturity range of the trade, focusing on a range in the curve where there is less of a carry disadvantage. This would also reduce the added cash requirement.
- *A more aggressive trade* would leverage up the position.

Conversely, if the UK Gilt curve is expected to flatten over the investment horizon, the investor who wishes to be insulated from parallel curve shifts would execute a duration-neutral curve flattener – that is, sell the short end of the curve (such as 1s) and buy a duration-matched amount of longer dated bonds (such as 10s).

This duration-neutral flattener benefits from a roll-down advantage and has the potential for positive carry if the yield curve has an upward slope. Intuitively, this trade replaces a bullet which has no roll and a yield disadvantage with a bullet at a yield gain and with roll. The carry

Table 10.6 Duration-neutral curve steepener trade

Profit:	significant curve steepening (also ↓ volatility)		
Loss:	curve flattening, possible negative carry, roll disadvantage		

Position	Structure	Weight	Matching
Long	Bullet 2s	+135%[a]	Duration
Short	Bullet 20s	−100% and −cash 35%	Duration

[a]These weightings are illustrative.

Table 10.7 Duration-neutral curve flattener trade

Profit:	curve flattening, possible positive carry, roll advantage (also ↑ volatility)		
Loss:	curve steepening		

Position	Structure	Weight	Matching
Long	Bullet 10s	+65% and +cash 35%[a]	Duration
Short	Bullet 1s	−100%	Duration

[a]These weightings are illustrative.

and roll provide a cushion which allows the investor to profit even if the curve should happen to steepen a bit or does not change shape at all. A sudden increase in volatility will also boost the performance of this trade (Table 10.7).

Pure shifts and pure pivots in the yield curve are rare. In fact, research suggests that the most common yield curve shifts are: (1) a downward shift combined with steepening ("bull steepener") where the interest rate decrease is largest at the short end of the curve and diminishes with maturity; and (2) an upward shift combined with flattening ("bear flattener") where the interest rate increase is largest at the short end of the curve and diminishes with maturity (Jones, 1991). Investors can manage these mixed exposures by taking simultaneous duration and maturity allocation positions that differ from the benchmark. The idea is to decrease (or increase) duration in anticipation of movements in market direction while at the same time concentrating exposure on maturity sectors that appear to offer the best returns over the investment horizon.

Irrespective of the type of steepener – pure steepener, bull steepener or bear steepener – the structure of the trade will be the same; that is, sell the long end and buy the short end. The difference will be in the relative magnitude of the purchases and sales, which will calibrate the duration. Similarly, irrespective of the type of flattener, the structure of the trade will be the same – that is, sell the short end and buy the long end. Again, the difference will be in the size of the long position taken relative to the size of the short position, all depending on the durational view.

10.3 YIELD CURVE BETS: RISING AND FALLING CURVATURE

Another type of change in the yield curve involves non-uniform changes in the slope of the curve – that is, changes in curvature.

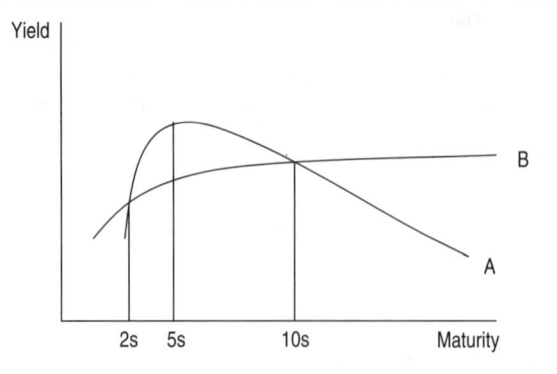

Figure 10.2 Decreasing curvature

Scenario 10.3

An investor has identified a suspected anomaly in the shape of the curve and suspects that this is just temporary. Specifically, 5s look cheap relative to 2s and 10s. In other words, the curve looks particularly concave (or humped) in this region (Figure 10.2).

- *The basic strategy* is executed using a duration-neutral butterfly which sells a barbell of short- and long-term bonds (in this case 2s and 10s) and buys a duration-matched bullet of an intermediate bond (5s). The cash generated from the sale of the barbell will be greater than the amount required to purchase the bullet; hence, the trade is not cash neutral. This trade protects the investor from parallel shifts (because of its duration neutrality). If the yield curve has a normal concave shape – that is, the rising slope increases at a decreasing rate – this trade also benefits from positive carry. Because this is not a cash-neutral trade, however, the carry advantage is not maximized.[5] Note that a sudden decrease in volatility will also improve the performance of this trade (Table 10.8).
- *A more conservative trade* would widen the maturity range of the barbell (to 2s and 30s); evenly space the maturity of the three securities (in order to reduce the correlation between their performance); or maximize the carry advantage with a cash-neutral (bullet overweight) trade.
- Carry-oriented investors or cost-saving issuers might focus on the cash-neutral version of this trade because it maximizes carry gains.

Table 10.8 Decreasing curvature trade

Profit:	↓ curvature, carry, roll (also ↓ volatility)		
Loss:	↑ curvature		

Position	Structure	Weight	Matching
Long	Bullet 5s	+65% and +35% cash[a]	Duration
Short	Barbell 2s and 10s	−100%	Duration

[a] These weightings are illustrative.

Conversely, the investor may believe that 5s look rich relative to 1s and 10s. At the same time the investor wishes to capitalize on this anomaly, the desire is to remain neutral with respect to duration. In this case, the appropriate trade would be a duration-neutral butterfly which sells an intermediate bullet of 5s and buys a duration-matched barbell of short- and long-term bonds (1s and 10s). The cash generated from the sale of the bullet will be insufficient for what is required to purchase the barbell; hence, the trade is not cash neutral (Table 10.9).

This trade suffers from negative carry and a roll-down disadvantage if the yield curve is concave.[6] Intuitively, this trade replaces a bullet which has carry and roll-down advantages with a barbell at a yield loss and less roll – putting the trade in a negative position at the starting point. In order to generate a profit on this trade, the capital gain earned from the change in curvature must at least offset the negative carry and roll-down disadvantage.

Yield curves with greater concavity (more curvature) have even larger negative carry and roll disadvantage – making the trade less attractive, particularly if the required change in yields is historically large. Hence, this trade requires a strong view – not just a firm belief that the curvature will increase, but also that the magnitude of the change in the curve will be large enough to generate a profit. A sudden increase in volatility, however, would boost the profitability of this trade because the barbell has a convexity advantage over the duration-matched bullet.

Table 10.9 Increasing curvature trade

Profit:	↑ curvature (also ↑ volatility)		
Loss:	↓ curvature, negative carry, roll disadvantage		

Position	Structure	Weight	Matching
Long	Barbell 1s and 10s	+105% and +30%[a]	Duration
Short	Bullet 5s	−100% and −35% cash	Duration

[a] These weightings are illustrative.

Although the logic of this trade is the mirror image of a decreasing curvature trade, execution is more complicated. First, the cash generated from the sale of the bullet may be insufficient to finance the purchase of a duration-matched barbell. Hence, the investor must either: (1) have available spare cash; (2) use cash as the short end of the barbell; or (3) be willing to leverage the position.

Second, the proportion of securities purchased for the barbell must mirror the relative durations of the wings. If the wings have durations that are equally distant from the bullet, duration neutrality is achieved by equally splitting the market value produced from the sale of the bullet into the purchase of each wing of the barbell. On the other hand, if the duration distances are asymmetric, a 50/50 split does not produce a duration-neutral trade.

10.4 SPREAD BETS

Thus far we have focused on trades that allocate positions along a single yield curve – that is, within a single segment of the fixed income market. We now expand our focus to consider positions allocated across different yield curves. Spread bets involve trades that adjust the allocation of securities in a portfolio across different segments of the fixed income market. If the investor believes the prevailing spread between two bonds is out of sync with fundamentals, for example, and believes the spread will realign by the end of the investment horizon, a spread bet is taken.

Spread positions can deviate from the benchmark allocation on a number of levels: (1) individual security; (2) industry (such as utilities versus industrial corporate bonds); and (3) bond market (such as government versus corporate bonds). Sector-rotation trades are another type of spread bet. Examples include: (1) rotation of fixed for floating rate securities as a function of inflation expectations; (2) rotation between cyclical and non-cyclical sectors as a function of economic weakness; and (3) rotation between dollar and non-dollar denominated debt as a function of currency weakness.

The allocation of positions across yield curves (i.e. "credit risk allocations") will depend on the anticipated change in spread ("credit spread change") and on the anticipated carry ("credit spread advantage"). Credit upside trades (or credit extensions) extend the credit quality of the portfolio into lower quality tiers in order to capitalize on potential credit-quality improvement (spread narrowing). For example, if corporate spreads are expected to widen over the near term, an investor might temporarily upgrade the average credit rating of the portfolio, await the anticipated spread changes, and reverse the trade at a later date. Note that a tight spread and low volatility environment makes it more difficult to discern relative value opportunities between two curves.

Carry is achieved by switching into higher yielding bonds. Yield spread pick-up trades (or yield extensions) seek to add yield within the duration and credit-quality constraints of a portfolio. In general, yield spread pick-up trades work best during periods of economic growth.

Scenario 10.4

An investor expects the spread between US corporate and government bond yields to narrow – a consequence of an overall improvement in the economy.

- *The basic strategy* is to sell a bullet of US Treasuries and use the proceeds to buy a duration-matched bullet of corporate bonds.[7] This trade profits from a narrowing in the yield spread and benefits from a yield pick-up (Table 10.10).
- *A more conservative trade* would use less risky spread products, such as agencies.
- *A more aggressive trade* might add yield curve exposure, or leverage the position.

Table 10.10 Spread narrowing trade

Profit:	narrowing credit spreads, positive carry		
Loss:	widening credit spreads		

Position	Structure	Weight	Matching
Long	Spread product	+100%	Cash, duration
Short	Benchmark bond	−100%	Cash, duration

Conversely, to profit from an anticipated widening in the spread, the trade would involve the sale of a bullet of US corporates and a purchase of US Treasuries of comparable maturity. This trade profits from a widening in the yield spread, but sacrifices yield. Hence, spreads must widen far enough to offset the loss from the yield loss. Investors that are particularly sensitive to the yield give up can add yield to their portfolios by overweighting agencies instead (Table 10.11).

Table 10.11 Spread widening trade

Profit: widening credit spreads
Loss: narrowing credit spreads, negative carry

Position	Structure	Weight	Matching
Long	Benchmark bond	+100%	Cash, duration
Short	Spread product	−100%	Cash, duration

10.5 VOLATILITY BETS

Volatility is a positive function of uncertainty. The larger the uncertainty, the larger the expected change in interest rates, and the less protection provided by a duration-neutral portfolio. During periods of high interest rate and spread volatility, the opportunity to boost performance is enhanced – due to greater mispricing opportunities, changes in the shape of the yield curve, and fluctuations in yield spreads. Note that volatility has a skewed nature – known as the "Up the staircase, out the window" phenomenon. More specifically, volatility tends to be higher when prices fall (when prices go down they collapse). In contrast, when prices rise, they tend to gradually grind higher.

Volatility bets – positions that deviate from the optionality of the benchmark – can be placed using a number of methods, including: (1) straight bonds (via convexity selection); (2) bonds with embedded options; (3) credit spread trades; (4) options; and (5) swaps. Long volatility trades (buying volatility) profit from rising volatility. Selling volatility means taking positions that will obtain profits in situations where the price is stable. Within all sectors there are bonds that perform well for a particular volatility forecast (Table 10.12).

For straight bonds (bonds without embedded options), the selection of maturity along the yield curve has important implications for volatility exposure as bonds of longer maturity offer a convexity advantage. Convexity, which increases with duration at an increasing rate, is highly valued when volatility is expected to be high. Hence, investors buy volatility at the long end of the yield curve and sell it at the short end. A long bond position is long duration and long convexity – that is, it is long volatility. Short-term bonds exhibit little convexity.

Expected volatility is an important component in the valuation of bonds with embedded options. Mortgage securities and callable corporate bonds generally contain embedded options and are, as a class, substantially affected by volatility forecasts. For bonds with embedded put options, an increase in volatility increases the value of the embedded option to put the bond to the issuer and increases the value of the bond (as the option benefits the investor). Conversely, an increase in interest rate volatility increases the value of the call option, but reduces the price of the bond (as the call option benefits the issuer instead of the investor). In other words, a call option is short volatility and a put option is long volatility. Hence, long positions in bonds with embedded call options are short volatility trades, while long positions in bonds with embedded put options are long volatility trades.[8]

An increase in volatility decreases the value of spread products such as corporates or mortgages because the market assigns a greater value to more liquid securities. Spreads between callable and non-callable bonds change as a result of expected changes in both the direction of interest rates and interest rate volatility. An expected drop/rise in the level of interest rates will widen/narrow the yield spread between callable and non-callable bonds as the prospect that

Table 10.12 Trades that execute volatility bets

Trade	Buy volatility	Sell volatility
Straight bonds	Long convexity	Short convexity
Bonds with embedded options	Long bond with put option	Long bond with call option
Options	Long straddle	Covered call, short straddle

the issuer will exercise the call option increases/decreases. An increase in interest rate volatility increases the value of the embedded call option and thereby increases the yield spread between callable and non-callable bonds.

Buying volatility means taking a long position in an option, while selling volatility means taking positions that will obtain profits in situations where the price is stable – that is, selling volatility by taking a short position in an option. A "covered call" – shorting a call option against a long bond position – outperforms when volatility falls; while a long straddle outperforms if volatility rises. Short volatility strategies are vulnerable to market stress situations, particularly extreme flight-to-quality events (where credit spreads widen and liquidity dries up as many try to close positions at the same time).

Scenario 10.5

Based on independent quantitative analysis as well as an increase in the SSSB Instability Index,[9] an investor anticipates an increase in interest rate volatility. As a result, the investor wishes to buy volatility (Table 10.13).

- Long volatility trades generated through the sale of an intermediate bullet and the purchase of a barbell of short and long bonds can be weighted such that the trade is cash as well as duration neutral.[10] This trade also profits from increased curvature between the two longer bonds, but has negative carry and a roll disadvantage which must be evaluated against the convexity pick-up.[11] The disadvantage is greater the more concave is the yield curve.
- Long volatility trades generated from the sale of callable corporate bonds have a yield disadvantage, as the coupons on callable bonds tend to be larger than coupons on comparable straight bonds.

10.6 SUMMARY

The potential for enhancing return is greatest if one can take advantage of multiple trading strategies – including positions on the yield curve, selections on sector, coupon, and issuer, as well as the use of derivative and synthetic securities – particularly when the prevailing market environment does not favor an individual strategy. Table 10.14 provides a summary of alternative trading strategies depending upon various expectations for market direction, curvature, spreads, and volatility. Thus far, we have learned what risk exposure we seek to have and how to achieve it. In Chapter 11 we examine a number of other considerations to take into account when building a portfolio.

Table 10.13 Long volatility trades

Profit: increased volatility
Loss: stable interest rates

Position	Structure	Weight	Matching
Straight bonds			
Long	Duration	+100%	Cash
Short	Duration	−100%	Cash
or			
Long	Barbell (wings)	+52% and +48%[a]	Cash, Duration
Short	Bullet (intermediate)	−100%	Cash, Duration
Bonds with embedded options			
Long	Straight bond	+100%	Cash, Maturity
Short	Callable bond	−100%	Cash, Maturity
or			
Long	Putable bond	+100%	Cash, Maturity
Short	Straight bond	−100%	Cash, Maturity
Options			
Long	Call and put option		

[a] These weightings are illustrative.

Table 10.14 Summary

Sector/forecast	High volatility	Low volatility	Lower rates	Higher rates
Corporates/ growth	Lower quality, non-callables	Lower quality, callables	Lower quality, non-callables	Lower quality, callables
Corporates/ recession	Avoid	High quality, callables	Avoid	Avoid
Governments/ growth	Barbell (long/short)	Bullet (intermediates)	Extend duration	Cash
Governments/ recession	Barbell (long/short)	Bullet (intermediates)	Extend duration	Cash

Source: Adapted from Dialynas and Rachlin in *Managing Fixed Income Portfolios*, F. Fabozzi (ed.), copyright © 1997. This material is issued by permission of John Wiley & Sons, Inc.

NOTES

1. Investors that are "structurally bullish" will take bull-steepener or bull-flattener positions.
2. The specific selection of maturities will depend on the shape of the yield curve. Look for the best carry and roll.
3. The appendix to this chapter discusses bullet, barbell, and butterfly structures in more detail.
4. Whether this trade has negative or positive carry depends on the ratio of the coupon rates and the DV01s. A steep curve would likely generate negative carry. For example, in the case of a 2-year bond with a coupon of 2% and duration of 4 and a 10-year bond with a coupon of 5% and a duration of 6, the duration-neutral steepener has negative carry of 2% ($= -5\% + (2\% \times 1.5)$). On the contrary, if the 2-year bond had a coupon of 4%, the duration-neutral steepener has positive carry of 1% ($= -5\% + (4\% \times 1.5)$).
5. The cash-neutral version of this trade – where the bullet is overweighted relative to the barbell – maximizes the carry advantage associated with a concave yield curve.
6. With a normal upward-sloping concave yield curve, the bullet has a yield advantage over the barbell. Hence, the sale of the bullet to finance a barbell purchase results in a yield loss (because the yield loss from the 5-year to the 1-year is greater than the yield pick-up from the 5-year to the 10-year). The 5-year also rolls down a steeper part of the curve than a 10-year, and a 1-year earns no roll because it has zero duration at the end of a 1-year investment horizon.
7. For bonds with embedded options, portfolios are positioned to take advantage of expectations as to how the OAS will change over the investment horizon – that is, buy the bond with the highest OAS and finance the acquisition by shorting a matched-duration Treasury.
8. Callable bonds are more negatively convex than straight bonds, while bonds with put options are more positively convex than straight bonds. Hence, an increase in volatility benefits putable bonds (which are long the option and volatility) and diminishes the price of callable bonds (which are short the option and volatility). In a stable yield curve environment, investors are willing to pay more for high-quality callable bonds compared to straight bonds of similar quality.
9. The Schroder Salomon Smith Barney (SSSB) Instability Index measures the degree of market distress using credit spreads, leverage and volatility. A sharp increase in the Instability Index implies higher volatility.
10. Since convexity increases as the dispersion of cash flows is increased, a barbell is more convex than a duration-matched bullet.
11. Convexity is more important at longer durations, while curve reshaping is more important at shorter durations (below 10 years). Narrower barbells have smaller yield give up and smaller convexity pick-up.

APPENDIX: BULLETS, BARBELLS, AND BUTTERFLIES

Two portfolios with the same duration may perform quite differently when the yield curve shifts. One key factor is the spacing of the maturity of bonds in the portfolio. This allocation of maturities is used to manage yield curve risk. The other key factor affecting performance is the type and magnitude of shift in the yield curve. Hence, investors with different curve expectations will select different maturity structures. The different maturity structures used to construct portfolios include bullets, barbells, and butterflies.

Bullets

A bullet[1] trade involves a position in a security at a single maturity point on the yield curve. A duration-neutral bullet has the same exposure to market risk as that of the benchmark. If the duration of the bullet differs from the benchmark, the bullet is a bet on market direction. The selected maturity point for the bullet will affect the performance of a portfolio depending on the type of yield curve shift. Over a one year investment horizon, the total return of a portfolio with securities all maturing in one year will not be sensitive to yield curve shifts because in one year the securities have matured. In contrast, the total return of a portfolio with securities all maturing in 30 years will be sensitive to how the yield curve shifts one year from now because in one year the value of the portfolio depends on the yield offered on 29-year securities (Fabozzi, 2000).

Barbells

A barbell trade involves a long (or short) position in two bonds with different maturities, usually at two extremes. Like bullets, barbell trades can be constructed to be duration-neutral relative to the targeted benchmark. A barbell may involve two bonds in different market sectors – such as a corporate bond at one end of the curve and a Treasury bond at the other end of the curve. In practice, barbell trades tend to be constructed relative to a particular bullet strategy.

When the yield curve shifts, a portfolio consisting of equal proportions of securities maturing in 1 year and 30 years will have quite a different total return over a 1 year investment horizon than two portfolios holding 1s and 30s separately. It is often stated that a bullet portfolio will outperform a barbell with the same duration in a steepening yield curve environment due to convexity. However, relative bullet-barbell performance depends on how the yield curve shifts and the magnitude of the shift. Intuitively, although it is better to have more convexity than less, the market charges for convexity in the form of a higher price (e.g. lower yield). In practice, the benefit of convexity depends on how much yields change. For small parallel shifts in the yield curve, a duration-matched bullet portfolio with smaller convexity may outperform. Although a barbell may outperform for any magnitude of curve flattening, it may also outperform if curve steepening is slight (Fabozzi, 2000). The point is that the characteristics of specific securities need to be analyzed using different yield curve scenarios in order to be sure of the exact nature of the exposure and impact on performance.

---

[1] This is not to be confused with "bullet bonds" which are non-callable bonds.

Butterflies

A butterfly trade consists of a bullet and barbell combination, where one is used to finance the other. Whether one is short the bullet and long the barbell or vice versa depends on anticipated changes in the yield curve. Butterflies have a number of uses, including the implementation of arbitrage strategies, the creation of synthetic options, and the placement of bets on volatility and yield curve shape.

11
Odds and Ends

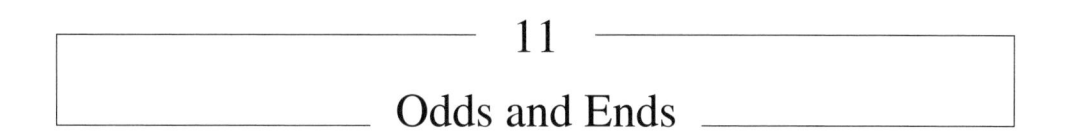

Thus far we have discussed how one forms a fixed income strategy and constructs trades that achieve the desired level of risk exposure. There are, nevertheless, some remaining details regarding the management of a fixed income portfolio that require further attention:

- Asset allocation
- Individual bond selection
- Leverage
- Risk management
- Strategy management.

11.1 ASSET ALLOCATION

Asset allocation has important implications for overall return and risk. Research indicates that 80–90% of portfolio returns stem from asset allocation as opposed to individual security selection or market timing (Brinson et al., 1986, 1991). Meanwhile, diversification – achieved through the selection of securities, sectors, or asset classes with returns that are imperfectly correlated – provides the primary method of risk management within a portfolio. Maintaining a diversified portfolio with allocation targets also helps to minimize the risk of market timing (being out of an advancing market).

Although past performance is not an indicator of future performance, it is nevertheless insightful to compare historical returns, risk, and correlations for different fixed income sectors.[1] Table 11.1 shows annualized mean returns and standard deviations for the period January 1991 to December 1997. During this period, US debt offered the lowest average return, while non-US debt offered the lowest risk. Meanwhile, emerging market debt generated the highest returns for the highest risk – not just in terms of fixed income, but all asset classes.[2] The US high-yield sector offered comparable double-digit returns to emerging market debt, but with much lower risk.

For US investors, crossing over into the global bond market creates opportunities for enhanced returns and lower overall portfolio risk. Faillace and Thomas (1997) illustrate the disparity between the best and worst major bond market performers during 1975–1996.[3] The average disparity in returns for the overall period was 24%. However, the disparity for 1986–1996 was much smaller (10.8%) compared to the average disparity (37.2%) in 1975–1985. The widest disparity in returns was between the UK and Canada (+64.51% versus −2.96%, respectively) in 1977. Meanwhile, the smallest disparity was between Japan and the UK (−0.91% versus −7.92%, respectively) in 1994.

The low correlations in returns shown in Table 11.2 suggest that these major bond sectors offer significant diversification benefits. For US investors, the combination of low correlations between bond sector returns and typically lower volatility in international bond returns (when

Table 11.1 Bond sector returns and risk, 1991–1997

	Mean return	Standard deviation
US	8.45	3.99
US high yield	15.61	5.20
Non-US	9.35	3.11
Emerging markets (EM)	18.91	14.46

Source: Enge and Goodwin (1998)

Table 11.2 Correlation of bond sector returns, 1991–1997

	US	US high yield	Non-US	EM
US	1.00			
US high yield	0.34	1.00		
Non-US	0.59	0.24	1.00	
EM	0.37	0.43	0.41	1.00

Source: Enge and Goodwin (1998)

hedged into US dollars) – together create particularly attractive opportunities to reduce overall portfolio risk. The low correlation of returns between non-US and US bond markets is attributed to asynchronous economic and interest rate cycles – the result of different cultural, structural, and political circumstances. In the event of increasing return correlations, international diversification could still be warranted, based on a desirable reduction in portfolio volatility.

The ability to outperform a benchmark requires an allocation of funds that differs from the benchmark. In addition to bond sector, alternative allocations might involve different maturities and credits within the government, corporate, and mortgage sectors. Expected changes in the level of interest rates will affect the allocation of funds within the corporate and mortgage sectors because the more attractive the call feature of a security, the worse it may perform in a declining interest rate environment due to negative convexity. By the same token, expected changes in the yield curve will affect the maturity selection within sectors. Anticipated changes in spreads affects allocation decisions within, as well as between, different bond market sectors (Fabozzi, 2000).

Asset allocation may follow a passive or an active approach. Passive asset allocation involves rebalancing the portfolio back to the target portfolio weights to ensure that the desired level of volatility and diversification is maintained. Rebalancing requires selling in bull markets and buying in bear markets (buy low and sell high).

Active asset allocation can take many forms: dynamic, tactical, or strategic. With dynamic asset allocation investors attempt to gain downside protection by selling as bond prices fall in order to make the portfolio less susceptible to further losses. Alternatively, bonds are purchased as prices are rising to increase the upside potential (buy high and sell higher). Tactical allocations attempt to capitalize on expected shifts in prices in the very short term. This is achieved by rotating into or out of a segment of bonds ahead of its outperformance or underperformance. Strategic allocations (positions held for one to three months or longer) take advantage of longer economic trends.

Like anything else associated with investment, allocation involves risk. Sector allocation risk is measured by the percent allocation to each sector and the option-adjusted spread (OAS) of each sector. As such, sector allocation risk is affected by changes in the OAS of sectors (Jones and Peltzman, 1997).

11.2 INDIVIDUAL BOND SELECTION

Of the important contributing factors to the return of a fixed income portfolio, duration management has had the greatest impact, followed by sector selection and then individual bond selection (Fong, 1997). Individual security selection can be accomplished either passively or actively. The key is to minimize transaction costs.

Selection under Passive Management

Individual issues can be selected using an optimizer that maximizes returns and diversification benefits of prescreened securities while either minimizing turnover or keeping it below a prescribed level.[4] Issues of the benchmark index might first be screened for liquidity and "cheapness". In Schroder Salomon Smith Barney's *Euro Area Model Portfolio*, for example, the "cheap" issues have favorable coupon-adjusted-spreads compared to their three-month averages. The optimizer in the *Euro Area Model Portfolio* maximizes rolling yield[5] subject to duration contribution targets.

Selection under Active Management

Active security selection presumes that exploitable inefficiencies exist at the individual security level which can be identified through skilled analysis. As such, active security selection is highly dependent on quantitative valuation models. At some stage, however, selection will likely involve the use of a screening device – such as an optimizer to identify the least-cost solutions that achieve targeted exposures.

Security selection within the corporate bond sector requires a combination of fixed income and equity analysis. Equity-type analysis involves an examination of financial statements, interviewing management, evaluating industry issues, reading indentures and charters, anticipating changes by rating agencies, and developing independent operating and financial forecasts – all of which are beyond the scope of this book.

A Note about Transaction Costs

Because of transaction fees (and slippage), you are behind before you even begin. Hence, an important part of enhancing return is implementing your view in a cost-efficient way. Even passive investors are in the market on a regular basis – rebalancing portfolios and reinvesting cash flows. The idea is to trade well when you must to improve the risk/return profile of the portfolio, and reduce unexpected transactions to avoid being forced to trade. Those with a long investment horizon have an advantage as they can avoid forced transactions.

Trading well means switching into cheaper bonds with the same or better risk-adjusted returns. Avoiding unexpected transactions requires being able to fund your liabilities in any economic scenario. Cheap bonds enhance the risk/return characteristics of the portfolio in all scenarios; hold these until they become rich.[6] In contrast, rich bonds enhance the risk/return characteristics in only a limited number of scenarios.

11.3 LEVERAGE

Leverage is directly related to the amount of money borrowed to finance bond positions beyond an investor's capital base. By increasing the size of positions, investors can magnify their potential returns as well as their potential losses. The most famous illustration of the use of leverage is that of Long-Term Capital Management (LTCM) – which employed leverage of 20–30 : 1 to generate impressive returns (185% profit after fees in 50 months) as well as catastrophic losses ($5 billion, or 92% from top to bottom) in the weeks following the Russian default in August 1998 (Lowenstein, 2000).

Leverage is created through borrowing (unsecured, secured, or on margin), repurchase agreements (repos), or the use of derivatives. Pyramiding, which is another technique, is the use of unrealized profits on an existing position as margin to increase the size of a position. Derivatives allow investors to replicate the value of a leveraged position in the cash market while at the same time circumventing the problems of managing a margin account. Moreover, the degree of leverage available to establish positions in futures contracts on margin is considerably greater than in the cash market.

Depending on the asset, market, broker, and applicable regulations, leverage can be obtained ranging from 5:1 to 30:1. The degree of leverage employed (usually by hedge funds and speculators) will depend on the circumstances. For example, fixed income arbitrage strategies involving government securities tend to be highly leveraged (10–25+ times the asset base) because of the small margins available for exploitation. When the variance of returns is larger or when capital is abundant, leverage tends to be reduced.

Leverage in falling markets can produce losses that are larger than the gains produced in rising markets as a result of the forced liquidation of positions when valuations fall (liquidity risk). Moreover, declines in the value of a leveraged position may far exceed the decline in the bond market because the unwinding of leveraged positions can quickly cause a ripple effect. When markets fall, for example, highly levered investors are required to pay down loans or meet margin calls. Those marginal investors with low liquidity are then forced to close positions and realize losses in order to raise the necessary cash for lenders. This selling can force the market to fall further, in turn prompting other lenders to raise collateral requirements, and forcing more leveraged investors to sell (Lavinio, 2000).

11.4 RISK MANAGEMENT

Fixed income strategy is all about offense (i.e. profit-focused), while risk management is all about defense (i.e. loss-focused). Whether you wish to survive or thrive, you must control your losses to stay in the game. As such, risk control is absolutely essential. Risk management is achieved in a number of ways – including position limits and stop loss orders. The careful selection of trades also serves to limit risk. It is important to keep in mind that if you are wrong, what you have to make back to break even is much bigger than what you have lost. For example, if the value of your portfolio falls 50% from 100 to 50, to get back to 100 you need to generate returns of 200%.

Position Size and Risk Limits

Position size limits define the maximum amount of cash at risk on any single trade. The purpose of position size limits is to enable you to sustain a string of losses without jeopardizing your capital base. As one rule of thumb, never risk more than 1–2% of the investment account on any single *trade*. As another rule of thumb, limit bets to less than 5% on any one *idea* (which could involve a number of individual trades); in this case, you can be wrong and/or unlucky more than 20 times. Size limits based on the idea (as opposed to the trade) are especially important if the risk of many trades is highly correlated.

Risk limits define the maximum exposure over a period of time. For example, one might be allocated 50 bps of risk in a year. As such, the idea is not to risk 50 bps on a single trade. Alternatively, risk limits might be specified in terms of explicit price movements. For example, the maximum allowed risk might be a 7% price decline.

Another technique is to keep position size proportional to market volatility. During periods of higher volatility, position size should be reduced sharply. If volatility is extreme, trading might even be temporarily suspended.[7] The idea is to minimize exposure until a more favorable price trend reappears.

Position size might also be sharply reduced after sustaining large losses or following an extended winning streak. In the first case, the idea is to preserve remaining capital and minimize exposure while trading at your worst. After an extended winning streak, one tends to become complacent and sloppy.

Conversely, if you are flush with profits, or if the market is more tranquil, or if all your signals are pointed in the same direction – positions might be increased. For example, if all your signals are pointed in the same direction, the size of your position might be five times larger than normal.

Exit Strategies

Establishing a position is only half of the process. The other half is getting out – or rather, closing the position.[8] Getting in is easy, but getting out is key. Before a position is taken, rigid limits are determined for stopping losses (if things go badly) and taking profits (if things go to plan or better). It is best to set the thresholds at the start, because it is difficult to overcome the emotions of greed and fear amidst the sharp twists and turns of the market. Exit orders commit you to getting out when the losses are small and reasonable. They can also keep you from adding to losing positions and help you to hang on to your profits.

You must stick with the winners so that they can pay for the losers. Hence, not having a predetermined profit objective allows you to continue with a trend for its full duration. One rule of thumb is to take profits in increments on the way up and fully close the position just as the market is coming down. Alternatively, a smaller position might have a wider stop, while larger positions might have narrower stops. Wider stops for profits avoid getting kicked out of a winning strategy. Note that it is always easier to get back in than to get out, especially if the position is large.

Successful poker playing offers insight into the skilled balance required between offense and defense. That is, fold the bad hands and forfeit the ante; play the good hands to the hilt when the percentages are in your favor. In other words, limit losses quickly when it's "wrong", and be aggressive when it's "right".

Table 11.3 Risk management rules of thumb

- Place a good-until-cancelled, stop-loss order to sell automatically should the price fall 25% from the purchase price.

- If you are up 30% in a position, sell one-third of it to lock in partial profits; sell the second third once it is up 50%; and hold the last third until technical indicators show serious deterioration.

- Diversify by holding a portfolio of 20–35 different bonds, with no single bond comprising more than 5% of the portfolio (3% recommended). The returns on these bonds should not be not highly correlated.

- Don't concentrate any more than 15% of your portfolio in any one theme or idea. Less than 10% is preferable. Avoid asset class myopia (e.g. don't overlook cash).

Source: Adapted from Dorsey et al. (2001), Gallea and Patalon (1998), and Schwager (1989).

Hold on to winners and cut losses

11.5 STRATEGY MANAGEMENT

Because the market is in a constant state of flux, strategies as well as the analytical tools underpinning the strategies must be continually reassessed in light of new developments.[9] Moreover, in a volatile environment, strategy may need to change frequently.

As we learned in Chapter 5, it is important that our investment decisions are as objective as possible. Decisions made in a frenzied atmosphere or panic are bound to be losers as greed and fear cloud our perceptions of opportunities and dangers. Hence, a strategy with clearly predefined trading parameters is needed to keep the emotions at bay. This also allows you to identify the source of your errors and avoid similar mistakes in the future.

Learning in this context requires record keeping. A record of each trade should include: (1) the reasons for entering and exiting the trade; (2) the date and price of entry and exit; (3) stops and all adjustments of stops; (4) maximum unrealized profits and losses; (5) before and after technical charts; (6) fees, execution, slippage and cost of carry; and (7) your emotional state. This record will help to identify repetitive patterns of success and failure, which will enable you to enhance what works and discard what doesn't.

* * *

We have now reached the home stretch of fixed income investment. Thus far, we have seen a plethora of specific techniques. Depending on your return objectives, risk tolerance, and investment horizon, some of these techniques will be more applicable than others. In the final chapter, we present key principals that are relevant to *all* types of investors.

NOTES

1. Note that different time periods will have different implications.
2. Research by Enge and Goodwin (1998) finds that emerging market debt (measured by the EMBI) outperformed all major asset class benchmark indices except US equities (measured by the Russell 3000), which it essentially tied during the period January 1991 to December 1997.
3. Performance hedged into US dollars.
4. There is always the possibility that the optimizer selects an unrealistic combination of instruments. In such cases, the optimization result (usually the notional amount) will need to be adjusted.
5. The rolling yield equals yield income plus roll-down return (assuming no change in the yield curve).
6. Grant (1997) notes that this happens much more slowly than price volatility may suggest.
7. In the case of emerging markets (where there are limited alternatives), a situation may arise where supportive fundamentals override the normal response (position reduction) to increased volatility taking you outside your allowed range.
8. For benchmarked investors with a long horizon, the implicit exit strategy is to neutralize an overweight position when it becomes "rich" relative to perceived risks (based on fundamental models).
9. Performance attribution – understanding the sources of excess returns (or losses) – is an important aspect of assessing strategies.

RECOMMENDED READING

Dembo, R.S. and Freeman, A. (1998). *The Rules of Risk: A Guide for Investors*. New York: John Wiley & Sons.

Lowenstein, R. (2000). *When Genius Failed: The Rise and Fall of Long-Term Capital Management*. New York: Random House.

12
Survival Principles for the Financial Battlefield

What is it actually like to trade fixed income? This chapter represents a synthesis of my own experience as well as a number of interviews with different types of market practitioners – including asset managers, hedge funds, pension funds, traders and supranationals – to get you as close to the trading floor as possible without actually being there.

Six themes emerged from this body of experience. These themes are applicable irrespective of your investment horizon and irrespective of whether you believe in efficient markets. Interestingly enough, this collective wisdom echoes key survival principles taught to the élite in the Special Forces. These principles essentially embody the control of risk and emotion.

The bond market is indeed much like a battlefield where victories are measured in profits and casualties are measured in losses. Each trade represents a skirmish where one investor takes money away from another. With each mission, a soldier puts his life on the line. With each trade, a practitioner puts his or her livelihood on the line. The survival of a soldier is ultimately the function of rigorous training, field experience, and a bit of luck. The same can be said of the successful fixed income practitioner.

12.1 SIX PEARLS OF WISDOM

[1] Plan your Moves

Wisdom from the Battlefield

Careful planning for every eventuality is essential. Plan your moves, contingencies, and exit strategies. Planning helps deal with Murphy's Law: "Whatever can go wrong, will go wrong." The unwary and unprepared end up dead. Remember the five P's: Prior Planning Prevents Poor Performance.

Wisdom from the Trading Floor

A sound and objective decision framework is an investing essential. Use money management and have a trading plan for each potential situation – before the markets open.

[2] Keep it Simple

Wisdom from the Battlefield

Although the plan should account for every last detail, it should be essentially simple. If success depends on a large number of factors coming together at the right time, this is a recipe for disaster. The less complicated the plan, the less there is that can go wrong (and the fewer opportunities for Mr Murphy to show up).

Wisdom from the Trading Floor

The key to profits is simplicity. The more rules you have, the more you will lose money. Also limit your focus to what you understand – as quantity is no replacement for quality.

[3] Never Assume

Wisdom from the Battlefield

Never assume that you have thought of every contingency and that reality will conform to the plan. Assumptions produce inflexible thinking and will get you killed. To survive you need to be flexible and able to improvise as situations unfold.

Wisdom from the Trading Floor

A rigid view can quickly become outdated. You need to be flexible and open minded. Successful practitioners adapt to changing circumstances; they listen and learn. Bias limits your field of opportunity.

[4] Use Common Sense

Wisdom from the Battlefield

Blindly following rules will get you killed. You need to be able to think "outside of the box".

Wisdom from the Trading Floor

There is no substitute for thinking for yourself. There are no absolutes and just sticking to formulas will lose you money. No consistently successful investor has substituted computer-generated analysis for common sense. This reflects the fact that models only work for so long.

[5] Keep a Clear Head

Wisdom from the Battlefield

Fear is your worst enemy. Fear and anxiety only produce mistakes. The more relaxed you are, the more you will be able to keep a clear head and retain self-control when Mr Murphy arrives on the scene. Good training helps to keep the panic at bay.

Wisdom from the Trading Floor

Your success or failure as an investor depends on controlling your emotions. Greed will get you "killed". Patience will allow you to wait for the right opportunity to come along and to ride with the trend.

Leave your ego at home. You may have been right for 10 years in succession, but don't get carried away by thinking you are invincible. A large ego short circuits risk control as well as the learning process – both of which are vital for survival.

It is the rare individual who can sit in front of a quote screen and make consistently good trading decisions day after day. Other components of your life affect your thinking, unless you adhere to a mechanical system with clear entry and exit points.

[6] Mind your Equipment

Wisdom from the Battlefield

If you take care of your equipment, it will take care of you. Otherwise, badly maintained gear will fail when you need it most. In the theater of war, the utmost care is taken to keep weapons clean and powder dry. Members of the Special Forces are taught to take extra precautions with their feet – because when everything else fails, you must be able to rely on yourself.

Wisdom from the Trading Floor

The value you add as a practitioner depends on your human capital – specifically, your ability to think critically. In this sense, your most important piece of equipment is your brain. So get a good night's rest, because bad decisions are made when you are tired. The nuclear accident at Chernobyl, the near meltdown at Three Mile Island, the disastrous oil spill by the *Exxon Valdez*, and the explosion of the US space shuttle *Challenger* all have one thing in common: They were all caused by people who made mistakes because they had not had enough sleep (Coren, 1996).

Even the loss (or addition) of a *single* hour can make a difference. For example, Coren (1996) finds that the shift to daylight savings time (the loss of one hour of sleep each spring) is associated with a 6% increase in accidental deaths and a 7% increase in traffic accidents as compared to the week before and after the shift. Similarly, the shift from daylight savings time (the gain of one hour of sleep each fall) is associated with a 7% decrease in the number of traffic accidents immediately following the change, with everything back to normal a week later.

*   *   *

Long-term survival – both on the battlefield and on the trading floor – takes discipline, endurance and courage. In terms of investment, this means trading your plan, managing your risk, and thinking independently. This advice may seem tiresome and obvious, but it is tried and true.

12.2 CONCLUDING REMARKS

The investment game is a complex one. The rules are in a state of flux and there is a lot of "noise" in the system. Moreover, the numerous positive feedback loops pose quite a challenge to our linear thinking. Amidst all the chaos, the challenge is to keep your eye on the ball. In terms of fixed income investment, this is all about managing risk and paring emotion from your decision making. In terms of strategy, this is all about understanding the constraints faced by investors and policy makers (economics), their motivations (politics and demographics), and the intensity of their sentiment (psychology). In other words, market dynamics are *social* dynamics. As such, the use of a single static relationship to predict the future will generate profits and losses at random. You may get a string of profits, but so does flipping a coin. If no single technique works well in all circumstances, surely the use of a number of techniques from different disciplines improves the odds of figuring out whether you are in a new trend or stuck in a range. Long-term success in an ever-evolving market requires dynamic thinking. This means that the learning process is ongoing.

Bibliography

Ahking, F.W. and Miller, S.M. (1985). "The Relationship between Government Deficits, Money Growth and Inflation." *Journal of Macroeconomics*, 7: 447–467.
Alesina, A., Cohen, G. and Roubini, N. (1992). "Macroeconomic Policy and Elections in OECD Democracies." *Economics and Politics*, 4: 1–30.
Alesina, A., Cohen, G. and Roubini, N. (1993). "Electoral Business Cycles in Industrial Democracies." *European Journal of Political Economy*, 23: 1–25.
Alesina, A. and Gatti, R. (1995). "Independent Central Banks: Low Inflation at No Cost?" *American Economic Review Papers and Proceedings*, 85: 196–200.
Alesina, A. and Summers, L. (1993). "Central Bank Independence and Macroeconomic Performance." *Journal of Money, Credit, and Banking*, 25: 151–162.
Asch, S.E. (1955). "Opinions and Social Pressure." *Scientific American*, 193(5): 31–35.
Bak, P., Paczuski, M. and Shubik, M. (1996). "Price Variations in a Stock Market with Many Agents." Santa Fe Institute Economics Research Program Working Paper, 96-09-078.
Barro, R.J. (1979). "On the Determination of the Public Debt." *Journal of Political Economy*, 87: 940–971.
BCA Research (2003). "Global Demographics: An Economic and Geopolitical Time Bomb." March.
Beck, N. (1987). "Elections and the Fed: Is There a Political Monetary Cycle?" *American Journal of Political Science*, 31: 194–216.
Benartzi, S. and Thaler, R. (1995). "Myopic Loss Aversion and the Equity Premium Puzzle." *Quarterly Journal of Economics*, 110: 73–92.
Bernard, V. (1992). "Stock Price Reactions to Earnings Announcements." In R. Thaler (ed.), *Advances in Behavioral Finance*. New York: Russell Sage Foundation.
Black, F., Derman, E. and Toy, W. (1990). "A One-Factor Model of Interest Rates and Its Application to Treasury Bond Options." *Financial Analysts Journal* (January–February): 24–32.
Bradley, M.D. and Potter, S.M. (1986). "The State of the Federal Budget and the State of the Economy: Further Evidence." *Economic Inquiry*, 24: 143–153.
Brinson, G.P., Hood, L.R. and Beebower G.L. (1986). "Determinants of Portfolio Performance." *Financial Analysts Journal* (July–August).
Brinson, G.P., Singer, B.D. and Beebower, G.L. (1991). "Determinants of Portfolio Performance II: An Update." *Financial Analysts Journal* (May–June).
Burdekin, R. and Laney, L.O. (1992). "Is Fiscal Policy-Making Constrained by an Independent Central Bank?" In R. Burdekin and F. Langdana, *Budget Deficits and Economic Performance*. New York: Routledge.
Burdekin, R. and Langdana, F. (1992). *Budget Deficits and Economic Performance*. New York: Routledge.
Burdekin, R. and Willett, T. (1992). "The Importance of Central Bank Independence." In R. Burdekin and F. Langdana, *Budget Deficits and Economic Performance*. New York: Routledge.
Campbell, J.Y. (1995). "Some Lessons from the Yield Curve." *Journal of Economic Perspectives*, 9: 129–152.
Canina, L. and Figlewski, S. (1993). "The Informational Content of Implied Volatility." *Review of Financial Studies*, 6 (3): 659–681.

Cassidy, D. (1999). "Why it is so Difficult to Sell." In L. Lifson and R. Geist, *The Psychology of Investing*. New York: John Wiley & Sons.

Chan, L., Jegadeesh, N. and Lakonishok, J. (1996). "Momentum Strategies." *Journal of Finance*, 51: 1681–1713.

Chen, P. (1986). "Mode Locking to Chaos in Delayed Feed-back Systems." Center for Studies in Statistical Mechanics Working Paper, University of Texas at Austin.

Chirella, C. (1986). *The Elements of Nonlinear Theory of Economic Dynamics*. PhD Thesis, University of South Wales.

Chopra, N., Lakonishok, J. and Ritter, J. (1992). "Measuring Abnormal Performance: Do Stocks Overreact?" *Journal of Financial Economics*, 31: 235–268.

Chopra, N., Lakonishok, J. and Ritter, J. (1993). "Measuring Abnormal Performance: Do Stocks Overreact?" In R. Thaler (ed.), *Advances in Behavioral Finance*. New York: Russell Sage Foundation.

Christensen, P.E. and Fabozzi, F.J. (1997). "Dedicated Bond Portfolios." In F. Fabozzi (ed.), *The Handbook of Fixed Income Securities* (5th edn). New York: McGraw-Hill.

Coren, S. (1996). *Sleep Thieves: An Eye-opening Exploration into the Science and Mysteries of Sleep*. New York: The Free Press.

Crescenzi, A. (2002). *The Strategic Bond Investor: Strategies and Tools to Unlock the Power of the Bond Market*. New York: McGraw-Hill.

Cukierman, A. (1992). *Central Bank Strategy, Credibility and Independence: Theory and Evidence*. Cambridge, MA: MIT Press.

Cunningham, A., Dixon, L. and Hayes, S. (2001). "Analyzing Yield Spreads on Emerging Market Sovereign Bonds." *Financial Stability Review* (December).

Cutler, D., Poterba, J. and Summers, L. (1991). "Speculative Dynamics." *Review of Economic Studies*, 58: 529–546.

Dialynas, C.P. and Rachlin, E. (1997). "Fixed Income Portfolio Investing: The Art of Decision Making." In F. Fabozzi (ed.), *Managing Fixed Income Portfolios*. New Hope, Pennsylvania: Frank J. Fabozzi Associates.

De Bondt, W. (1991)."What Do Economists Know About the Stock Market?" *Journal of Portfolio Management*, 17 (2): 94–91.

De Bondt, W. (1993). "Betting on Trends: Intuitive Forecasts of Financial Risk and Return." *International Journal of Forecasting*, 9: 355–371.

De Bondt, W. (1998). "A Portrait of the Individual Investor." *European Economic Review*, 42: 831–844.

De Bondt, W. and Bange, M. (1992). "Inflation, Money Illusion, and Time Variation in Term Premia." *Journal of Financial and Quantitative Analysis*, 27 (4): 479–496.

De Bondt, W. and Thaler, R. (1985). "Does the Stock Market Overreact?" *Journal of Finance*, 42: 793–805.

De Bondt, W. and Thaler, R. (1987). "Further Evidence on Investor Overreaction and Stock Market Seasonality." *Journal of Finance*, 42: 557–581.

Dialynas, C.P. (1997). "The Active Decisions in the Selection of Passive Management and Performance Bogeys." In F. Fabozzi (ed.), *The Handbook of Fixed Income Securities* (5th edn). New York: McGraw-Hill.

Dialynas, C.P. and Rachlin, E. (1997). "Fixed Income Portfolio Investing: The Art of Decision Making." In F. Fabozzi (ed.), *Managing Fixed Income Portfolios*. New Hope, Pennsylvannia: Frank J. Fabozzi Associates.

Dorsey, T.J. and the DWA Analysts (2001). *Tom Dorsey's Trading Tips: A Playbook for Stock Market Success*. Princeton: Bloomberg Press.

Drazen, A. (2000). *Political Economy in Macroeconomics*. Princeton: Princeton University Press.

Edwards, W. (1968). "Conservatism in Human Information Processing." In B. Kleinmutz (ed.), *Formal Representation of Human Judgment*. New York: John Wiley & Sons.

Eichengreen, B. and Frieden, J. (1993). "The Political Economy of European Monetary Unification: An Analytical Introduction." *Economics and Politics*, 5: 85–104.

Einhorn, H.J. and Hogarth, R. (1978). "Confidence in Judgment: Persistence in the Illusion of Validity." *Psychological Review*, 85 (5): 395–416.

Elder, A. (1993). *Trading for a Living*. New York: John Wiley & Sons.

Enge, B. and Goodwin, T. (1998). "Emerging Market Debt: A New Class for Asset Allocation?" *Russell Research Commentary* (March).

Evans J.L. and Archer, S.H. (1968). "Diversification and the Reduction of Dispersion: An Empirical Analysis." *Journal of Finance* (December): 761–767.
Fabozzi, F.J. (1997). *Fixed Income Mathematics: Analytical and Statistical Techniques* (3rd edn). New York: McGraw-Hill.
Fabozzi, Frank J. (2000). Bond Markets, Analysis and Strategies (4th edn). Upper Saddle River, NJ: Prentice-Hall.
Faillace, A.L. and Thomas, L.R. (1997). "International Fixed Income Investment: Philosophy and Process." In F. Fabozzi (ed.), *Managing Fixed Income Portfolios*. New Hope, Pennsylvania: Frank J. Fabozzi Associates.
Fair, R. (1978). "The Effect of Economic Events on Votes for President: 1980 Results." *Review of Economics and Statistics*, 64: 322–325.
Fama, E. (1970). "Efficient Capital Markets: A Review of Theory and Empirical Work." *Journal of Finance*, 25: 383–417.
Fama, E. (1984). "The Information in the Term Structure." *Journal of Financial Economics* (December): 509–528.
Fama, E. (1998a). "Efficiency Survives the Attack of the Anomalies." *GSB Chicago* (winter): 14–16.
Fama, E. (1998b). "Market-Efficiency, Long-Term Returns, and Behavioral Finance." *Journal of Financial Economics*, 49 (3): 283–306.
Fama, E. and French, K. (1998). "Value versus Growth: The International Evidence." *Journal of Finance*, 53: 1975–1999.
Festinger, L. (1957). *A Theory of Cognitive Dissonance*. Stanford, CA: Stanford University Press.
Fong, H.G. (1997). "Bond Management: Past, Current, and Future." In F. Fabozzi (ed.), *The Handbook of Fixed Income Securities* (5th edn). New York: McGraw-Hill.
Foot, D.K. and Stoffman, D. (1998). *Boom, Bust & Echo 2000: Profiting from the Demographic Shift in the New Millennium*. Toronto: Macfarlane Walter & Ross.
Frey, B. and Schneider, F. (1978). "An Empirical Study of Politico-Economic Interaction in the United States." *Review of Economics and Statistics*, 60: 174–183.
Froot, K. (1989). "New Hope for the Expectations Hypothesis of the Term Structure of Interest Rates." *Journal of Finance*, 44: 283–305
Gallea, A.M. and Patalon, W. (1998). *Contrarian Investing: Buy and Sell When Others Won't and Make Money Doing It*. New York: New York Institute of Finance.
Garrett, G. (1993). "The Politics of Maastricht." *Economics and Politics*, 5: 105–123.
Gibson, L. (1997). "Managing Market Risk at Long-Term Investment Funds." In F. Fabozzi (ed.), *Managing Fixed Income Portfolios*. New Hope, Pennsylvania: Frank J. Fabozzi Associates.
Gladwell, M. (2002). *The Tipping Point: How Little Things Can Make a Big Difference*. New York: Little, Brown & Company.
Grilli, V., Masciandaro, D. and Tabellini, G. (1991). "Political and Monetary Institutions and Public Financial Policies in the Industrial Countries." *Economic Policy*, 13: 341–392.
Hagstrom, R.G. (2000). *Investing: The Last Liberal Art*. New York: Texere.
Grant, K.E. (1997). "Improving Insurance Company Portfolio Returns." In F. Fabozzi (ed.), *The Handbook of Fixed Income Securities* (5th edn). New York: McGraw-Hill.
Hakkio, C.S. and Rush, M. (1991). "Is the Budget Deficit 'Too Large'?," *Economic Inquiry*, 29: 429–445.
Hamilton, J.D. and Flavin, M.A. (1986). "On the Limitations of Government Borrowing: A Framework for Empirical Testing." *American Economic Review*, 76: 808–819.
Haugen, R.A. and Baker, N. (1996). "Commonality in the Determinants of Expected Stock Returns." *Journal of Financial Economics*, 41: 401–439.
Haynes, S. and Stone, J. (1989). "Political Models of the Business Cycle Should Be Revived." *Economic Inquiry*, 28: 442–465.
Heisler, J. (1994). "Loss Aversion in a Futures Market: An Empirical Test." *The Review of Futures Markets*, 13 (3): 793–822.
Henderson, C. (2002). *Currency Strategy: The Practitioner's Guide to Currency Investing, Hedging and Forecasting*. Chichester: John Wiley & Sons.
Howe, J.S. (1986). "Evidence on Stock Market Overreaction." *Financial Analysts Journal* (July/August): 74–77.
Ilmanen, A. (1995a). "Convexity Bias and the Yield Curve. Understanding the Yield Curve: Part 5." *Portfolio Strategies*. Salomon Brothers (September).

Ilmanen, A. (1995b). "A Framework for Analyzing Yield Curve Trades. Understanding the Yield Curve: Part 6." *Portfolio Strategies*. Salomon Brothers (November).

Ilmanen, A. (1996). "The Dynamics of the Shape of the Yield Curve: Empirical Evidence, Economic Interpretations and Theoretical Foundations. Understanding the Yield Curve: Part 7." *Portfolio Strategies*. Salomon Brothers (February).

Ilmanen, A. (2000). "Convexity Bias and the Yield Curve." In N. Jegadeesh and B. Tuckman (eds), *Advanced Fixed-Income Valuation Tools*. New York: John Wiley & Sons.

Ilmanen, A., Byrne, R., Gunasekera, H. and Minikin, R. (2001a). "Seasonals – Are There Any?" *European Debt Strategy Update*. Schroder Salomon Smith Barney: DE10 (31 August).

Ilmanen, A., Byrne, R., Gunasekera, H. and Minikin, R. (2001b). "More Seasonal Regularities." *Government Bond Research*. Schroder Salomon Smith Barney: DE159 (24 September).

Ilmanen, A., Byrne, R., Gunasekera, H. and Minikin, R. (2001c). "Seasonal Patterns in Euro Government Bond Performance." *European Debt Strategy Update*. Schroder Salomon Smith Barney: November.

Ito, T. (1990). "The Timing of Elections and Political Business Cycles in Japan." *Journal of Asian Economics*, 1: 135–156.

Iwanowski, R. and Chandra, R. (1995). "How Do Corporate Spread Curves Move Over Time? An Empirical Study of the Salomon Brothers Corporate Bond Index." Salomon Brothers.

Jaeger, L. (2002). *Managing Risk in Alternative Investment Strategies: Successful Investing in Hedge Funds and Managed Futures*. London: FT Prentice Hall.

James, W. (1907). *Pragmatism*. Indianapolis, Indiana: Hackett (republished 1981).

Janis, I. (1972). *Victims of Groupthink: A Psychological Study of Foreign Policy Decisions and Fiascoes*. Houston: Boston.

Janis, I.L. and Feshbach, S. (1953). "Effects of Fear-Arousing Communications." *The Journal of Abnormal Psychology*, 48: 78–93.

Jegadeesh, N. and Titman, S. (1993). "Returns to Buying Winners and Selling Losers: Implications for Stock Market Efficiency." *Journal of Finance*, 48: 65–91.

Joines, D.H. (1991). "How Large a Federal Budget Deficit Can We Sustain?" *Contemporary Policy Issues*, 9: 1–11.

Jones, F.J. (1991). "Yield Curve Strategies." *Journal of Fixed Income* (September): 43–48.

Jones, F.J. and Peltzman, L.J. (1997). "Fixed Income Attribution Analysis." In F. Fabozzi (ed.), *Managing Fixed Income Portfolios*. New Hope, Pennsylvania: Frank J. Fabozzi Associates.

Kahn, M.N. (1999). *Technical Analysis: Plain and Simple*. London: FT Prentice-Hall.

Kahneman, D. and Tversky, A. (1973). "On the Psychology of Prediction." *Psychological Review*, 80: 237–251.

Kahneman, D. and Tversky, A. (1974). "Judgment under Uncertainty: Heuristics and Biases" *Science*, 185: 1124–1131.

Kahneman, D. and Tversky, A. (1979). "Prospect Theory: An Analysis of Decision under Risk." *Econometrica*, 47: 263–291.

Kane, E.J. (1988). "Fedbashing and the Role of Monetary Arrangements in Managing Political Stress." In T.D. Willett (ed.), *Political Business Cycles: The Political Economy of Money, Inflation, and Unemployment*. Durham: Duke University Press.

Katz, E. and Lazarsfeld, P. F. (1955). *Personal Influence: The Part Played by People in the Flow of Mass Communication*. Glencoe, Illinois: Free Press.

Kazdin, A.E. (ed.) (2000). *Encyclopedia of Psychology*. Oxford: Oxford University Press.

Klaffky, T., Nozari, A. and Waldman, M. (1997). "New Duration Measures for Risk Management." In F. Fabozzi (ed.), *The Handbook of Fixed Income Securities* (5th edn). New York: McGraw-Hill.

Kremers, J.J.M. (1988). "Long-Run Limits on the US Federal Debt." *Economics Letters*, 28: 259–262.

Kremers, J.J.M. (1989). "US Federal Indebtedness and the Conduct of Fiscal Policy." *Journal of Monetary Economics*, 23: 219–238.

Lakonishok, J., Shleifer, A. and Vishny, R. (1994). "Contrarian Investment, Extrapolation, and Risk." *Journal of Finance*, 49: 1541–1578.

Lavinio, S. (2000). *The Hedge Fund Handbook: A Definitive Guide for Analyzing and Evaluating Alternative Investments*. New York: McGraw-Hill.

Lewis, J.E. (ed.) (2002). *The Mammoth Book of The Secrets of the SAS and Elite Forces: How the Professionals Fight and Win* (Revised). London: Constable & Robinson Limited.

Lewis-Beck, M. (1988). *Economics and Elections*. Ann Arbor: University of Michigan Press.
Lifson, L.E. and Geist, R.A. (1999). *The Psychology of Investing*. New York: John Wiley & Sons.
Lombra, R.E. (1988). "Monetary Policy: The Rhetoric versus the Record." In Willett, T.D. (ed.), *Political Business Cycles: The Political Economy of Money, Inflation, and Unemployment*. Durham: Duke University Press.
Lopes, L. (1987). "Between Hope and Fear: The Psychology of Risk." *Advances in Experimental Social Psychology*, 20: 255–295.
Loucks, M.M., Penicook, J. A. and Schillhorn, U. (2002). In F. Fabozzi and E. Pilarinu (eds), *Investing in Emerging Fixed Income Markets*. New York: John Wiley & Sons.
Lowenstein, R. (2000). *When Genius Failed: The Rise and Fall of Long-Term Capital Management*. New York: Random House.
Mackay, C. (1841). *Extraordinary Popular Delusions and the Madness of Crowds*. New York: Three Rivers Press (reprinted 1980).
Madsen, H. (1980). "Electoral Outcomes and Macroeconomic Policies: The Scandinavian Cases." In P. Whitely (ed.), *Models of Political Economy*. London: Sage.
Malvey, J. (1997). "Global Corporate Bond Portfolio Management." In F. Fabozzi (ed.), *The Handbook of Fixed Income Securities* (5th edn). New York: McGraw-Hill.
McCallum, R.T. (1984). "Are Bond-Financed Deficits Inflationary: A Ricardian Analysis." *Journal of Political Economy*, 92: 123–135.
Meyers, T.A. (1989). *The Technical Analysis Course*. Chicago: Irwin.
McDougall, A. (1999). *Mastering Swaps Markets: A Step-by-Step Guide to the Products, Applications and Risks*. London: FT Prentice-Hall.
McEnally, R.W. and Boardman, C.M. (1979). "Aspects of Corporate Bond Portfolio Diversification." *Journal of Financial Research* (Spring): 27–36.
McEnally, R.W. and Jordan, J.V. (1997). "The Term Structure of Interest Rates." In F. Fabozzi (ed.), *The Handbook of Fixed Income Securities* (5th edn). New York: McGraw-Hill.
McGuire, W. J. (1969). "Attitudes and Attitude Change." In G. Lindzey and E. Aronson (eds), *Handbook of Social Psychology*. Reading, MA: Addison-Wesley.
Miller, G.A. (1956). "The Magical Number Seven Plus or Minus Two: Some Limits on Our Capacity for Processing Information." *Psychological Review*, 63 (2): 81–97.
Mossavar-Rahmani, S. (1997). "Indexing Fixed Income Assets." In F. Fabozzi (ed.), *The Handbook of Fixed Income Securities* (5th edn). New York: McGraw-Hill.
Odean, T. (1998). "Are Investors Reluctant to Realize Their Losses?" *Journal of Finance*, 53: 1775–1798.
Osler, C.L. (2001). "Currency Orders and Exchange Rate Dynamics: Explaining the Success of Technical Analysis." *Federal Reserve Bank of New York Staff Report*, No. 125 (April).
Parkin, M. (1986). "Domestic Monetary Institutions and Deficits." In J. M. Buchanan, C.K. Rowley and R.D. Tollison (eds), *Deficits*. Oxford: Basil Blackwell.
Ploeg, F. van der (1985). "Rational Expectations, Risk and Chaos in Financial Markets." *Economic Journal*, 96.
Rasmussen, D.R. and Mosekilde, E. (1988). "Bifurcations and Chaos in a Genetic Management Model." *North European Journal of Operational Research*, 35.
Rogoff, K. (1985). "The Optimal Degree of Commitment to an Intermediate Monetary Target." *Quarterly Journal of Economics*, 100: 1169–1190.
Rosenberg, M.R. (1997). "International Fixed Income Investing: Theory and Practice." In F. Fabozzi (ed.), *The Handbook of Fixed Income Securities*, (5th edn). New York: McGraw-Hill.
Ross, K. (2002). "Market Predictability of ECB Policy Decisions: A Comparative Examination." *IMF Working Paper*, International Monetary Fund, WP/02/233.
Rouwenhorst, G. (1997). "International Momentum Strategies." *Journal of Finance*, 53: 267–284.
Sargent, T.J. and Wallace, N. (1981). "Some Unpleasant Monetarist Arithmetic." *Federal Reserve Bank of Minneapolis Quarterly Review*, 5: 1–17.
Scharfstein, D. and Stein, J. (1990). "Herd Behavior and Investment." *American Economic Review*, 80: 465–489.
Schwager, J.D. (1989). *Market Wizards: Interviews with Top Traders*. New York: New York Institute of Finance.
Sharpe, W.F. (1975). "Likely Gains from Market Timing." *Financial Analysts Journal* (March–April): 60–69.

Shefrin, H. (2000). *Beyond Greed and Fear: Understanding Behavioral Finance and the Psychology of Investing*. Boston: Harvard Business School Press.

Shefrin, H. and Statman, M. (1985). "The Disposition to Sell Winners Too Early and Ride Losers Too Long: Theory and Evidence." *Journal of Finance*, 40: 777–790.

Sherif, M. (1937). "An Experimental Approach to the Study of Attitudes." *Sociometry*, 1.

Shermer, M. (2000). *How We Believe*. New York: W.H. Freeman.

Shiller, R.J. (1987). "Investor Behavior in the October 1987 Stock Market Crash: Survey Evidence." National Bureau of Economic Research Working Paper 2446, reprinted in Robert Shiller, *Market Volatility* (1989).

Shiller, R.J. (1988). "Portfolio Insurance and Other Investor Fashions as Factors in the 1987 Stock Market Crash." *NBER Macroeconomics Annual 1988*, 287–296.

Shleifer, A. (2000). *Inefficient Markets: An Introduction to Behavioral Finance*. Oxford: Oxford University Press.

Statman, M. (1994). "Tracking Errors, Regret, and Tactical Asset Allocation." *Journal of Portfolio Management* (Spring).

Steward, C.B. and Lynch, J.H. (1997). "International Bond Portfolio Management." In F. Fabozzi (ed.), *Managing Fixed Income Portfolios*. New Hope, Pennsylvania: Frank J. Fabozzi Associates.

Steward, C.B. and Greshin A.M. (1997a). "International Bond Investing and Portfolio Management." In F. Fabozzi (ed.), *The Handbook of Fixed Income Securities* (5th edn). New York: McGraw-Hill.

Steward, C.B. and Greshin A.M. (1997b). "International Bond Markets and Instruments." In F. Fabozzi (ed.), *The Handbook of Fixed Income Securities* (5th edn). New York: McGraw-Hill.

Thaler, R.H., Tversky, A., Kahneman, D. and Schwartz, A. (1997). "The Effect of Myopia and Loss Aversion on Risk Taking: An Experimental Test." *Quarterly Journal of Economics*.

Trainer, F.H. (1997). "Active Bond Portfolio Management: An Expected Return Approach." In F. Fabozzi (ed.), *Managing Fixed Income Portfolios*. New Hope, Pennsylvania: Frank J. Fabozzi Associates.

Trehan, B. and Walsh, C.E. (1988). "Common Trends, the Government's Budget Constraint, and Revenue Smoothing." *Journal of Economic Dynamics and Control*, 12: 425–444.

Tufte, E. (1975). "Determinants of the Outcomes of Midterm Congressional Elections." *American Political Science Review*, 69: 812–826.

Tufte, E. (1978). *Political Control of the Economy*. Princeton, NJ: Princeton University Press.

Turnovsky, S.J. and Wohar, M.E. (1987). "Alternative Modes of Deficit Financing and Endogenous Monetary and Fiscal Policy in the USA 1923–1982." *Journal of Applied Econometrics*, 2: 1–25.

Tvede, L. (2002). *The Psychology of Finance: Understanding the Behavioral Dynamics of Markets* (Revised). Chichester: John Wiley & Sons.

Williams, J. (1990). "The Political Manipulation of Macroeconomic Policy." *American Political Science Review*, 84: 767–795.

Willett, T.D. (ed.) (1988). *Political Business Cycles: The Political Economy of Money, Inflation, and Unemployment*. Durham: Duke University Press.

Willett, T.D., Banaian, K., Laney, L.O., Merzkani, M. and Warga, A.D. (1988). "Inflation Hypotheses and Monetary Accommodation: Postwar Evidence from the Industrial Countries." In Willett, T.D. (ed.), *Political Business Cycles: The Political Economy of Money, Inflation, and Unemployment*. Durham: Duke University Press.

Woolley, J. (1986). *Monetary Politics: The Federal Reserve and the Politics of Monetary Policy*. Cambridge: Cambridge University Press.

Index

active management 122, 153–5, 156–60, 163, 178–9
adaptive attitudes 85, 91–4, 186
age issues 77–83, 129
agencies 142–4
aggregate demand 40–1
aggregate supply 40–1
alternatives 39–43, 141–61
   bonds 141–61
   economic issues 39–43
ambiguities 86
AMG Data Services 115–16
anchoring concepts 85, 87
annual effects, seasonal analysis 120
anxieties 85, 90–3, 129–30, 182–3, 186
arbitrage 34, 87, 152, 157–8, 180
Argentina, crises 74
asset allocations 141–61, 177–9
asset classes, concepts 3–5, 177–9
asset managers 122, 152, 153, 156–60
asset-backed securities (ABS) 142, 146
asset-liability management *see* structured portfolio management
assumptions, dangers 186
at-the-money options 29–30
attitudes 85, 86, 88–92, 127–32, 136, 149–53, 186
   actions 91–2, 186
   concepts 85, 86, 88–92, 186
authoritarian regimes 67
avalanche theories 96

Baby Boomers 78–83
Bank for International Settlements 142, 147
banks
   central banks 45–8, 68–9, 71–3, 131, 135, 150
   commercial banks 152–4
   interest rate swaps 35–6

barbell portfolios, yield curves 12, 158, 170–5
Barron's Confidence Index 112
battlefield analogies 185–7
bear markets 58, 73, 89–93, 99, 101–9, 111, 157–8, 165–7
behavioural finance 84–98, 182–3, 186, 187
   see also psychological insights
benchmarks
   EMH 59
   passive management 154–5, 178–9
   portfolio strategies 154–5, 178–9
bets
   market direction 165–7
   spread bets 171–3
   yield curves 167–71
bias, decision making 84–93, 94–6, 130, 133–4
bid-ask spreads, liquidity risks 14, 54–7, 159
biology analogies, markets 93–4
Black-Derman-Toy pricing model, options 30
Black-Scholes pricing model, options 29–32
bond futures *see* futures
bonds
   see also callable bonds; putable bonds
   alternatives 141–61
   convertible bonds 145–6, 158
   high-grade issuers 19, 144
   high-yield issuers 19, 118–20, 144, 148
   issuers 3, 19, 34–5, 50, 118–20, 142–9
   pricing 3–15, 19, 22–7, 58–9, 83–115, 127–9
   risks 13–15, 177–9
   selections 177–83
   statistics 141–2, 177–9
   types 142–61
   warrants 146
   yield curves 9–13
Brazil 82
break-even yield change 16
breakout, technical analysis 101–2
bucket duration *see* partial duration

budget deficits, Monetary policy 67–73, 118–20
Buffett, Warren 59
bull markets 58, 89, 90–3, 99–109, 157–8, 165–7
bullet portfolios 12–13, 166–76
Bush, George W. 66, 83
business cycles 43–4, 54–5, 60–1, 65–7, 128–32
butterfly shifts
   RV analysis 124–5, 157–8
   yield curves 11–12, 124–5, 169–71

call options 19, 22–7, 29–32, 56, 110, 174–6
call-to-put ratio (CPR) 110
callable bonds 19, 22–7, 29–32, 56, 145
   concepts 19, 22–7, 29–32, 145
   interest rates 22–5, 29–32
   non-callable bonds 23–4, 56
   OAS 25–7, 179
   portfolios 25
   pricing 19, 22–5, 29–32
Canada 177–8
capital gains 15–16, 22–3
carry concepts 15–16, 20–1, 53–4, 172–3
cash flows
   concepts 3–4, 21–2, 25–6
   interest rate swaps 34–6
cash-neutral duration extension/shortener trades 166–7
CDs 152–3
central banks 45–8, 68–9, 71–3, 131, 135, 150
certainty effects 90–1
Challenger disaster 187
change
   dynamic markets 113, 133, 187
   flexibility requirements 126–8, 137, 186
   resistance factors 85–7
chaos theory 59–60, 187
charts 96, 99–115
Chernobyl disaster 187
Chicago Board of Trade (CBOT) 109, 118
China 82
Citigroup's Instability Index 55
cognitive dissonance 85–6, 89, 93
commercial banks 152–4
Commitments of Traders (COT) 110–12, 116–8
Commodity Futures Trading Commission (CFTC) 110–11, 116–8
common sense 186
complex adaptive systems 59–60
complex instruments 3, 19–37
'Concorde' fallacy 89
Confidence Index 112
confirmation bias 85, 88
conservatism heuristic 85, 87
contrarians 109–11
convertible bonds 145–6, 158

convexity
   concepts 5–8, 15–16, 21–7, 166–76
   strategies 5–8, 166–76
   volatility 7–9, 16, 21–5, 173–6
Coren, S. 187
corporations 19, 20, 118–20, 142–9, 152, 173
   demands 152
   issuers 19, 20, 118–20, 142–9
   security types 144–6
   spread curves 57, 173
correlation breakdown risk 122
country considerations 14, 16, 148–9, 166
   see also emerging markets
coupon, concepts 3–5, 15–16
covered option positions, hedging 30–2, 148–9, 174
credit default swaps 13
credit qualities
   concepts 9–10, 13, 16, 19, 158–9
   risks 13, 16, 19, 158–9
   spectrum 19
   yield curves 9–10
credit ratings 9–10, 13, 16, 19–21, 34–5, 54, 55, 144, 148
credit risks 13, 16, 19–21, 25–6, 54–7, 129–30, 147, 158–9, 171–3
   approximation equation 21
   concepts 13, 16, 19–21, 25–6, 54–7
   measurements 20–1
   pricing 19–21, 129–30
   strategies 21
credit spread trading 158, 173–6
crises
   behavioural finance 59, 93–4, 182–3
   disasters 187
   politics 74, 129
critical mass 93
currency considerations 14, 16, 148–9
'cutting losses and letting winners run' 85, 89, 94, 181–2

data 134
   see also information
death cross 103
debt
   budget deficits 67–73, 118–20
   concepts 3–17, 67–8, 146
   US risks/returns 175–6
decision making
   behavioural finance 84–98, 182–3, 186, 187
   emotions 84–94, 113, 127–32, 136, 182–3, 186, 187
   market bias 84–93, 94–6, 130, 133–4
   planning requirements 185
   psychology insights 74, 77, 83–115, 127–30, 135–6, 182–3, 186

rest benefits 187
sleep benefits 187
survival principles 85, 89, 94, 180–3, 185–9
tool selections 130–2
dedication strategies 155–6
default risks *see* credit risks
demand and supply laws 39–43, 49, 51, 55, 99, 118–20
demand technicals, short-term analysis 119–20
demographic factors 77–84, 129–32, 136, 187
Denmark, government policies 65–7
derivatives 13, 19, 22–36, 146–7
   see also futures; options; swaps
   concepts 13, 19, 22–36, 146–7
   credit risks 13
   embedded options 19, 21–7, 56, 173–6
   interest rate derivatives 19, 27–36, 146–7
directional duration, concepts 12–13
directional strategies 157
discounted cash flows, concepts 3–4, 21–2
distressed debt 144
divergences, MACD 103, 106–8
diversification concepts 177–8
   see also portfolios
Dow theory 100–2
downgrade risks *see* credit risks
downside risks, evaluations 133
duration
   concepts 7–8, 15–16, 20–1, 25–6, 28, 155, 159–60, 163–5
   credit risks 20–1
   interest rates 7–8, 15–16, 28, 163–5
   mean reversion 124–5, 159–60
   portfolios 9, 13, 28, 155–60, 165–7
   prices 7–8
   strategies 8–9, 155–60, 165–7

economic issues 20–1, 36, 39–62, 65–75, 127–9
   alternatives 39–43
   building blocks 39–44
   business cycles 43–4, 54–5, 60–1, 65–7, 128–32
   chaos theory 59–60
   concepts 20–1, 36, 39–62, 65–75, 127–9
   crises 68, 74, 129
   cycles 43–4, 54–5, 60–1, 65–7, 128–32
   fiscal policies 40–3, 57–8, 65–8, 129, 136
   forecasts 44–58, 60–1
   GDP 40–1, 46–50, 100
   government policies 40–3, 45–9, 53–4, 57–8, 65–75, 129
   growth 40–1, 46–50, 65–6, 68, 100, 136
   ideologies 41–3, 45–9, 65–75
   inflation 40–2, 44–54, 65–7, 100, 136
   interest rates 20–1, 36, 43–62
   Keynesian school 42–3, 49

laws of supply and demand 39–43, 49, 51, 55, 99, 118–20, 131
limitations 61
Monetary policy 40–3, 45–9, 53–4, 57–8, 67–73, 136
optimization scenarios 39–40, 61, 68, 155
politics 41–3, 45–9, 65–75, 128, 187
quantitative analysis 114, 121–36, 179
risk premiums 54–7
spread products 20–1, 54–5
thought processes 39–40
volatility 57–8
effective convexity 26–7
effective duration 25–6
efficient market hypothesis (EMH), concepts 59–60, 99–100, 128
ego-defensive attitudes 85, 86, 88–9, 93, 95–6, 186
elections, government entities 66–7, 73–4
Elliot wave analysis 100
embedded options 19, 21–7, 56, 173–6
   see also callable bonds; putable bonds
   returns 22–3, 26
   strategies 27
emerging markets 21, 56, 59, 82–3, 132, 135–6, 148–9, 177–8
   demographic factors 82–3
   politics 135–6, 148–9, 177–8
   sovereign bonds 21, 56, 59, 148–9, 177–8
emotions, decision making 84–94, 113, 127–32, 136, 182–3, 186, 187
endowment funds 150
enhanced indexing 155
equilibrium market interest rates 49–50
equipment requirements 187
equities
   concepts 3, 145–6, 148, 158
   convertible bonds 145–6, 158
EUREX 109, 116
euro 71–3
Euro Area Model Portfolio, Schroder Salomon Smith Barney 179
Eurobonds 21
Eurodollar 33–4, 112
European Central Bank (ECB) 71–3, 135, 166–7
European Monetary Union (EMU) 72–3
European options 29–30
European Union (EU) 71–3, 116, 142
   demographic factors 80–1
   open interest data 109, 116
   world shares 142
event risks 14, 159
exchange rate risks 14, 16, 148–9
exchangeable bonds 145–6
exit strategies 181–2

expectations
  inflation 44–51, 54
  markets 136–7
  yield curves 50–4
experiences, trading floor 185–7
exposures 85, 88, 148, 160, 165–76
extreme positions 111, 136
Exxon Valdez 187

false consensus effects 85, 88, 93, 94–5
Fama, E. 58–9
Federal Open Market Committee (FOMC), US 69, 116, 137
Federal Reserve, US 69–71, 117, 135
feedback loops, complex adaptive systems 59–60, 93, 132
filters 85–6, 135
fiscal policy 40–3, 57–8, 65–8, 129, 136
The Five P's 185
fixed income basics 3–17, 19, 85, 89, 94, 180–3, 185–9
fixed income derivatives *see* derivatives
fixed rates, swaps 32–6
floaters 146
floating rate notes (FRNs) 36
floating rates, swaps 32–6, 146
flow analysis 114, 115–18, 127–30, 136
Foot, David 77–80
forecasts
  demographic forecasting 77–83
  economic issues 44–58, 60–1
  inflation 44–51
  interest rates 44–58, 137
  magical thinking 86
  Monetary policy 45–9, 53–4, 57–8, 69–73
  risk premiums 54–7
  technical analysis 86, 88, 93, 96, 99–114
  volatility 57–8
  yield curves 50–4
forward rates 50–1
frame dependence 89, 94–5
France 65–7
fundamental analysis 93–4, 99–100, 114, 121–32, 135–6
funding costs, interest rate swaps 34–5
futures 19, 27–32, 108–9, 137, 146–7, 157–8, 165–7
  concepts 19, 27–9
  hedging 28–31
  open interest 108–9, 116
  options on bond futures 30–2
  pricing 27–9
  risks 28–9
  strategies 28–9, 146–7
  technical analysis 108–11
  uses 28, 30–1

Gallea, A.M. 88, 95, 134
gamblers' fallacy 85, 87
game concepts 63
GDP 40–1, 46–50, 100
Generation X 78–80
geometric progressions, markets 93–4
Germany 65–7, 68, 72–3, 105
  crises 68
  EMU 72–3
  government policies 65–7, 72–3
  hyperinflation problems (1919-1923) 68
Gestalt psychologists 86, 91
Gilts 142, 157–8, 168–9
golden cross 103
government entities 3, 13–14, 15, 19, 63–75, 129, 142–4
  agencies 142–4
  concepts 3, 13–14, 15, 19, 65–75, 142–4
  ECB 71–3, 166–7
  elections 65–7, 73–4
  Federal Reserve 69–71, 117, 135
  policies 40–3, 45–9, 53–4, 57–8, 65–75, 129
  regulations 118–20
Graham, Benjamin 59
greed 90–3, 182–3, 186
Greenspan, Alan 70
group behaviour 77–85, 91–5, 129–30
groupthink 85, 91–5, 129–30
guaranteed investment contracts (GICs) 151–2

head and shoulders pattern 104–6
hedge funds 153–4
hedging 19, 27–36, 130, 145, 152
  see also derivatives
  convertible bonds 145–6, 158
  covered option positions 30–2, 148–9, 174
  credit risks 13
  flat yield curves 53
  futures 28–31
  interest rate swaps 34
herding tendencies 91–5, 110, 113, 129–30
heuristics 85, 86
high-grade issuers 19, 144
high-yield issuers 19, 118–20, 144, 148
hindsight bias 85, 88, 89–90, 92–3, 96
holiday effects, seasonal analysis 121
human factors 55, 74, 77–98, 127–9, 182–3, 186, 187
  see also investors
  age issues 77–83, 129
  attitudes 85, 86, 88–92, 127–32, 136, 149–53, 186
  behavioural finance 84–98, 182–3, 186, 187
  bias issues 84–93, 94–6, 130, 133–4
  decision making 74, 77, 83–98
  demographic issues 77–83, 129–2, 136, 187

Index   199

emotions 84–94, 113, 127–32, 136, 182–3, 186, 187
  group behaviour 77–83, 91–5, 129–30
  herding tendencies 91–5, 110, 113, 129–30
  pattern formations 85–6, 128–9
  population issues 78–83, 129–30
  psychology insights 74, 77, 83–115, 127–30, 135–6, 182–3, 186
  sociological insights 77–98, 129–30, 187

IBM 55
immunization strategies 15, 155–6
implementation considerations 139–83
implied volatility 27, 29–30, 121
in-the-money options 29
index trackers 122, 153–5
Indonesia 74
inflation 40–2, 44–54, 65–7, 100, 136
  ECB 71–3
  economic issues 40–2, 44–54, 65–7, 100, 136
  expectations 44–51, 54
  Federal Reserve 69–71
  forecasts 44–51, 54
  German hyperinflation problems (1919–1923) 68
  measurements 46–7
  PBC effects 66–7
  risks 14, 16
  under-reaction bias 51
  unemployment levels 65–6
inflation-indexed securities 45, 143
information
  behavioural finance 84–98
  bias 84–93, 94–6, 133–4
  cognitive dissonance 85–6, 89, 93
  management 134–5
  pattern formations 85–6, 128–9
  processing characteristics 84–8
Instability Index 55, 174
institutional investors 113–14, 116–17, 149–53
insurance companies 150–2
integrated approach 127–38
interdisciplinary model 127–38
interest rate derivatives 19, 27–36, 146–7
  see also derivatives
  concepts 19, 27–36, 146–7
  speculation 28, 30–2
  strategies 28–9, 32
interest rate swaps 19, 32–6, 55, 147, 163–5, 173–6
  see also swaps
  concepts 32–6, 147
  pricing 32–6
  uses 34–6

interest rates
  budget deficits 67–73
  callable bonds 22–5, 29–32
  central banks 45–8, 68–9, 71–3
  concepts 3, 4, 5–13, 15–16, 203, 39–62
  demographic factors 80–3
  ECB 71–3, 166–7
  equilibrium market interest rates 48–50
  Federal Reserve 69–71
  forecasts 44–58, 137
  law of supply and demand 39–43, 49, 51
  monetary policy 40–3, 45–9, 53–4, 67–73
  risks 4, 5–13, 15, 19, 28, 159
  theories 44–58
  volatility 3–4, 7–9, 15–16, 26, 30–2, 52
intertemporal budget constraints 67–8
investors 55, 63, 74, 77–98, 113–14, 149–53
  see also human factors
  attitudes 85, 86, 88–92, 127–32, 136, 149–53, 186
  behavioural finance 84–98, 182–3, 186, 187
  bias 84–93, 94–6, 130, 133–4
  concepts 55, 63, 74, 77–98, 113–14, 149–53
  decision making 74, 77, 83–98
  demographic issues 77–83, 129–32, 136, 187
  emotions 84–94, 113, 127–32, 136, 182–3, 186, 187
  group behaviour 77–83, 91–5, 129–30
  herding tendencies 91–5, 110, 113, 129–30
  institutional investors 113–14, 116–17, 149–53
  objectives 149–53
  pattern formations 85–6, 128–9
  psychological insights 74, 77, 83–114, 127–30, 135–6, 182–3, 186
  risk-aversion 55, 136, 149–53
  sociological insights 77–98, 129–30, 187
  types 113–14, 116–17, 149–53
issuers, fixed income securities 3, 19, 34–5, 50, 118–20, 142–9
Italy
  demographic factors 80–1
  government policies 65–7

James, William 85–6
Japan
  crises 74, 93
  demographic factors 80, 83
  government policies 65–7, 119
  open interest data 109
  statistics 142, 177–8
  world shares 142
JP Morgan
Fleming's LCPI 55
Sentiment Flow Index (SFI) 111
junk bonds 19, 144

key rate duration *see* partial duration
Keynesian school 42–3, 49

law of supply and demand 39–43, 49, 51, 55, 99, 118–20, 131
learning approaches 95–6, 187
legal risks 14, 61, 159
leverage uses 28, 153–4, 180
  concepts 28, 153–4, 180
  futures 28, 153, 180
  hedge funds 28, 153–4, 180
Lewis, John 134
life insurance companies 151–2, 154
liquidity (risk premium) hypothesis 52–3, 54, 56
liquidity risks 14, 16, 25–6, 52–4, 56, 149–53, 159
logic checks 133
London Interbank Offered Rate (LIBOR) 32–6, 116
London International Financial Futures and Options Exchange (LIFFE) 109, 116
Long-Term Capital Management (LTCM) 87–8, 180
losses
  aversion 85, 88–9, 95–6, 130
  survival principles 85, 89, 94, 180–3, 185–9
Lynch, Peter 59

MacKay, Charles 91
magical thinking 86
management issues
  see also strategies
  active management 122, 153–5, 156–60, 165, 178–9
  asset managers 122, 152, 153, 156–60
  information 134–5
  passive management 122, 153–5, 178–9
  risk-management strategies 180–2, 187
  structured portfolio management 153–4, 155–6
manias, markets 93–4
market bias, decision making 84–93, 94–6
market risks
  see also interest rates; risks
  concepts 4–13, 15–16
  coupon size 4
  maturity 4–5
  measurements 7–9, 12, 121
market-neutral strategies 157–8, 167–71
market-timing strategies 157, 177
markets
  battlefield analogies 185–7
  behavioural finance 84–98, 182–3, 187
  biology analogies 93–4
  directional bets 163–5
  expectations 136–7
  integrated approach 127–38
  manias and panics 93–4
  psychological insights 74, 77, 83–114, 127–30, 135–6, 182–3, 186
  sectors 141–61, 177–9
  survival principles 85, 89, 94, 180–3, 185–9
  tool selections 130–2
  trading-floor experiences 185–7
mean reversion 122–3, 159–60
measurement
  credit risks 20–1
  inflation 46–7
  market risks 7–9, 12, 121
  yield curve risks 12–13
mental accounting 85, 89, 92–3
mental models 86
Meriwether, John 87
Merton, Robert 87
mispriced securities 59, 122, 125
models 86, 126–38
  data needs 134
  inflexibility problems 126–8, 137
  interdisciplinary approaches 127–38
  risks 16, 25–6, 122–6, 159
modified duration, concepts 7–8, 12–13
momentum indicators 103, 106–8
momentum strategies 159–60
monetary policy 40–3, 45–9, 53–4, 57–8, 67–73, 136
  budget deficits 67–73, 118–20
  forecasts 45–9, 53–4, 57–8, 69–73
money market 142–4
money supply 47–9, 68–9, 129
Monte Carlo simulations 133
month effects, seasonal analysis 120–1
moods 88–91
mortgage-backed securities (MBS) 19, 22–7, 142–4, 146
moving average convergence-divergence (MACD) 103, 106–8
moving averages 102–5
Munger, Charlie 95
municipal bonds 142–4, 151
Murphy's Law 185
mutual funds 152, 154–5

naked option positions, interest rate speculation 30–1
NASDAQ 134
necklines, head and shoulders pattern 104–6
negative feedback loops 59–60, 93, 132
New Zealand 65–7
Nixon, Richard 66
noise filters 85–6, 95, 115–8, 187
non-callable bonds, callable bonds 23–4, 56
non-life insurance companies 150–1

objective processes, behavioural finance 84–96, 182
open interest, technical analysis 108–9, 112, 116–8
open market operations (OMO) 47–8
optimization scenarios, economic issues 39–40, 61, 68, 155
option-adjusted spread (OAS) 25–7, 179
options 19, 21–7, 29–32, 147, 173–6
   see also callable bonds; putable bonds
   Black-Derman-Toy pricing model 30
   Black-Scholes pricing model 29–32
   concepts 19, 21–7, 29–32, 147
   embedded options 19, 21–7, 56, 173–6
   open interest 108–9, 116
   options on bond futures 30–2
   OTC 147
   strategies 27, 30–1, 32, 147, 173–6
   time values 29–30
options on bond futures 19, 30–2
out-of-the-money options 31
over-the-counter options (OTC) 147
overconfidence bias 85, 87–8, 93, 95–6
overreaction bias 85, 86–7, 130

panics, markets 93–4
parallel shifts, yield curves 10, 13, 25–6
partial duration, concepts 12–13
passive management 122, 153–5, 178–9
Patalon, W. 88, 95, 134
pattern formations 85–6, 128–9
pearls of wisdom 185–9
pension funds 150, 151, 154
performance issues
   future/past performance 177–8
   RV analysis 121, 123–6, 157–8
   yield curves 9–13
persuasion effects 91
'plain vanilla' swaps 32–3
political business cycle (PBC) 65–7, 131
political economy perspectives 65–9
politics
   central banks 68–9, 71–3, 131, 150
   crises 68, 74, 129
   economic issues 41–3, 45–9, 65–75, 129, 187
   elections 65–7, 73–4
   emerging markets 135–6, 148–9, 177–8
   government policies 40–3, 45–9, 53–4, 57–8, 65–75, 129
   risks 14, 61
population issues 78–83, 129–30
portfolios 9–13, 25, 28, 114, 121–6, 149–74
   callable bonds 25
   concepts 9–13, 121–6, 149–74
   duration 9, 13, 28, 155–60, 165–7

   management 153–81
   quantitative analysis 114, 121–6, 179
   risk exposures 160, 165–76
   risk-management strategies 180–2
   size limits 181
   trading strategies 165–76
   yield curves 9–13, 153–60
positions 115–18, 148–9, 153, 165–76, 181–2
positive feedback loops 59–60, 93, 132
practical experiences 185–7
preferences 51–3, 61, 77, 83
preferred habitat hypothesis, yield curves 51–3
premiums
   determinants 54–6
   forecasts 54–7
   risks 44, 52, 54–7
prepayment risks, MBS 19, 22–7, 56, 146
pricing
   bonds 3–15, 19, 22–7, 58–9, 83–114, 127–9
   callable bonds 19, 22–5, 29–32
   charts 96, 99–114
   credit risks 19–21, 129–30
   EMH 58–60, 99–100, 128
   futures 27–9
   interest rate swaps 32–6
   MBS 22–7, 146
   putable bonds 19, 22–5, 29–32
   mispriced securities 59, 122, 125
   price-yield relationship 5–13, 22–3, 26
   psychological insights 83–114, 127–30
   risks 3–17
   spread products 20–1
   technical analysis 86, 88, 93, 96, 99–114
proprietary traders 153
prospect theory 85, 88–9
protective puts 31–2
psychological insights 74, 77, 83–114, 127–30, 135–6, 182–3, 186
   see also human factors
   behavioural finance 84–98, 182–3, 186, 187
   concepts 74, 77, 83–114, 127–30, 135–6, 182–3
   investors 74, 77, 83–114
   technical analysis 99–114
   trends and reversals 92–4, 99–114
put options 19, 22–7, 29–32, 110
putable bonds 19, 22–7, 29–32, 145
   concepts 19, 22–7, 29–32, 145
   pricing 19, 22–5, 29–32

quantitative analysis 114, 121–36, 179
quarter effects, seasonal analysis 120–1

randomness issues 59–60, 85, 87, 128–9, 137
   chaos theory 59–60
reactive strategies 159–60

record-keeping needs 182–3
regret theory 85, 88–9, 92–3
regulations, supply and demand analysis 118–20
reinvestment income 5, 15
reinvestment risks 14–15, 22–3
relative demand 54, 55
relative strength index (RSI) 106–8
relative value (RV)
   quantitative analysis 121, 123–6
   strategies 157–8
repo rates 15–16
representativeness heuristic 85, 86–7, 92–3
resistance 101–2
returns 3–5, 15–16, 22–3, 177–9
   components 3–17
   embedded options 22–3, 26
   EMH 58–9, 99–100, 128
   interest rate swaps 34–5
   portfolio strategies 154–60
   roll-down returns 15–16
   statistics 177–9
reversals
   psychological insights 92–4, 103–14
   technical analysis 103–14
rich/cheap effect 16
RiedThunberg and Company 116
'risk-free' rates 15, 19–21, 29–30, 34, 44–5
risk 3–17, 25, 122, 133, 150–3, 159, 165–82
   see also market risks
   appetite 54, 55, 136, 149–53
   assessment distortions 89–91
   concepts 3–17, 19, 28, 150–3, 159, 163–77
   credit risks 13, 16, 19–21, 25–6, 54–7
   embedded options 19, 21–7
   exposures 85, 88, 148, 160, 165–76
   futures 28–9
   management strategies 180–2, 187
   maximum-pain approaches 133
   portfolio-building 160, 165–76
   premia 44, 52, 54–7
   quantitative analysis 114, 121–6, 179
   sources 4, 13–15, 16, 25, 165
   statistics 177–9
   types 4, 13–16, 25, 122, 133, 150–3, 159
   volatility 7–9, 21–7
   yield curves 9–13, 15–16
roll-down return 15–16
rules
   technical analysis 101–12
   of thumb 86
Russia 180

scarce resources 39–43
Scholes, Myron 87
Schroder Salomon Smith Barney 179
seasonal analysis 120–1, 127–8, 131, 136
sectors, fixed income investments 141–61, 177–9
securitized debt, concepts 3–17, 146
selective exposure 85, 88, 149
selective perception 85, 88
self-fulfilling dynamics, technical analysis 113
selling bias 95
SFI see JP Morgan's Sentiment Flow Index
short-term analysis 86, 88, 93, 96, 99–138
   flow analysis 115–18, 127–30, 136
   quantitative analysis 114, 121–36, 179
   seasonal analysis 120–1, 127–8, 131, 136
   statistical limitations 125–6
   supply and demand analysis 118–20, 131
   technical analysis 86, 88, 93, 96, 99–114, 127–36
   tools 100–38
size limits, positions 181
smart money 111–14
social comparisons 91–2
sociological insights 77–83, 93, 96, 131–2, 187
   see also human factors
   demographic factors 77–83, 129–30, 187
   investors 77–98
spread bets 169–71
spread convexity 21
spread curves 20–1, 54–7, 171–3
   concepts 20–1, 54–7
   corporations 57, 173
   economic issues 56–7
spread duration 20–1, 25–6
spread products 20, 54–5, 158
   see also credit risks
spread risks see credit risks
SSSB Instability Index 174
statistics 141–2, 177–9
stochastic oscillator 107–8
stochastic-process hypothesis, yield curves 52
stock market crashes
   US 1929 93
   US 1987 59, 93
Stoffman, D. 78–80
Stone and McCarthy Research Associates 116
straddle 32, 172
straight bonds, concepts 19, 22–5, 173–6
strangle 32
strategies 5–8, 27–32, 135–6, 146–7, 153–81, 187
   see also management issues
   active management 122, 153–5, 156–60, 165, 178–9
   concepts 5–8, 26–32, 135–6, 146–7, 153–83, 187
   convexity 5–8, 166–76
   directional strategies 157
   duration 8–9, 155–60, 165–7
   embedded options 26–7, 173–6

Index   203

enhanced indexing 155
exit strategies 181–2
futures 28–9, 146–7
immunization strategies 15, 155–6
interest rate derivatives 28–9, 32, 146–7
momentum strategies 159–60
options 26–7, 30–1, 32, 147, 173–6
passive management 122, 153–5, 178–9
reactive strategies 159–60
risk-management strategies 180–2, 187
RV strategies 157–8
structured portfolio management 153–4, 155–6
templates 135–6
trading strategies 31–2, 165–76, 185–9
structured portfolio management 153–4, 155–6
structured securities 145–8
structures, fixed income securities 19–27, 141–61
subjective processes, behavioural finance 84–96
sunk cost fallacy 89
supply and demand
    laws 39–43, 49, 51, 55, 99, 118–20, 131
    short-term analysis 118–20, 131
supply technicals 118–9
support levels, technical analysis 101–2
survival principles 85, 89, 94, 180–3, 185–9
swaps 13, 19, 27, 32–6, 55, 146–7, 165–7, 173–6
    see also interest rate swaps
    concepts 13, 19, 27, 32–6, 147
    spreads 34
synthetic securities 28, 30–2
system checks 133–5

taxes 14, 20, 56–8, 65–6, 129, 143–4, 159
technical analysis 86, 88, 93, 96, 99–114, 127–36
    concepts 86, 88, 93, 96, 99–114, 127–30
    contrarians 109–11
    Dow theory 100–2
    extreme positions 111, 136
    head and shoulders pattern 104–6
    limitations 113–14
    MACD 103, 106–8
    mixed signals 132–3
    momentum indicators 103, 106–8
    moving averages 102–5
    open interest 108–9, 112, 116–18
    RSI 106–8
    rules 101–12
    smart money 111–14
    speculators 110–11, 115–16, 130
    tools 100–9
TED spread trades 158
templates, trading 135–7
term structure of credit spreads *see* spread curves
term structure of interest rates *see* yield curves
Three Mile Island disaster 187

time horizons, tool selections 130–5, 153
time value of money 3–4, 45
options 29–30
Tokyo International Financial Futures Exchange (TIFFE) 116, 109
trading strategies 31–2, 165–76, 185–9
trading-floor experiences 185–7
transaction costs 156–7, 179–80
Treasuries 13–21, 28, 34, 54–9, 66–71, 102, 107–9, 112, 135, 142–4, 173
Treasury duration 20–1
trends and reversals
    Dow theory 100–2
    psychological insights 92–4, 99–114
    technical analysis 86, 88, 93, 96, 99–114
Twain, Mark 99

UK
    Gilts 135, 142, 157–8, 168–9
    government policies 65–7, 119
    open interest data 109, 116
    regulations 119
    statistics 177–8
underreaction bias 51, 85, 87, 130
unemployment 65–6
universe, fixed income investments 141–9
US
    agencies 142–4
    CFTC 110–11, 116–18
    debt risks/returns 177–8
    demographic factors 78–83
    Federal Reserve 69–71, 117, 135
    FOMC 70, 116, 137
    government policies 65–7, 69–71, 83
    market composition 142–4
    open interest data 109, 112, 116–18
    population issues 78–83
    TIPS 143
    Treasuries 13–21, 28, 34, 54–9, 66–71, 102, 107–9, 112, 135, 142–4, 173
    world shares 142
utility maximization 39–40

Value-at Risk analysis 133
vicious circles, business cycles 43–4
virtuous circles, business cycles 43–4
volatility 3–4, 7–9, 15–16, 21–6, 30–2, 52, 135–6, 166–76
    bets 171–2
    convexity 7–9, 16, 21–5, 166–76
    economic issues 57–8
    embedded options 19, 21–7, 173–6
    forecasts 57–8
    implied 27, 29–30, 121
    interest rates 3–4, 7–9, 15–16, 27, 30–2, 52
    maturity 26

volatility (*cont.*)
  risks 7–9, 21–7
  seasonal analysis 121
  trades 31–2, 173–6
volume, technical analysis 99–114

warrants 146
wedges 103
weekday effects, seasonal analysis 120
weighted average duration *see* directional
    duration
wildcard factors 127–8, 133, 136

year-end effects, seasonal analysis 120–1
yield curves 10–13, 50–4, 135–6, 154–60, 165–76
  bets 165–73
  butterfly shifts 11–12, 124–5, 169–71
  classic shapes 8–9, 15–16, 50–4
  concepts 9–13, 50–4, 135–6
  demographic factors 83

expectations hypothesis 50–4
  forecasts 50–4
  liquidity (risk premium) hypothesis 52–3
  parallel shifts 9–10, 13, 25–6
  portfolio strategies 9–13, 153–60, 165–76
  preferred habitat hypothesis 51–3
  risks 9–13, 15–16
  roll-down returns 15–16
  shapes 8–9, 15–16, 50–4, 166–76
  shifts 9–13, 50–4, 169–71
  steepness measures 10–11, 54, 135–6, 166–76
  stochastic-process hypothesis 52
  trades 167–73
yield spreads, credit risks 19–21, 25–6, 135–6
yields 5–13, 22–3, 26, 44–50
  components 44–5
  concepts 5–13, 22–3, 26, 44–50
  price-yield relationship 5–13, 22–3, 26

zero coupon bonds 14

Indexed compiled by Terry Halliday